Survivor

Survivor

A TRUE STORY OF SURVIVAL

RF Heeney

Copyright © 2016 R. F. Heeney
All rights reserved.

ISBN: 1530757533
ISBN 13: 9781530757534

I have recently finished reading this book and I cannot recommend it enough. I found it captivating, compelling, and funny in parts and I could not put it down. Congratulations to the Author, and I'm quite sure it will be a winner. Only sad thing about it is..It's a True story.

M Maher

I have just finished reading this book and I could not put it down until I reached the last page.

It is funny in places but overall it is a powerful testament to the lives of children in Irish society who were put into the care of the" UNCHRISTIAN" Christian Brothers. A must read book, and congrats to the author for sharing the horrors of his young life with us.

Rick Lee

A harrowing story told brilliantly. Here is nature's survival of the fittest in its natural form. Some people are born to survive and succeed and little Frank Heeney is definitely one of natures selected.

Fortunately I am not old enough to remember what it was like 'back then', it seems like an alien world to me but I for one are relieved that the catholic church no longer has its vice like grip about the Irish people's throats.

They no longer are a force to be feared and what a mighty fall from grace they're taking. Thankfully no one is keeping their filthy little secrets anymore. The legacy they've left behind is nothing but hurt, betrayal, disgust, hatred, vengeance……….

I cannot help but think of my own children and wonder would they have coped with what this child had to deal with.

Young Frank was a very clever, resourceful, insightful and brave young man. His strongest asset was definitely his stubbornness and I've no doubt that without it he wouldn't be here today.

I really enjoyed this book; the writer encapsulated the reader and brought us on his journey. I could feel his pain, sadness, anger and rare bouts of happiness and joy.

Ciara McKenna

Just read the book and I'm wondering why these people are not being hunted to the ends of the earth like the Nazis still are for their crimes,
Its incredible to hear one boys story in detail rather than the usual watered down snippets we don't really pay heed to on the news every now and then.
It took a lot of guts I'm sure to re-live the horrors I've read by scum that are still walking free to this day.
It boils the blood no end, but I hope also the courage and human spirit that prevailed throughout will serve some good, be it to any of the other hundreds/thousands of victims out there or just to create more awareness of what our government and religious systems are capable of.
Well done Frank

David Murrary

*Although this book is a true testament of my life
Names have been changed to protect the guilty.*

Dedicated to my Mom and Dad who gave me life

**Parts of this edition were included in my first book
In My Own Words [Still Running]
Under the pen name of Mickey Finn.**

Foreword

St Joseph's Industrial School. Letterfrack. Co Galway.

As an Irish National, it gives me no pleasure to assist in the recording of an account of the heartbreaking tribulation of those boys who, largely through no fault of their own, were sent to St Joseph's Industrial School in Letterfrack, County Galway. The road to hell being paved with good intentions, this monstrous and now notorious penal institute for children, let's call a spade a spade, began life and for some, death, as a Quaker-inspired school in 1887.

Through the passage of time it transformed into what was euphemistically called an industrial school (*Scoileanna Saothair*) for young boys. Under the Industrial Schools Act (1888) their purpose was to 'care for neglected, orphaned and abandoned children.' In essence they were a dumping ground for children who found themselves on the fringes of society. In 1964 there were three classes of boys placed in Letterfrack's St Josephs: The Homeless and those guilty of criminal offences, the destitute sent by local authorities in accordance with the Public Assistance Act and those voluntarily admitted by parents and guardians. In respect of those committed for criminal acts it should be remembered these unfortunates were extremely young and their 'offences' petty in the extreme. From its conception St Joseph's Industrial School was mismanaged by the Congregation of Christian Brothers.

It is a sobering thought that within our lifetime conditions at this school find their equal only in 18th Century English judicial barbarism. The nearby Fields of Athenry are poignant enough for most people's stomachs.

For many of the unfortunate boys who endured St Joseph's, transportation might well have been a blessing. The 'school's' notoriety was founded upon the abuse and extreme physical and mental punishments inflicted upon defenseless children by a largely psychotic mob of cassocked ecclesiastic wardens. No fewer than 147 children died whilst under their tender mercies. Many of these brothers may be presumed to be practitioners of the dark arts. Only the devil could have been inspired to inflict such miseries on defenseless waifs. Only darkness could have conspired a whole community to turn aside from the wailing of hundreds of children through those dark decades of its existence. Some of the dreadful scenes are reminiscent of the scenes depicted in medieval tapestries in which the excesses of hell are defined.

'Survivor' is the testimony of R.F. Heeney, himself an inmate from the age of twelve to sixteen. It is also an authentication, a memorial and recognition for each of the adolescent victims of those men of the cloth and their collaborationists. His account of life in this dreadful institution will give many pause for thought as to the iniquities of man. It immortalizes the cold ethos of the judiciary. Readers will also be inspired by the selfless acts, rebelliousness and inborn stoicism of young boys in the face of extreme hostility.

CHAPTER 1

'Jesus!' I thought to myself as I awoke during the dark hours of the early morning, 'What is that sticky stuff on my leg?'

The smell in the airless room was fetid. Hardly surprising as it was home to an entire family. I was in bed with my half-brother, although I was still half asleep. I could feel something on my leg which my mind interpreted as skutry shite.

'Has someone shit the bed?' I muttered to myself in the darkness.

Like a foul-smelling blanket the oppressive night air desensitized my senses. Drifting off again was the preferred option given the only other thing I could do was check the unwanted sensation out. I was so tired.

'Fuck it,' I thought, 'I will see what it is in the morning'.

As I drifted between wakefulness and slumber I heard someone moving about in the darkened room. Someone was going to use the piss bucket. Pssssssssssssssssssssss, you could clearly hear the stream gushing out of my Da's bladder. His dropping the bucket's lid did nothing to remove the stench of urine and body odor. I was struggling to get back to sleep but eventually I drifted off.

Our family lived in one room in a terraced tenement situated in North Great Georges Street in Ireland's capital city, Dublin. It was a four-storey building with the ubiquitous basement somehow holding it all up. There were five of us, children that is, then there was me Ma and Da. Where we were living, or rather existing now was probably the sixth place we had lived since I was ushered into the world and I was not yet eleven years old.

This place was what you get when you have been evicted from your home by Dublin Corporation, the great Irish Housing Authority, who is a law unto itself and is controlled by lowly civil servants, who do not seem to answer to any authority outside of their own little circle.

This was 'Rejects Ville' with all its attendant baggage of poverty, the bowed and the broken, the debris of Ireland's lower classes.

The foul and cramped tenement was owned by one of the largest estate owners in the Irish Republic, the religious orders of God. Could there be anyone on earth so religious as to consider their charity so generous, charging rents for a single room accommodating no less than seven impoverished family members? A manger in a stable would be a major step upwards, anything but this. Here they expect the grateful, pious residents to live not in squalor but in harmony. Yes, for them it is our privilege to be able to get to our feet when the first bars of the Irish national anthem are played following the 11.30 a.m. mass. Suffer the little children, from those pious brethren who afterwards retreat to their overburdened tables in the opulent mansions of ecclesiastical benevolence. Wouldn't your heart go out to the piety?

Our room was 16ft by 12ft, wall to wall just four strides apart. The room's bleak landscape was broken only by two burlap flour sacks keeping the light and the cold winter air on the outside. If you pulled the sacking aside and peered out you would gaze out over a tiny backyard set against a factory wall. In the room itself there were three beds, two chairs, a small table, and a sink unit with a couple of presses atop it.

My half-brother and I shared a single bed. He was much older and had recently returned from an industrial school, a euphemism for a house of correction for juvenile offenders. I had just a vague recollection of seeing him on earlier occasions; I think when I was about six-years old. There was little bonding between us. I hardly understood the brogue he had adopted, which hadn't improved since his return.

He, I was led to believe, was taken from his mother at birth by the heavenly Nuns, at the Navan Road mother and baby home and placed into various institutions for the first sixteen years of his life. My other brother was about five-years old.

Our two sisters shared their single bed with him. They were ten and seven-years old whilst Ma and Da had the comfort of the remaining double bed. When we kicked our bare feet out in the mornings we were reminded of the coldness of the torn linoleum partly covering the bare floorboards. The wallpaper, no doubt resplendent when long ago it was applied, was stained with damp and in parts was already showing the effects of gravitational pull. Hanging precariously from the grey ceiling was a single un-shaded light bulb. The bucket-loo could be dispensed with during the day as there was a small communal toilet in the backyard used by those privileged to live in such salubrious accommodation. The commode was far too good for a priestly backside.

Our home was at least central to Dublin's bars and perhaps as a reminder of our saintly heritage just a short walk away from the internationally famous O'Connell Street and the other Irish 'Saint' Parnell (Street). Both should be spinning in their graves having had their names attached to such human wretchedness and vice.

I was awake now or at least conscious of the clattering of the teapot that told me Ma was preparing the morning ritual pot of tea. My spirits lifted for the sticky stuff I had felt on my bare leg seemed a figment of my sleep-filled imagination, nor was there a stain to be seen.

'Ma, I felt some sticky stuff on my leg in the night. It woke me up as well as did Da when he was pissing in the bucket.'

Ma was wearing a worn and stained dressing gown and even though her blond hair was yet to be brushed and combed she looked ethereally beautiful to me.

Ma looked at me with those bright green eyes of hers.

'Sure, it was only a bad dream you were having. We all get them from time to time.'

I wasn't entirely persuaded and I was not sure she was convinced by her own reassurances either. Her unease was noticeable and I could almost read her mind.

'Oh, God. I hope it isn't what I think it is, the oldest of my sons playing with himself despite his sharing the bed with his younger brother. What's to be done? I haven't a spare bed for him.'

There weren't many options for the hard-pressed mother. With five children to feed and clothe on my Da's meager wages there was little enough left to feed the insatiable appetite of my father's drinking and gambling habits. She herself was third or fourth down the pecking order whilst the moneylender could go and whistle. When we heard him knock on the door we would all be quiet in the hope he would go away. My Da seemed able to find him when he wanted money, but was never here when he would call to be repaid. Such women managed.

Da was up and about now and at the sink, which he routinely washed and shaved himself in. It seemed far too small for his large frame as he bent over it. There was the alternative larger bowl in the yard outside he sometimes used for a proper wash. The emptying of the night bucket was below his dignity though. This chore was left to me or my sisters. His having helped to fill the pot seemed to have no bearing in the matter. In some ways the socialist philosophy of all for one and one for all was lost on him, when he chose, and this was often.

So off we trotted, my sister and I, each holding our own side of the bucket's wire handle. It occurred to me as we stepped out into the dark hallway leading to the steps descending to the yard that this morning it seemed heavier than usual.

All was going perfectly well until I slipped on something, perhaps a puddle of piss or some other piece of rubbish, that would often litter the stairway. Unable to catch myself my sister screamed a warning but losing my balance I was horrified to see the bucket and its contents tumbling and spilling down the staircase. Above the din of the falling bucket cascading its contents down the stairway was my sister's shrill warnings that Da would kill both of us for letting the bucket slip.

My attempts at hurriedly cleaning up the mess were futile. I had neither the means nor the will on account of how great the mess was. Nor did I have the time for I could already hear the threatening tread of Da coming down the stairs in response to the noise. Wham! I felt the thud of a damp cloth strike the nape of my neck, almost knocking me off my feet. The brief pause only heralded the follow up slap, this time across my face.

'Are you mad or what?' Bawling with his eyes popping with annoyance he demanded to know which of us had spilled the bucket.

'Out of my way, you useless pair of gobshites,' he exclaimed, 'I will sort this out.'

His uttered oaths brought some relief as surely he didn't have time to clean the mess up, kill me, and go to work. We pair ran as fast as our legs could carry us towards the back yard's washing and toilet area. Even there, the smell of urine was persistent. Fresh air was at a premium in these tenements.

There was a sit down toilet but the seat had disappeared to God knows where a long time ago. Beside it was a small enamel sink set against the wall. The concrete floor was bare of any comforting linoleum or rug. The toilet door no longer locked and there being no light at all, there was plenty of evidence that previous visitor's aims were a little hit and miss. Occasionally, Ma put bleach into our night bucket and also splashed it everywhere around the toilet. She did her best to make it clean but the stench persisted.

As my sister and I were using the facility Da roughly barged in on us both.

'Are you two finished yet? I have my work to go to. Move over, you daft pair.'

Our Da drove a coal lorry so no amount of washing was going to scour his skin clean. The use of cold water could hardly help for the soap hardly sudded up at all. Happily there was no discrimination against the hard working poor in the pub he frequented and it was the one place where he was at peace with himself. His truck was a tipper that carried its spare wheel under its rear axle. When he tipped the deck the coal slithered down to fill up the hub of that spare wheel, the contents of which he sold too. For this bonus he had ready customers and it was what he called his little nixer.

With the morning's mishap behind us I called goodbye as I set my feet towards Marlborough Street School, just a five minute schoolboy's amble away. My mood was carefree for today's lessons would be taken by Mr. Cleaney. He had a pleasant and patient temperament and hadn't any favorites. He treated the kids from the poorer backgrounds with patience and understanding. The school itself was imposing, a rather grand stone brick affair that was home to the Irish Language School too. I was fond of my school where my own class of about 40 pupils was situated on the first floor. It was a light airy room with three vast windows and an impossibly high ceiling.

It must have been about eleven o'clock one morning; all was studiously calm when the silence was broken by a big bang from the back of the classroom. Jesus! There was a mad scattering, kids ducking and weaving in every direction. Surely there was a mad gunman in the school? I thought as I dived under my desk out of the way.

Mr. Cleaney was the model of calmness and I had no doubt his kind calmly sang hymns from the stern of the Titanic when it sank below the waves.

A youngster sitting at the rear of the classroom, having found a live bullet had brought it to school with him. With a schoolboy's natural curiosity he had been probing the bullet with a heated pin when it detonated. The result was that two of his fingers ended up somewhere distant in the classroom. Needless to say there was little work done for the rest of that day.

There were times when the school would give us 'poor boxes' so that we might make collections on the school's behalf. My own contribution was to learn adeptness at opening them with a butter knife, for weren't we poor too? We also targeted a nearby bakery in order to help make ends meet. It wasn't beyond our wit to liberate a few loaves of bread for me Ma's empty table. Batch loaf being me Da's favorite. Those whose courage failed to desert them could venture even further into the bakery to lay their thieving little hands on the cakes that were baked there.

The sharpest tool in the box was a boy named Redser. He was a dab hand at locating where the bigger chocolate gateaux were shelved. In fact he was so good at it that we became sick of chocolate cakes. Emboldened by his growing reputation as a sneak thief, he moved onwards and upwards. One day he slipped into the egg carrier's van and made off with a small bag of the man's takings. Redser later appeared, flaunting £10, £5 and £1 notes, booty from which I was given a total of £20.

Unfamiliar with such wealth I hid it and kept the notes for two weeks. I wasn't quite able to perceive their value but the egg carrier surely had and the heat was on. The word had got around and local shopkeepers were keeping their eyes open for youngsters using notes to make their purchases. When I finally decided to spend the money it was to a local shop called The Mullingar. The owners I thought were from Cork County.

My purchasing a pennyworth of sweets with a £5 pound note aroused immediate suspicions and in no time at all the Garda was upon me. This was to be my first encounter with the stalwart culchie, the police force known in Ireland as The Gardaí. With little choice in the matter, for I was handcuffed to a police officer, I was ushered into the patrol car with another of the officers holding me by the scruff of the neck. He had noticed the handcuffs were far too large for me and feared I might take to my feet. In no time at all I was being pushed through the doors of Store Street Garda Station. Terrified by my surroundings and the manner of the police officers I confess to wetting my pants.

Taking me through to an ante room there was much to alert me to the gravity of the situation. The room was bare except for a table and two chairs. Both the table and its two chairs were screwed to the floor. I was motioned to sit on one, an officer towered above me. I think had I stood up my head might just have reached his belt buckle.

'Where did you get all that money from you fucking little bastard? And don't lie to me.' He growled.

By this time the tears were flowing freely and I was screaming for my Ma.

'You'll get your Ma alright. You'll get your Ma alright,' he swore. 'Now tell me, lad. Where did you get that fucking money?'

I felt a blow to the back of my head that nearly knocked me from the chair.

'Speak up, where did you get that fucking money from?' he kept repeating over and over again, hitting me until I began to lose track of time or even see an ending to the torment.

My head was swimming with fear and confusion. I had no idea how to respond. Eventually paperwork was brought in and I was charged with theft. From what or who they never did say. It seemed my being unable to account for the money was my only crime.

Leaning over close enough for me to feel his hot breath he told me there had been a spate of burglaries from gas meters.

'Why not admit to some of them?' he said. 'Admit it, son, and the judge will go more leniently on you.'

I was an eleven-year old skinny runt of a lad; hardly the Al Capone of Dublin but the policemen didn't seem to notice the difference. Maybe it takes a special kind of person to be a copper. They tarred everyone as a criminal regardless of age or circumstance. They seemed to have no sense of proportion. I often wonder how many juveniles they turned to criminality through their over zealousness and brutality. I had the occasional cuff off my Da but never a beating as such. My Ma was a loving soul no matter what the circumstances. Only time would tell the effects of what these two uniformed pillars of society were to inflict on such a young child. They saw it as just another arrest, the banality of routine. I saw it as my genesis and they provided the baptism of a life, the story of which I will leave the world to decide.

CHAPTER 2

THE INEVITABLE COURT CASE LOOMED and I was to appear in the Children's Court deep in the heart of Dublin Castle. I was looking my best and dressed in my Sunday clothes, and my Ma was also getting herself ready, as though she was going to church and it was true to say a few prayers were being said. 'Son,' she said 'I hope this will teach you a lesson and that you will never steal again.'

'I never stole anything, ma,' I protested. 'Redser did and he gave it to me. They never got the rest of the money, Ma. I hid it under a slate of the roof outhouse, in a little tin box.'

A tramp I knew had helped me to change it to smaller denominations after he had taken his share of it.

To get to the Castle we walked down O'Connell Street and on to the Quays. From there we crossed the Halfpenny Bridge, up Parliament Street and into the courts. Inside there were many children, most with their mothers and fathers hanging around outside the Court House. Some of them were dressed in their Sunday best. It was these parents who knew the score and knew that the better they presented themselves and showed respect to the courts the lighter the sentences would be. The less knowing were badly dressed and I supposed I was somewhere in the middle. All there was left to do was wait until one's name was called. So we just hung around outside the main door, surrounded by young kids smoking fags as if their life depended on it.

I could see the copper who was dealing with my case standing in the background. It was to him I owed this dilemma. There were also other boys I knew, among them. I could see Redser, Jobo and Hatchet.

'What are you doing here?' Jobo asked plaintively.

I told him I was up for theft but I hadn't thieved from anyone. Redser did know why I was there but he was keeping quiet. I had never squealed on him, nor had I told anyone where I got the money from. The three of them were in court for an unrelated offence. They had been caught stealing from a large department store in the city centre.

Hearing my name being called I allowed myself to be led into the court by a court clerk who with the passage of time I was to get to know better. Inside the dark paneled court, filled with the curious, court reporters and functionaries sat a woman judge. I was the centre of unwanted attraction as I was instructed to stand facing the judge with my Ma standing just a little behind me.

The Clerk of the Court read out the charge made against me, the theft of £5 from a person or persons unknown.

The judge held my gaze and her words seemed frozen in the court's silence. 'Did you steal this money, young man?'

'No, I got it for my birthday.'

'And your birthday, when was it?'

'Last year,' said I.

There was a sniggering from around the court as my piping voice gave her my explanation.

Exasperated, the judge then enquired as to whether or not I had a mother and father. The policeman standing in the witness box confirmed I had both parents. She asked if the father was known to the policeman, to which he replied he was not. Her next question, again directed to the policeman, was to ask if my father was a working man.

'I believe so, ma'am.'

'That being the case I am fining you ten shillings and you have one month to pay. Next case please.'

Uncomprehendingly I turned to my Ma: 'what's happening, Ma?'

She told me to shush and added that she would explain a little later. As we walked from the court the assembled boys were filled with curiosity.

'What did you get?'

'A fine. I got fined ten shillings.' I told them.

'You lucky bastard,' said Redser, which was ironic considering that it was his fault that I was there at all.

Outside in the fresh air I felt some self-confidence returning. As we headed towards home, Ma said to me 'I will take you past Hector Greys and get you a little something.'

Hector Greys was a shop in Liffey Street that was like an Aladdin's Cave full of goodies that all kids love.

It seemed everything was going in the opposite direction to the one I had imagined. The shop was crammed with children's toys. This was the shop to which Uncle William; my godfather had taken me on my 10th birthday. He had invited me to choose anything from the window. I had chosen a cowboy outfit, which fitted me perfectly. I imagined myself to be the perfect likeness of the Lone Ranger. Ma's suggestion that I buy a yo-yo wasn't quite as generous but the unexpectedness more than made up for it.

Having been dealt with by the court I soon learned that as a rite of boyish passage I now had what is called 'form.' This had consequences that would never be welcome. It meant the Garda could pick me up as and when they pleased. By my misdemeanor I had exposed myself as a potential criminal. They also had the power to visit our home as and when they wished and they did, they would stop you any time they saw you on the street and body searched you.

They wasted little time in putting their advantage to what they might call good use. Returning home from school a week later I was pounced upon by a Garda in plain clothes. The reason for his stopping me was my having stuffed my school satchel up my pullover.

'What have you got up there, you little shite?' he barked as he roughly pulled the bag from under my school jumper.

There was disappointment written large on his face as he searched through the bag only to find school books. Contemptuously spilling them over the pavement he kicked the now empty bag across the pavement.

This was observed by passers-by, one of whom rushed over and confronted him. He could clearly see I was frightened and upset by the encounter.

'You fucking idiot, you rozzer,' the man said with measured disdain for the police officer. 'He's only a child for God's sake. Why don't you pick on someone who's your own size you big thick?'

As the policemen snorted and strode on his way, I realised I was now a marked kid.

CHAPTER 3

Things at home weren't looking too good either. Da had lost his job and was already ranting that there was no way he would be able to pay the ten shilling fine. Ma, at her wits end, said she would try to find the money. She was equally determined I wouldn't be taken away from her. I was confused by the fuss and unclear as to what being taken away meant. More important to me was Redser telling me that as I had not squealed to the rozzers I was welcome to become one of his trusted inner circle.

But I remembered that I still had some of the money hidden in a tin in the back yard, but would it be wise to produce it? To pay the fine? I thought it was better not to mention it.

Redser now had a more daring plan that involved taking money from the bakers' vans rather than just bread and cakes. As I was small I was given the task of hanging around the bakery's gates and to act as an observer. No one was going to take much notice of a youngster. Redser told me that I was to note when the firm's drivers returned from their rounds and to note their routine on parking their vehicles. After three days of this, I was feeling discouraged. I couldn't see there being any likelihood of their leaving their takings in the vans. Redser didn't appear too pleased at my disappointment and feeling deflated we left things at that. Already their wayward minds were focusing on other victims.

Redser, Jobo and Hatchet were pupils at a school known as the redbrick slaughterhouse, situated at the top of Summerhill. Each day they went to the school just for an hour during which time their names were registered as being present. Then, during the mid-morning break, over the wall they went to spend their day as they wished.

The teachers knew well what was going on, perhaps they were equally glad to be rid of their wayward charges, or feared their elder brothers who were adept at intimidation.

I did go to school each day and stick to the routine but I was under pressure from Redser's group to join them in their daily shenanigans. I seemed to be getting more involved but being so young I couldn't figure my way out of their influence. It wasn't long before I too was mitching from school with them.

The first occasion I did so I hid my schoolbag in a derelict building in Gardiner Place. As I did so I saw a man eying me up and down from a balcony of a block of flats nearby but it didn't concern me. A schoolbag was hardly likely to be of any interest to him. That day we spent at St Stephen's Green. There wasn't much to do except wander, chat between ourselves and look at the park's ducks. The only excitement was when on our way back we each grabbed an apple from a barrow boy's stall and ran like the wind, a great craic.

The fun ended when returning to the derelict building where I had left my schoolbag I found it had been taken. Fuck! I was in the shite big time, I thought to myself. What do I do now? Ma was getting the dinner ready when I arrived home without my bag and being distracted by her chores she failed to notice. 'How was school today?' she called.

'Great, Ma.'

'Tell me, what did you learn today?'

'I don't know, Ma. I am not sure.'

'Typical kids,' she said to no one in particular. 'Go out and play awhile but don't go too far away. I will call you in when your dinner's ready.'

Playing was the last thing on my mind as I sat on the steps with my chin on my knees moodily contemplating my predicament. Fuck, where the hell was I going to get another bag and books? Dejected I forgot my mother's advice that I stay close to home. Wandering down Parnell Street to Gardiner Street I hoped to see Redser who could perhaps come up with something to get me out of the mess. Again I was in trouble because of my association with my wayward friend.

Walking past Hill Street I bumped into skinny Sally who asked me how I was. I told her that I am grand though I was sure I don't look it. Sally was a bit older than I, perhaps fourteen but I couldn't be certain. A bit of a hussy with blonde mousey hair she was making the most of her prepubescent curves. The skirt she was wearing revealed what she had for lunch that day but the attention she got was clearly what motivated the girl.

'Maybe you want to go for a walk then.' she said invitingly. 'We could just walk up to Mountjoy Square and maybe lie on the grass for a little while?'

Jesus! Lie with Sally on the grass? There is no way I was going to fall for that one, me being not too sure of what she would want to do in the park when we got there. Some of the lads said she was gamey, whatever that means. There was no way I was going to find out either as telling her I was on a message for my Ma I took to my heels.

My next encounter was much more promising. Redser and Hatchet were standing on the corner of Gardiner Street with cigarettes and looking cool.

'You want a drag?' Redser asked as he offers me his cigarette.

I didn't smoke of course but thinking maybe I should do so I took it from him.

Taking a big drag in imitation of them my head began to spin, a queer feeling similar to feeling sick came over me and involuntarily I began to cough my guts up. My reaction had the boys' in fits of laughing, they could hardly control themselves. They were like those cartoon characters holding their bellies and guffawing.

Wiping the tears from my streaming eyes with my sleeve I wondered how they can smoke these things without reacting the same way.

'What's the story anyway,' asked Redser after the coughing fit had subsided and I had recovered my wits.

It was the opportunity to tell him about my lost bag and books. He agreed that it was a sad outcome to our day's adventures.

Hatchet had an idea: 'Maybe you can get to school early in the morning and rob someone's bag, get the books from it dump the bag, and then all you have to do is get a new bag.'

It seemed a good idea and would leave just the minor problem of arranging each book's dust cover. My mum had used wallpaper, I wondered if she had any left. I was fast learning the arts of resourcefulness.

'We're going on a job later,' added Redser: 'Come with us if you want to. We need someone to keep nix.'

'What's happening,' I asked.

'Well,' he said: 'We've got a trolley and we want to get a couple of bags of turf. We can get two bob for them.'

The trolley was made from a couple of wooden planks nailed together, with pram wheels or ball bearings attached to make it mobile. We would often take it in turns to ride down Hill Street on such trolleys. I agreed to go with them, it seemed innocent enough.

Going to the depot at the Diamond and running down the twenty seven steps we could see groups of men stacking sacks of turf. The bags looked heavy to me but I held my tongue. Creeping unnoticed to the side of the shed I took a peek to make sure the coast is clear. It was and whilst I was peering out Redser and Hatchet grabbed two bags of turf between them. Loading them on to the trolley we ran together, pulling the trolley in unison with me desperately trying to stop the two bags of turf from falling off.

'Geronimo!' screams Hatchet having successfully made our getaway as we boys turned into Sean Mac Dermott Street.

At No. 14 there was a Mr. Knobbly who was something of a Fagan and always prepared to buy what Redser has to offer. Each of my friends received one shilling each whilst I received nothing for my part.

'You have to learn more about the job before you are cut in,' explained Redser.

All I could think of is that I am a mug. My Da was right when he said I was a little gobshite. Telling the two I was off for my dinner I headed back by way of the Tuggers Market, a street famous for its second-hand clothes sales. They were spread out on stalls and hung from the railings on a Saturday morning. It isn't an activity one admits too and when going from stall to stall buyers kept an eye open for anyone who might recognize them so they could disappear unnoticed into the throng.

Our family got a lot of its clothes from the St Vincent de Paul handout centre, which is found at the corner of Mountjoy Square. It was there that I got my communion suit and shoes.

'Tuggers Market is for the poor people,' Ma told me.

It was made clear to us that we were never to tell anyone we had shopped there, to tell them instead that we had bought our clothes from Guiney's department store.

Dinner this eventful day was spam and mashed potatoes, which I wolfed down. Outside I had noticed working men unloading 45 gallon oil drums and couldn't wait to see what was going on. I found myself recalling my younger days, if there was any such thing for an eleven-year old boy. My thoughts returned to when we lived in Railway Terrace in one of Granda's homes. I was at a bonfire and one of the barrels on it was well alight and throwing plumes of acrid smoke and flames into the night air. A kid tried getting its lid off and received massive burns to his hands, which were covered in burning tar. I shall never forget his screams as he was rushed off to the hospital.

By the time I had my dinner inside me and scampered down the tenement steps to the street below there was no end of children running across the tops of the standing barrels. Each had their lids on and the tar contents were going to be used for resurfacing the road. As I crawled among the barrels, which to me appeared like a maze, I spotted skinny Sally amongst the playing children.

'Sally. Where are you?' I yelled.

'I'm here. What do you want?'

'Come over here, I am in the middle.'

I could hear her feet stepping over the barrel tops as she searched for me. She couldn't even see me when straddling the two barrels above my hiding place.

'Can you see me?' she called out.

'Sure I can. I can see you have no knickers on and I now know what you had for lunch.' I cheekily called out.

My insolence didn't faze Sally at all.

'Do you want me to squeeze down there with you then?'

I was thinking to myself, 'God, no. I do not want you here with me.'

My prayers were answered when she added 'It might be too tight and too dark.'

Telling her I would come out and join her at the steps she agreed that was a better idea. I must admit to being a little nervous. She was older than me and had got a bit of a reputation with the boys, but I was now eager to learn fast even if it was a nail-biting ride. Acting what I hoped would appear cool I asked her how she was as she joined me on the tenement steps.

'I'm fine,' she said 'I hear you're hanging around a lot with Redser. Is that right?'

'Yea. Why not?'

'He has a bit of a reputation you know. He is a bit of a rogue and everyone knows it. He might get you into trouble. You go to Marlborough Street school don't you?'

Nodding my head I listened as she told me that her brother, Mucker went there too.

'Do you know him?'

I told her I did not but had heard of him but he doesn't attend school all that often so we don't see him much.

'No, that's right. He just can't be bothered going. He would rather collect empty jam jars and bottles and sell them to the rag and bone man. He says that pays, going to school doesn't.'

As I listened to her the penny dropped and I was thinking what a good idea. Maybe I could do the same.

'Where does he sell them?' I asked her.

Sally was perched on the step beside me and looking thoughtful.

She replied 'Dominic Street I think, he said something about it but I can't quite remember.'

Dominic St? This rang a bell and started to bring back memories. Dominic Street was where I went to school when I was about six years old. It was a time when my Ma and Da had been doing a lot of fighting and had separated. As a consequence I had been placed in a nearby orphanage, St Joseph's. I seemed to recall that it wasn't far from the Plaza cinema either. It was at the top left hand corner of Parnell Square. I seemed to recall it was an imposing Georgian building with a Red door and steps leading up to it.

Her words brought back mixed memories. I remembered clearly the woman who used to bathe me. She was tall with long brown hair, always with a Consulate cigarette in her lips as she scrubbed me clean. Often she would blow the smoke into my face and I had recollections of its sweet perfumery smell.

It was while I was at the orphanage that I attended Dominic Street School where the Orphanage uniform was the required wear for us.

That caused problems because it marked us out as posh gits, the results of which were several beatings from local boys. I had no idea at the time that my Ma was living with her sister, my Auntie Rosie. I did think she was living in Bluebell and was already planning my escape to rejoin her. My younger sisters and brother were also in some type of home or orphanage at this time

It was on a day when arriving back at the orphanage and changing into my day clothes the lady who bathed me came into the room. I found it disconcerting when she started to rub my bare bum for I could see no reason for her to do so. I wasn't sure I liked it either. After she left the room I dressed myself and then fled down the stairs and out of the orphanage's front door, determined to get to my Auntie Rosie's. I had only the vaguest of ideas as to which direction I should take.

Turning left I followed my feet along to Parnell Square and on to Parnell Street. I recalled it was a lovely summery day with a great many people about. Taking a right turn I passed Moore Street where all the market traders were selling their fruit and vegetables. As I walked through the din of raised voices, bantering and bartering I kept my head held high, turning occasionally to make sure no one was following me. Breathless, I passed a lane I knew led to Dominic Street School and then walked a little faster. I chose the route through Capel Street where there were many more people and less chance of my being spotted. I was hoping that if by chance I bumped into the Garda they would think I was heading home from school.

Which way now, I thought as I turned right on to The Quays. By this time I was a long way from the orphanage and somehow knew I had to get to the big court buildings without my being noticed. Luckily I didn't seem to be drawing attention to myself.

I was tired and thirsty but knew I had little choice but to stick to my plan to reach Auntie Rosie's home where I would find my Ma. Keeping to the Quays I turned left over Kings Bridge. Taking another right I headed past the railway station along St. Johns Road heading in the general direction of Inchicore district. It did occur to me to go into my Auntie Peggy's shop but thought better of it. She owned a shop on Inchicore Road. At this stage I had already been walking for close on two hours. I must keep soldiering on was my only thought. I took a left turn into Tyrconnell Road hoping I was going in the right direction.

Somehow my instincts proved right and it was with relief that this six-year old wanderer found himself at Auntie Rosie's front door in Bluebell. My sharp rapping at the door's knocker quickly brought her to the door and wasn't her face a treat when she saw me? Her jaw dropped and she seemed speechless, as if she was seeing an apparition.

'What on earth are you doing here, young man?' she finally asked.

Calling her husband I heard him shouting 'what is it?'

'It is Maureen's young lad.'

'Come in,' she said ushering me inside, as agitated as a flummoxed hen. 'Where is your Ma, child?' she said as she directed me down the hallway and into the small living room.

At this point the anxieties and the tiresome journey began to have its effect on me. Mixed with the relief of finding someone who knew and cared for me brought a swelling up of emotion followed by cascades of tears.

'Oh, you poor wee mite,' she said as I sobbed my heart out.

'Here, let me put the kettle on. It is a nice cup of sweet tea you will be needing before any explanations. Where on earth have you been coming from now?' she asked as she filled the kettle at the tap.

'From the orphanage,' I cried, wiping the tears from my face with the sleeves of my jacket.

I tried to tell her what was happening, how I felt in between the sobs.

'The orphanage,' she said: 'What orphanage are you talking about then? Are you out of your mind? Are you making this up?'

In between the sobs I tried to tell her what was happening, unclear as to whether I was making any sense or not.

'You just settle yourself down, you poor wee mite. I will get you a sandwich and I won't be very long. Here, wipe your face,' she added as she passed me a warm wet cloth after holding it beneath the kitchen tap for a moment.

My auntie was hardly out of the door when she appeared again, this time with the sandwich and then another. I was still wolfing it down when there was a sharp rat-a-tat-tat at the door. The next moment two uniformed Gardaí were in the room.

'There you are, young man. Come along, you have a home to go to.'

The tears came flowing again but this time were added to by wailing 'I want my Ma, I want my Ma. I can't go back there, I want my Ma.'

'Now kid,' said one of the Gardaí with a note of sympathy in his voice 'You're going to be alright there. They will look after you.'

'I just want my Ma,' I wailed as another flood of tears came and the sobbing continued.

As the two officers took me towards the police car I managed to free myself and made a dash for it. Running like a little steam engine I flew over the garden fences, falling and stumbling through the shrubs. I was not going back there I was thinking. I was too small and not as fast as I thought I was. Within moments one of the coppers had me by the scruff of my neck.

Lifting under his arm I was carried towards the car with my two small legs pounding the air. As they pushed me into the patrol car my auntie came rushing out to tell me she would be in touch with my Ma and would tell her what had happened.

'Okay, lad, there's no use in you crying. You're going back and you will be well looked after. There is nothing for you to be crying about.'

'I don't want to go there,' I wailed: 'The woman who bathes me rubs my bum and I am afraid of her.'

At hearing this one of the policemen started to laugh: 'that's okay, lad, we all need our bums rubbing from time to time.'

Crestfallen and bowed I was deposited back at the orphanage to the delight of the long haired Consulate smoking woman, but not for too long. Early the following morning Ma arrived to take me home. It was then I only found out it was at my aunt's in Sheriff Street she was staying and not in Bluebell.

'Wake up, lad. Have you been dreaming,' Sally asked with a friendly shove at my shoulder. 'You've been in another world and I have been yapping away to myself like an eejit. Anyway, I have got to go now. It's getting late and my Da says I have to be in by eight o'clock. He thinks that all bad things happen after this hour.'

'Okay' I murmured, 'I'll see you again then, Sally.'

By now my thoughts had already turned to thinking how I could find jam jars and bottles. This could be a nice little earner I was thinking to myself. I vowed that the following morning I would be up with the lark.

I was and the first words out of Ma's mouth 'You're up early. What's got into you this morning?'

'I am meeting one of my mates and we are walking to school together,' I lied.

The truth is I could hardly sleep thinking of my new career in bottle selling.

There was a house I knew at the top of the road on the left hand side. It was once used by some kind of drama group, the members of which left empty bottles in the backyard. I made my way there or rather to the disused site next door that was full of debris and collapsed walls and we lads used to play here.

Climbing through the opening in the rusted sheet of tin covering one of the building's windows, I already knew my way around. I had played there before. It was a four storey building that had been left to rot and had been vandalised over the years. All the inner stairs had disappeared along with the building's back wall. This meant I could get through to the back yard, easily climb a wall and get into the yard of the building used by the drama group.

There I found crates of empty bottles. I could already see myself rich beyond my dreams as I looked around for something suitable to carry my booty in. There in the yard I found an old wicker basket lying under a window sill and it was soon filled with empty bottles. I had about fourteen in all and the weight wasn't beyond me as I manhandled my booty back the way I had come. It took me about half an hour to get back to Dominic Street where I found the rag and bone man going about his day's work.

'What have you got there, lad?'

'Bottles!'

Peering at my haul he grimaced that he could give me two pence for them.

'Jesus, that's great, mister,' I said as I handed the bottles over to him.

It seemed my dreams had been answered. I had a career ahead of me, financial independence beckoned. As I headed back towards the drama school I felt like I was walking on air, the cock o' the walk. Stopping at The Mullingar shop I asked the shopkeeper for gob stoppers and jelly babies. She wanted to know how much I have to spend as she peered at me over her spectacles.

'Tuppence worth,' I answered her whilst thinking to myself, 'you old biddie.'

'Here you are,' she said kindly. 'Are you off school sick?'

'Sick?' I asked.

'Well, shouldn't you be in school?'

Shite I found myself thinking.

'No, I have a day off to look after me Ma. She is pregnant again and I am going to help her get the baby.'

Telling me I am a good boy she asked me if I would like it to be a brother or sister I will be getting.

'I think it is going to be a brother cause me Ma has got a big head of cabbage that she is eating, and boys come from heads of cabbage.'

I was so proud to know this and couldn't understand why she was laughing as I left the shop. My thoughts were already focused on rising as early as I could the following morning.

On this occasion things didn't move quite as smoothly. I was once again filling my wicker bag when the back door burst open and a man careered through.

'What the fuck are you doing here?' he screamed. 'Get the fuck out of here or I will call the Gardaí.'

Shite. I was over the wall like a scalded cat and with heart in mouth and covered in builder's dust I careered straight into my Ma who was coming the other way.

'Now, what are you up to?' she demanded to know. 'Where's your schoolbag and why are you coming down the street like that? Why aren't you in school?'

I am stuffed now, I thought to myself as I tried to dodge her grasp. Not quick enough, she grabbed me by my arm.

'Young man, don't try to get away, you'll only make matters worse for yourself. Where's your schoolbag and why aren't you in school? Answer me.'

Bursting into tears at the futility of it all I told her what I had been up to. Rather than give me the expected clip across the ear she took me in her arms and hugging me said we had better not let Da know what's been going on.

'Come on,' she said. 'We shall get you to school and go and see your master, see what he can do.'

Somehow I was reminded of the occasion when a little younger I had desperately wanted to go to the cinema. I couldn't afford to pay so on arrival at the cinema I started to cry and telling them I was lost and my Ma was inside. They allowed me through into the darkened picture house. I must have been in there for hours, thoroughly engrossed in whatever the movie was, before I ventured outside again. By this time it was dark, the first time I had ever been out on my own in the dark and it terrified me.

Not surprisingly my mother was out of her mind by the time I got home, a priest was with her and he wanted to take me away, or so I thought. He was there to giving me a good telling off, just to put the fear of God in me.

It was just as well my Da wasn't home. He was at sea having secured a rating berth on a ship. Such were my recollections as Ma got me to school where she had a quiet word with the teacher about acquiring a new set of books. On reaching home I found there was a new schoolbag waiting for me too. The evening was spent putting wallpaper dustcovers on each of the books.

'Son,' Ma said as we folded and pasted the dustcovers. 'You need to go to school, it is so important you do so. I know you don't think it very important but everything you learn will be useful to you in later life.'

I was hardly the only child not to take too much notice of a mother's words of advice.

CHAPTER 4

Saturday mornings were something we all looked forward to. It was the Saturday matinee at the flicks as the cinema was then called. It was our habit to go to the Electric Cinema in Talbot Street under the railway bridge and join the 'four penny' rush. In 1964 this got you two movies but you had to sit on hard wooden benches from where you could hardly hear yourself thinking with the rest of the kids hollering. The movie must have made an impression because we all emerged as either cowboys or Indians. The movies certainly fired a child's imagination. I had already made my mind up to make my way to America and be a cowboy when I grew up. It was either that or carry on as we were, using the weekends up by playing in half demolished tenement houses.

This activity was perhaps even more dangerous than that of being a cowboy. I once stood on a rusty nail, which merited a trip to the hospital. I had to be checked out for blood poisoning. It was an accident waiting to happen as we couldn't afford shoe repairs and a sole-sized piece of cardboard being inserted into the shoe would usually put matters right, until it rained and then the cardboard was rendered useless.

Childhood urban myth had it that if you cut your hand between the first finger and thumb you could get lock jaw, an ailment that terrified us. It didn't help that, apart from the obvious, no one seemed to know what lock jaw led to or how long it lasted or what it really was.

A welcome break had been the annual summer holiday to Balbriggan organised by one of the religious groups. A particularly memorable holiday was when during my eighth year I was chucked into the sea by the older boys. Still wearing my clothes I was floundering and terrified but it was great fun to them, especially as I was a non-swimmer.

I was petrified and screaming. Salt was rubbed into the wounds when on reaching the shore and still spluttering I saw the outline of a figure in the window of the nearby building, it was one of the sisters wearing her white robes. From the window she had watched the entire episode and later, calling me over, scolded me for leaping into the sea with my pants and vest on. She made it clear I would be sent straight home if I were to repeat such foolishness. What a silly old bat, I thought to myself. It was past time she had her spectacles replaced. Surely she had seen that I had been thrown in?

On this present Saturday morning after the movies I decided to take a walk, to see if I could catch up with things by tracking Redser and the lads down. I knew where to find them; they were as usual on the corner of Summerhill and Parnell Street.

'What's the story then?'

'We're going on a job,' Redser told me. 'You're in on it if you want.'

I remembered the earlier escapade when we stole the turf and I was cut out so I was not about to be taken for another ride. I told them I had to get home.

'C'mon you little shite, we'll cut you in this time.'

'What's the score then?' I asked.

'We're going to the Town and Muck he says with a slight lifting of the lip, as though relishing the opportunity to challenge the status quo once again.

The Town and Muck was reference to the Town and Country Club. It was where all the country boys and girls would go to dance and meet. The boys stood on one side of the hall and the girls on the other eying each other up before asking each other to dance I was led to believe.

Looking at me carefully he said 'There's a way in, through the back of the maternity hospital. We got in there last week; it's full of crates of lemonade, bags of crisps and bars of chocolate. It's a gold mine.'

Deciding to join them, we trotted off down Parnell Street until we reached the social club, which was surrounded by railings far too high for us to climb over but we were able to manage it by climbing on to each other's shoulders.

There was a back door which had hardboard covering over its glass window that had previously been broken. It seemed to be an open invitation, a marker placed by an earlier rogue, Redser no doubt.

With practiced ease Redser jerked on the hardboard panel and each of us in turn disappeared through the aperture. Inside it was dark and smelled strongly of stale smoke. I could feel the stickiness of the carpet under my feet.

'This way,' whispered Redser: 'The drinks are over here.'

Soon my eyes began to adjust to the darkness and in the gloom I could now make out the stage and saw the bar on its right towards which Redser was heading.

'Fuck! What's this?'

He had discovered a steel box and we could see him shaking it and distinctly hear the rattle of coins inside.

'Fuck the lemonade,' he said, his voice shaking. 'There's money in here, let's get the fuck out of here.'

Rushing for the door through which we had made our entrance Jobo flew through it. As he disappeared through the opening his velocity was hastened with the assistance of a person outside grabbing the collar of his jacket and roughly dragging him out into the daylight.

'Shite, it's the rozzers,' cried Hatchet. 'We're well and truly fucked now.'

Panic stricken we dashed back into the bar itself, desperately looking for somewhere to hide or an alternative escape route. There wasn't one to be found and after dashing behind the stage I attempted to make myself as small as possible curling up in a ball. I could already hear footsteps approaching and then a man's voice:

'Come out, you little bastards. The game's up. Come on out because if we come in and find you we're going to tan your fucking hides off.'

'Fuck off!' shouted Hatchet.

'Shhhhh,' whispered Redser. 'Let me think for a moment will you? There has got to be another way out of here. Keep quiet while I think.'

As he spoke he was tugging on a fire exit door bar. Suddenly there was a clattering as the double doors flew inwards and Redser went flying back to land on his backside. I nearly burst out laughing seeing the state of him and the money box spilling its contents across the floor. As Redser fell three huge rozzers come running into the hall. One scooped up my roguish friend with one arm and leaning down picked up the money box. Seeing the game was up I emerged from behind the stage, theatrically with my hands up whereupon I too was roughly grabbed by the scruff of the neck.

Hatchet for his part had taken refuge behind the bar from which he was now hurling empty bottles at the rozzers.

'You culchie bastards won't be taking me,' he screamed at the top of his lungs. He had been watching too many gangster films.

'Here, take this eejit,' said the rozzer holding me as he passed me to the Garda holding Redser firmly in his grip. The other two police officers then went about their task of getting Hatchet from behind the bar from where he was still mouthing obscenities and throwing bottles, none of which hit their target. He must think he is Geronimo or is scared out of his wits.

He kept bawling 'You'll never take me, never.'

In the meantime Redser and I were taken out to the police car where Jobo was already in the rear seat looking shamefaced. Moments later, we three were joined by 'no surrender' Hatchet who had been hauled out from behind the bar by the scruff of his neck. He was still defiantly kicking and screaming.

There were two police cars outside the club so we boys were evenly divided between them. Both Redser and I were squeezed between two giant Gardaí and I could smell the strong pong of mothballs and stale cigarette smoke from their uniforms.

'Right, lads. You're well and truly caught so there'll be no fucking fairy stories when you get to the station.'

'Fuck off, you div,' Redser said. 'We were only walking by and this geezer says do you want to come in and help us arrange the chairs and tables for a function later today. We've done nothing wrong and I want my Da at the station, you hear.'

'You'll get your Da alright,' said the driver as we pulled in to the confines of Store Street Garda Station. 'No doubt he'll be in Cusack's pub having his drop of the relic.'

Separated from Redser, I found myself in a room now familiar to me, the room where the table and the chairs were bolted to the floor. There I was confronted by two lethal looking uniformed policemen.

'Right, you little fucker,' said the bigger of the two. 'Tell us about the little robbery sprees you have been on for the last few weeks and no fucking lies as we know all that you have done.'

'I don't know what you are talking about.' I truthfully told him.

My retort earned me a smack across the back of my head.

'Don't be clever, you little shite. I said we know what you have been up to.'

'I haven't been up to anything,' I snuffled.

My ears were ringing in my head from the smack I had just received, snot was running from my nose in rivulets and drops splattered across the table as yet another hand slaps me across the back of my head. The force of the blow shot my head forward so it hit the table's corner. It was then the blood began to spurt.

'You little gobshite,' the bigger of the two exclaimed angrily. 'Now we have got to make a report as to how you fell over and hurt your head.'

The smaller of the two policeman said it would be alright as he left the room. By this time I was sobbing. Nothing had prepared me for this. It was just as well. Had I anticipated their being so rough I would have shit myself in the police car. My head was throbbing with the pain and I felt sick. Had I had any bravado, it had long since evaporated.

'I want my Ma, I want my Da,' I cried piteously.

At this point the smaller Garda came back into the room. He was carrying some jack's roll and a cup of tea. Leaning over he used a lump of the jack's roll and tried to stem the flow of blood from the wound on my head.

'Drink the tea there's plenty of sugar in it for you lad. Do you want a fag?' The bigger policeman offered a pack of John Players navy cut.

I sobbed that I didn't smoke and I wanted my Da and my Ma. Pushing the cigarette pack towards me he smirked 'You might as well start now as never.'

My hand was shaking as I reached out and drew one of the cigarettes from the open packet. As I placed the ciggie in my mouth the policeman leaned towards me and lit it with a match. As I nervously pulled on the cigarette I started to cough and wretch, which added to my whining and sniveling and only made me feel much worse. The slightly built copper had in the meantime muttered something about my wound having stopped bleeding but my head felt like a kicked football and it was throbbing like mad.

'Okay, we're going to write up a statement for you to sign,' one of them said 'You can hold on to these he added as he passed me the cigarettes and box of matches.

His attention was then turned to scribbling down the statement, which claimed that all four of us burgled the Town and Muck on two occasions, today and the previous Sunday.

As he finished reading it out to me he pushed it across the table top and glowered 'Sign it!'

'I can't and I will not,' I said having found some of my wits. 'I was only there today and I cannot sign for the other three.' Young as I was I was under no illusions as to my standing in the community if I grassed on my mates.

'Okay! We'll fucking change it then won't we,' he snarled with obvious distaste at my poor attempt at rebellion.

The revised statement was nearer the truth, but not the truth. It stated simply that I broke into the hall and stole minerals and a money box. Signing it, I pushed it back towards him, after which I was led out to the front desk to find my Ma waiting for me. Her expression told me she wasn't too happy to see me but I was delighted to see her.

Taking one look at my appearance she started to shout at the guards, demanding to know what they had been doing to me. Emphatically she wanted to know the reason for my bloodied and bruised head.

'He fell over when he was trying to get away from us,' the smaller of the two policemen said without a blink of his lying eyes.

I gathered that was the matter satisfactorily dealt with as they knew well that a policeman's version of events counted far higher than that of a slip of a kid. Ma's expression was one of contempt. She clearly didn't believe a word they said and perhaps rightly believed that one was as bad as the other, me and the policemen. Snatching my hand, she wheeled around and led me out of the police station. The police had their man, all in a day's work.

'Why do you do it? You don't have to get in these scrapes and you are never the better off for it. You always end up worse off.'

All the way home she kept repeating herself ranting and raving. Half the time she was talking to me and the rest of it she was talking to herself. All I wanted to do was get home. My head was throbbing with the pain from the blow and the sweet oblivion of sleep was all I yearned for.

On the following day I looked for the lads and found them but they were in no mood to see me. Each of them was scowling as they watched my approach.

'What did you tell the fucking coppers?' Redser roared. 'I am going to kill you, you little fuckin shite.'

'Nothing, I told them nothing,' I wailed as I waited for the expected blows to fall.

They didn't come but Hatchet's words were as stinging.

'They said you were singing like a canary,' he grimaced.

'No, no,' I cried. 'I never said anything about you three. They charged only me for doing the job. They tried to get me for doing both Sundays but I wouldn't do it, I only admitted to this Sunday. I was out with my auntie last Sunday and could prove it.'

'Did you plead guilty to it then?'

'I had to.' I told Redser. 'We were in the fucking Town and Muck when we were grabbed. What was the point in saying I wasn't there?'

'You never plead guilty,' he snarled. 'Even when you are caught red-handed. Us three have been let go as we're only kids and wouldn't admit to it so you're the eejit that will go away on your own for doing it, you thicko. Now fuck off as we can't be seen with a robber,' he added laughing.

His words more than anything else haunted me through the rest of my life. Those words expressed the ultimate betrayal and what made it worse was they had betrayed me whilst accusing me of betraying them. It was a lesson learned. That was how friends could treat you. I would look at people in a different light from there on.

My case was due to be heard tomorrow and I was mortified my Da wouldn't be able to be there with me. He had just started a new job and there being no way he could take a day off it was once again left to my Ma to take me to court. My case was to be heard at the same Children's Court in Dublin Castle. It was my heartfelt wish that the same judge wouldn't be hearing my case as I still hadn't paid the ten shilling fine from my last appearance.

Despite it being June the rain was coming down in stair rods as we set out. It was nine o'clock and we had to be there for the hour of ten. Ma assured me there was plenty of time.

'Get here, under the umbrella,' she said. 'You'll be getting your good clothes wet.'

We trotted on our way, Ma holding my hand tightly. Little did I know it would be nearly two years before I would again see North Great George's Street?

As we approached the forbidding court buildings with their black soot-laden sandstone blocks I could see a lot of youngsters hanging around outside. Ma pulled me inside the doors and into the hallway to escape the rain outside. Others were crowded in there for the same reason and among them all I could see the bigger of the two policemen who had taken my statement. As soon as he set eyes on Ma and me he came over.

As though it was a mere pleasantry exchanged between us he told us that my case should be dealt with by eleven o'clock. Had I but realised what my fate was to be the wait would have been much longer for I would have been out of that court building like a scalded cat.

As we waited for my name to be called a woman emerged from the court room and she was crying piteously.

'My poor Jacko. My poor Jacko. He is being sent to Dangein for four years and he is but twelve years old the wee mite. I hope that woman judge rots in hell, the fucking toffee-nosed bitch. Rot in hell for sending children to industrial schools for years. All he was doing was trying to feed his brothers and his sisters, bless him.'

'Ma,' I wailed: 'What is happening? What's Dangein?'

'Shush, son. It's okay. He must have done something really bad.'

I noticed Ma looked pensive and was biting her bottom lip in anxiety. It was then I heard my name being called out.

We went through the doors. It was the same court and looked exactly the same except this time it smelled of stale clothing. Perhaps it was the effect of the rain sodden clothes people were wearing that morning. As I took my place as directed the female judge peered at me over her rimless glasses. She studied me intensely for a moment as though trying to read my thoughts and guess my background and wasn't looking too kindly at me at all.

Turning to the Guard she said in an educated voice 'He has pleaded guilty to the charge laid before him?'

The guard nodded 'Yes, your honour.'

'Well now,' the judge said as she paused for effect 'This is a most serious case. Does the child have his parents in court?

Again the guard nodded and told the judge my mother was with me as he looked in her direction.

'Step up, madam,' her honour called to my Ma.

As my Ma respectfully stood in the dock beside me the judge addressed her directly 'Can you explain to the court how your son happens to be growing up the way he is? Do you not have any control over him, and where is the child's father?'

My Ma tried to explain that I got into the wrong company and that I was easily led but I have promised her faithfully I will never play with the boys again and the unfortunate lapse will never be repeated. She went on to explain firmly that my Da was working, it was a new job and it wasn't possible for him to take the time off to attend court.

Turning again to the guard standing beside me the judge asked if I had form. He replied that I had and that I have an outstanding fine yet to be paid. I stood there shaking as they talked about me. I had no excuses to make but in mitigation I was only eleven-years old.

She addressed me directly: 'I sentence you to Letterfrack Industrial School. There you will remain until you are sixteen-years old.'

Immediately she had spoken she turned to ask the court clerk if I might be taken the same day. Rummaging through a few papers on her desk the clerk replied all was in order for me to do so. With that I was taken away and hadn't the slightest idea what was going on.

As I disappeared I could hear my Ma pleading for leniency. 'Please, he is only a child, can't you see? Give him a chance; he won't do it again, your honour.'

The judge sternly rebuked Ma, telling her the case was over and asked her to remove herself from the court.

'Next case,' the clerk shouted as I was taken out of the courtroom to another room situated at the rear of the building. Ominously it had a heavy steel door and had a barred window set too high to be of any use to me. Inside were two other kids about the same age as I was. Looking around I took in the bare green walls. Inside I was collapsing. I hadn't the faintest idea what was going on. One of the other two children was crying whilst the other was looking nervous whilst he pulled on a cigarette.

'What did you get?' he said looking directly at me.

'Three years and six months I think,' I told him as he looked at me coolly.

'You jammy bollix,' he says: 'I've got four years in Dangein and yer man here has got a month in Marlborough House.'

'Will I be able to see me Ma?'

'Don't know. They wouldn't let me see mine.'

I was overwhelmed by anxiety. I wanted to burst into tears as the other child was doing but being eleven years old I felt I must show some self-restraint. I had a terrible sick sensation in the pit of my stomach. I couldn't stop myself from shivering but it was through nerves, not cold. Oh God! What was to become of me? I was terrified. Would I ever see my family again? Where is Letterfrack? My mind was just a chaotic jumble of questions that could not be answered. Amidst it all, I kept wordlessly repeating to myself I must whatever happens be strong, I must be strong.

The other child had stopped his crying and from somewhere I can hear my Ma calling my name over and over again.

'Frank, Frank, Son. Son can you hear me? It's alright, son, it is okay. I will write to you. You will be alright. Be strong, be brave, you will be alright'

'I know, Ma,' I called back. 'I will be alright.'

Thank goodness she could not see me for I was still trembling and wanting to be sick. My stomach was churning in terror. But I reminded myself, I was not a baby any more and I would stick up for myself. Today and from here on, I was an eleven-year old man. Such were my thoughts when I heard again my name being called, this time by a guard.

I was led outside to the police car and looking around there was no sign of my Ma at all. She must have gone on home. The rain had eased off a little but the skies were heavy and leaden and there was a chill in the air.

'In the back, boyo,' the Garda officer said as he opened the car's rear door.

The seat seemed so big. He must hardly be able to see the small boy huddled in its corner. It seemed neither of the boys in the cell was going with me. Before the door had clunked shut I was already planning my escape. I would be straight out of there at the first set of traffic lights. It was then I noticed the doors have no door handles on the inside. Fuck! There was no way out.

'Well, my boyo,' the officer said. 'You will be having a lovely time where you are going. You will be cutting hay, digging up the bog. You will also learn to read and write, and how to use a knife and fork.'

He seemed amused by his own wit.

The big mutton head I was thinking how would he know what type of a time I was going to have? How would he know what I was about to endure or did he know?

As the car sped along it passed the Guinness Brewery at St. James' Gate. I had no idea where I was being taken but I was sure to find out soon. In no time at all the police car pulled up outside Kingsbridge Railway Station, a big imposing building. As the Garda came around to open the car's rear door he warned me against doing anything stupid as he took me firmly by my arm.

'We are going to meet someone who will take you by train to Galway,' he said as we entered the huge ticket hall where by the office I could see another guard.

As we approached him I saw he was a much older, a grey-haired man with a pot belly. He too was wearing the uniform of the Garda and had a raincoat draped over his arm. He was also carrying a brown leather box with a handle on it.

'Only the one today?'

'Sure, no bother at all,' said the policeman who brought me here from Dublin Castle as he produced a sheet of paper for him to acknowledge 'custody of the body'.

Survivor

I am not dead yet I was thinking to myself as the first guard walked off whistling a merry tune.

'Now, my bucko,' my new guard said to me, 'We have quite a long journey ahead of us today and it is best for you to know you can make it easy or hard for yourself.'

I had no idea what he was talking about. He then asked if I want to use the lavatory, saying we have a few minutes to spare. I nodded silently.

'You need to poo or pee? I will come with you.'

'No, just a piss, sir.'

'A piss you say, there'll be none of that kind of language,' he muttered as the back of his hand slapped my head.

The tears well up at his unnecessary harshness but I was determined not to cry. He was standing right behind me as I did a wee.

'Shake it, lad, shake it now.'

We walked along. The railway platform seemed endless and the train itself seemed to be as long. My guardian seemed to be looking for a carriage that was empty and eventually he found one. Telling me to make myself comfortable, he took a newspaper from the box he was carrying.

I sat up against the window with him sitting right next to me, barring the way to the door and freedom. Anyway, I was jammed in by the small table in front of us. Any chance of fleeing went out of the window as the train pulled away and the station platform slipped by quicker and quicker. I had been on a train just once before. That was when we went to Balbriggan for our summer holidays with the Religious society.

As the train gathered speed I gazed at the passing landscape without giving it too much thought. I was trying to concentrate, hoping for the best whilst willing myself to be strong in the face of anything. How things could change so quickly? It was only hours since I slept in my bed and breakfasted with my brothers and sisters. Now I was in a train with a strange man not knowing where I was going or if I would ever see my family again.

Placing my crossed arms on the table I laid my head on them and giving in to exhaustion was soon fast asleep. I later awoke to the sound of squealing brakes, metal set against metal and a juddering from the train as it pulled to a halt. Shaking my head I wondered where we were as the guard asked me if I wanted a cup of tea. I nodded that I did then followed him out to the crowded café on the station platform. I was conscious of the stares our presence was generating, a boy with a policeman.

'Two teas, two ham sandwiches,' he said to the lady serving at the counter.

After paying he added sugar to my own cup and carried our lunch back to the compartment. More passengers had joined our train and there were people in our compartment now. When I took my seat I stared at the lady sitting opposite to us. She looked elegant, a bit posh and had fox furs around her neck even though it was summer. Clearly seen were the fox's claws and on view too the needles piercing her hair. Her suit was plaid and she carried a large black handbag, which was a contrast to her flame-red lipstick. My guard acknowledged her with a nod that was returned by a faint smile.

Sipping my tea and nibbling my sandwich I listened to the clackety-clack of the train's wheels as it picked up speed.

'Where would you be taking the young lad?' asked the lady passenger.

'He is a juvenile delinquent.' he said. 'I am taking him to Galway and from there he will be taken to Letterfrack, an Industrial School that is for his type.'

She looked at me with a mixture of compassion and curiosity.

'And by the looks of him you wouldn't think butter would melt in his mouth,' she said.

Silly woman, I thought to myself. Now what exactly would I be doing with butter in my mouth? Meantime the two of them kept up their conversation about the weather and the country in general, which concerned me not at all. I was off into a childish reverie and my thoughts largely centred on - I was in the shit, how do I get out of this mess and get home again?

After what seemed to be a long time we arrived at Galway station. Saying his goodbyes to the chance encounter he took me, not ungently by the arm.

'Okay, boyo. There's not long to go now and if you're having any ideas about running forget them.'

Ten minutes later and we were traipsing down the corridor of a Garda station. It was an old building and its mustiness evoked centuries of usage.

Behind the reception desk was a florid faced policeman seemingly awaiting our arrival?

'Hello, is this the lad we're expecting, the one for the bog?'

'The one and the same,' said my uniformed companion to which the policeman gruffly responded by lifting the counter lid to allow me through.

'I will look after him until the brothers arrive.'

'Brothers,' I wondered 'what are Brothers?' I would quickly find out.

As he glanced at me thoughtfully I tried reading his thoughts but they were impenetrable. I sat and watched silently as he took the sheet of paper from my former custodian who asked the policeman to sign it.

Then, with a cheery salute he went on his way having explained he had no wish to miss the train home. At least he is going home thought I. God alone knew where my home was going to be.

The uncle-like policeman offered me a chair and it was a relief to know I was not in jail as such. I was not locked in but there was nowhere for me to go to anyway. There was little for me to do but to sit forlornly behind the counter as the policeman turned his back on me and scribbled away at some paperwork. On the far wall there were some presses with a long table beneath each of them. I couldn't help but notice the paintwork was bilious green and peeling.

'You want a cup of tea, lad?' He asked after a while.

The policeman lit his pipe and studied me as he asked his question. Nodding my head I silently mouthed, 'yes please.'

I couldn't help but wonder at what was going on in his head. Did he have children, perhaps a son my age? He had a gas ring from which I could hear a comforting sound, it had already bought the kettle to the boil or rather it was singing. It was a whistling kettle and when the boiling water was added to the tin cup its contents looked as dark as Guinness. It was so strong you could stand your spoon up in it.

'You'll want milk and sugar I suppose,' said the policeman.

I noticed the three stripes on his arm but could only guess at his rank. I thought to myself that he wasn't an ordinary copper. As I watched in silence he poured a little milk into the cup and then taking an old jam jar near filled with sugar he added two spoons before stirring the brew. His tea was as thick as stew but I daren't say anything that might be interpreted as being ungracious.

'Here you are, son. Get this down you. You'll need it after that long journey.'

His words brought me back to thinking about the distance that lay between me and my Dublin home. I might just as well have been on the dark side of the moon.

'You'll be wanting to go to the lav' then? The brothers will be here to collect you soon and it is quite a long drive where you are going.'

Without waiting for me to reply he ushered me out to the station's backyard. The smell was something else and something I will never get used to. I tried to hold my breath while I was pissing but the stench will stay with me, becoming a part of the fabric of my clothing. There will be no easy escape from it. Nor will there be any escape from where I was destined. But I was not to know that at this time.

Outside I could hear a car pulling up against a backdrop of dogs barking. This was followed by what I would come to know as a Christian Brother entering the police station, peering around as he did so. God help us but Christian brothers they were most certainly not. He was of average size with grey hair trimmed short, a grey beard and with a portly belly wearing a black cassock and a priest's dog collar. His dark eyes examined me.

'Is this the one then?' He asked the Garda.

'It is, brother. And if you will kindly sign for him you can soon be on your way.'

I felt as a slave must have felt as my guardianship changed hands from the uniformed police office to the cassock-wearing brother. The paperwork signed and with a curtly recognition of my presence he ushered me out to his car, telling me as he did so that we had a fair drive ahead of us.

'Best of luck to you, bucko,' I heard the guard say as I exited the police station door. In the street outside was the brother's estate car. I recalled it was a bright evening and as I climbed into the car's backseat I heard its door slamming shut behind me. This time I was not on my own, in the rear of the car, separated by wire mesh were two large dogs. They were Irish red setters.

'Be a good lad and they won't bite you,' said the Christian Brother. His reassurances carried little weight.

I had never been so close to such large dogs before and neither of them looked very friendly. Such was my predicament as the car made its way out of Galway City and from there on drove along narrow country lanes bordered by hand-built stone walls on either side. The land was ever so green and conscious of the two hounds in the back as they balefully looked at me I tried to read their thoughts. Was I merely a curiosity or a new member of the pack? For some reason I noticed the absence of trees.

There were many sheep in the fields and we occasionally passed stone cottages set a little back from the road. I don't recall seeing villages, only occasional smallholdings and cottages. At no point in the journey did the brother speak to me, not a pleasantry nor anything to suggest his being curious as to me as a person or my reason for being there. I was in a dream world but hardly a pleasant one as I idly wondered what awaited me. By now the two dogs had settled down and were asleep.

Rounding a bend I could now see a large imposing fortress-like building and thought that at last we had reached our destination. It looked like a castle but I later learned it was Kylemore Abbey, a private school for girls. A further half hour passed before we reached a village and it was there that the brother swung the wheel and we turned up a small lane.

I could make out some buildings over on my right, we drove until we ran out of lane and then pulling hard on the handbrake we came to a stop. Welcome to Letterfrack thought I to myself.

As we stepped out of the car another brother of the order approached us. There was still daylight and from where I stood in the chill evening air I could see we were on the top west side of a square. There was a row of neat cottages running behind us to the east, and a big yard overlooked by two grim buildings, one to its left and the other straight ahead. On my right was a high wall and a smaller building.

The approaching brother was again smallish. I couldn't help but notice the blackness of his hair and his pointy chin. He was also wearing a black cassock with dog collar and his hands were buried deep under his brother's cassock. It was this brother who led me through a doorway and around the side of the building to what was a very big kitchen.

'There is some bread and milk for you, child. Eat it up as you will not be getting any more this side of morning.'

The milk was in a tin mug. The bread was in the shape of a small loaf and the butter was there but without a knife with which to spread it. Breaking the bread in half I simply slapped the butter in between the two halves and wolfed it down whilst gulping the milk. I hadn't realised just how hungry I was, the last I had eaten was the sandwich on the train.

The brother waited patiently, watching me with some interest until I had finished the meal. Only then did he instruct me to follow him and so off we went, into a yard, across it and through a door. We climbed a flight of stairs and from there into a washroom.

There my clothing was removed and I stood there naked as he handed me a nightshirt, a towel and a toothbrush.

'Wash and clean your teeth,' was all he muttered.

Having done as I was told he then took me through a door into a dormitory that was filled with what looked like endless rows of beds. Soon I found myself standing next to a bed on the right side of the hall situated about a third of the way up from the door to the washroom.

'This is where you now sleep.'

I could see the bedclothes were all neatly folded at one end of the bed.

'Make your bed now and go to sleep.' He said

Disappearing through a door at the top of the dormitory I could see a light flicker through where I could see a hatch of sorts. Making my bed I felt as miserable as could be imagined, especially when I again heard the mocking echoes of Redser, Jobo and Hatchet's voices. As I lay in empty loneliness I was thinking of the day's cruel series of events, not the least the callousness of the presiding judge. I filled up but fought back the tears as I pulled the sheet up to my chin.

Somewhere in the gloom I could hear the sounds made by other boys who were sleeping, light snores and snuffles and the occasionally creaking of a bed when a boy moved restlessly in his sleep. But not a whisper of welcome did I hear. I tried to sleep but there was too much on my mind. I instinctively felt I was at the beginning of a heartbreaking journey and wondered how I was going to manage my way through it.

CHAPTER 5

JUNE 1964.

'WAKE UP, YOU SHOWER. WAKE UP!'

The sharply spoken commands were accompanied by much clapping of hands. Jerking awake I asked myself what is going on. I felt as though I had been asleep for just an hour or so. Beyond my bedclothes I could make out the brother tramping up and down the dormitory constantly clapping his hands and barking, wake up. He was the same one who directed me to my bed the previous evening.

'Stand by your beds, all of you,' he shouted.

I half stepped, half fell out of my own bed then realising I was on the wrong side of it I scrambled over to its furthest side. From somewhere behind me I could hear sniggering. Glancing over my shoulder I saw a big lad with jet black hair chuckling. He recognised I was new. Further up the line of beds the brother was coming nearer and nearer, placing his hand under the sheets of each blanket as he approached.

He was looking for wet beds and seeming to know where he was looking it wasn't long before he found one.

Nausea swept over me at the sound of the perfunctory slaps that rained down on the hapless boy's head and face. These were followed up by a kick at the lad's backside. My shoulders hunched with revulsion as the child fell to the floor wailing and crying.

'You dirty little pissy bastard,' the brother screamed at the figure hunched on the bare floor: 'How dare you piss your bed, how dare you?'

'I'm sorry, brother,' the youngster sobbed 'I thought it was only a bad dream I was having.'

'Dream? Dream you say? I'll give you dream,' yelled the brother fuming with incandescent rage. 'Fold your bed and dry your sheets.'

Each holding our breath, we waited as the brother commenced checking each of the beds for a telltale sign of dampness but he found no others.

Reaching my bed he glared at me 'I don't want any more pissy beds. Do you understand me? Now go and wash.'

'Welcome to hell' I thought.

This then was clearly the way the Christian Brothers dealt with boy problems, with slaps, oaths, anger, fists and kicks. Under no illusions I realised that I had to learn quickly but cautiously. I held back whilst the other boys used the wash basins. I knew my place in the pecking order and had no desire to upset anyone. The ritual afterwards was to get ourselves dressed, return to our beds and to stand by them.

From where I was standing I could see the bed that had been pissed in, which was still unmade. The covers had been folded back over the bed's end and the sheets stretched out so they could dry better, they would not be changed for fresh bedding.

By nightfall they would be dry but carry the smell of the previous night's involuntary bed wetting.

'Okay. All of you in a straight line.'

The order was broken by chattering. Whack! A smack descended on the head of the lad seen talking.

'Don't speak before line-out in the yard, you fucker,' the brother shrieked.

The brother's name I later found out was Chinney.

Following the other boys as they trooped silently down the stairway to the yard I saw another group emerging from the same door who then form a line behind us. A head count took place and in rows of two we walked up to the church.

This was for 7.30 a.m. mass and would be a daily ritual come rain, hail or snow. We boys took our places in the pews to the left of the church facing the altar. The villagers from the surrounding areas were on the right of us. During the week there were only a few elderly ladies present but on Sunday that side of the small church was filled to capacity.

After mass we again filed down to the yard in a two-abreast column and on getting there I learned that we could sit around and talk among ourselves. I was instantly approached by two lads who seem welcoming. I wasn't sure what they meant when one of them told me I would be alright here, the brothers like the pretty ones they said as they walked away sniggering. I was soon to find out what they meant.

Once again there was a loud clapping of hands and it seemed to me that this was more often done than hands being held together in prayer.

This time it was a well-built brother who reminded us all of Friar Tuck. He was rotund though hardly jovial with patches of dark wispy hair pulled over his balding head.

Okay,' he shouted. 'Form a line, you know the drill.'

We did so and again in a column we disappeared into the dining hall, which was through the same main doors leading to the stairway and to the dormitories but set off to the left on the ground floor. I felt the gaze of Friar Tuck.

'You wait, boy. You will be shown to your place so just stand to the side and wait.'

As soon as the others found their places at their table and stood silently at them the brother took me to the first table on the left nearest to the kitchen door and placed me at the inside head of it with my back to a window.

'Grace.' He barked to the assembled lines of youngsters.

The lads having given the Lord thanks for what they were about to eat immediately began to chat among themselves, a bedlam punctuated by the sharp scraping of chair legs on bare floorboards.

Set before each of us were mugs of tea, a bowl of porridge and bread. I was to learn that the food we would receive would never be enough it was dished out in small meager amounts and you would feel constantly hungry. The boys fell on the fare ravenously, each trying to talk to their mates as they wolfed their breakfasts down. I gazed around my table but looked in vain for a face that might be familiar to me. I was starved and my plate was soon lick-clean,

I had no idea when I would next eat. Once again I was plucked out by Friar Tuck.

'You'll be working with me today, boy.' He said without any friendliness in his voice.

Outside in the yard there was a set of scaffolding adjacent to the outside walls of the building. The entire apparatus was on wheels so it was mobile, able to be shunted along the walls from task to task. By the time the boys had dispersed, Friar Tuck turned to me and told me to start climbing. He told me we will be painting the guttering.

I was terrified of heights. I often had nightmares in which I was falling from insecure heights and had never before been as high as the eaves of the roof. From up there I could see sheep grazing in the nearby fields and in the distance a solitary man with his dog. My legs were shaking like jelly; my nervousness wasn't helped by the apparent shakiness of the scaffolding, which I could only hope was secure. The brother could see I was so terrified I was likely to be useless at the tasks he had in mind for me.

'Are you alright, lad? You look sickly, pale.'

'I am terrified of heights.' I told him.

'Sure, you will get used to it,' he said. 'The best way to do that is just to get your mind off it by painting the guttering.'

You're a load of fucking bollix I thought to myself. I'll paint your fucking head if you keep me up here much longer. By this time I was trying my best to wield the paintbrush but my hands and legs were shaking with anxiety. There was a light wind which moved the scaffolding adding to my nervousness. To me the breeze seemed like a tempest. I could not stay up here. I was scared shitless.

Hearing my words he told me I would be scared if I get the feel of his hand and that I was up here for the day. I was left in no doubt that I had no choice but to grin and bear it and from that day to this my fear of heights has remained. The experience wasn't something to allay my fears.

Friar Tuck was hardly the worst of the brothers it was all still tough on a child so young.

We later stopped for lunch taken in the dining room where again I was directed to the same place as I had my breakfast. On this occasion we were given bread with jam, and a mug of tea. The room was quite empty though as most of the boys were working either at the farm or they were at the bog. Those who shared the tables with me had been working in the tailoring shop, as carpenters, in the laundry or on general maintenance work as I was. A few of the others were attending school.

Lunch over I returned to the scaffold. The wind had dropped a little but still failed to alleviate my nervousness. I was given to understand, instinctively and by example, the brothers' policy was to break the boys' spirits so they would become compliant with the regime. This they believed would make us men, like them. I hoped not. They were nothing other than an assemblage of sick perverts only too quick to abuse the power they held and to turn a blind eye, cover up for their accomplices in sin.

It had been said that not all of the brothers were wicked; there must have been some good ones who were driven by the ideals of their calling. This was not based on my experience. Furthermore, Letterfrack was a close community and no brother or lay person who worked at St Joseph's or lived in the village could honestly say they were unaware of the abuses that were prevalent there. Such abuses occurred on a daily basis, were routine and random. There was no one, person or authority to which a child could turn to. The Christian Brothers had a free hand in an isolated region and knowing it they abused it.

After work you went to the jacks to wash your hands where the stench of shite was unreal. There were only two wash rooms for over one hundred boys and they were on more occasions blocked than freely running. After this you went to the yard to wait until teatime. The same routine was followed day in and day out. Two single files would form and the column would then disappear into the dining hall. All meals were bread based; the youngsters were fed to the extremes of asceticism.

Breakfast would consist of one and a half slices of bread and a cup of tea or cocoa and on the odd occasion porridge.

Lunch two spuds a sliver of meat or chicken, peas, or carrots, fish on Friday mostly Mackerel. Rice and raisins, Sago.

Tea one and a half slices of bread and tea or cocoa.

Christmas or Easter roast meat or chicken spuds and veg.

After supper, if the weather was fine the boys would go into the yard until bedtime. If the weather was poor then it was the hall. The custom was, early to bed, early to rise will make the brothers wealthy but never wise. Depending on the time of the year and the Christian calendar, you could have on a nightly basis the Rosary or Stations of the Cross.

I dreamed a great deal. It was a form of nocturnal escapism from the constant threat posed by the brothers and the unrelenting ritual of work and conformity to prison-like procedures. During one such night I dreamt of a time when I was six-years old. It was when we lived at Sandymount and in my dream I visualised my Da returning home the worse for drink. Then too I had been asleep but it was his screaming at my Ma that had woken me up.

'I will fucking kill you. I will chop your fucking head off and you will be running around this room like a headless chicken, you bitch.'

Neither of them noticed me as I stood there in the doorway trying to make sense of what was happening. My Ma was screaming back at him, reminding him that he had left us no money for food or for anything else. We were destitute.

'How are we supposed to live at all when you are drinking and gambling our money away? There is no money to pay the rent and feed the children? I am leaving, I can't stand this anymore. I am not coming back.'

It was then my Da saw me standing at the door:

'Fuck off then, and take that little brat with you,' he snarled.

'Oh God, please be to God, leave the child out of it will you? Come here, son,' she said to me. 'I will get you dressed.'

Turning on my father she called him a bastard and told him to leave the house immediately, that he was a disgrace who should be ashamed of himself.

He set his jaw 'I am going nowhere. You get the fuck out now.'

Dressing me quickly my Ma took my hand and we left our home, pulling the door shut behind us. I was the only child at home at this stage as the others are in a home for a couple of weeks. Outside it was very dark and raining. I asked my Ma where we were going. She told me we will be going to grannies to see if we can stay with her.

A long walk was ahead of us with my Ma holding tightly on to my hand. As we walked through the darkened streets of Sandymount, Irish Town and on to Ringsend I was doing my best to stay warm and dry but it was futile, the rain was persistent and the night air cold. With my hand firmly held I had little choice but to keep up with Ma as we made our way along the river and towards Ringsend Park Cottages.

This was where my grandma lived with her man. I know him only as Ned and not as Granda, which I found a little confusing. This wasn't helped by my uncle and aunt also living there with them.

It seemed several minutes passed between Ma rapping the door knocker and the light going on inside. I can hear grandma calling who's there.

'It's me,' my Ma replied through the letterbox.

Moments later the door opened and my grandma was standing there. She had long white hair and had pulled about herself a long dark housecoat.

'What on earth is wrong,' she said as she peered at the pair of us on the darkened doorstep glistening in the rain. 'What do you want at this hour?'

'It's himself,' my Ma replied 'He is at it again. I had to run off with the lad before he killed the both of us.'

'Well you can't stay here. We told you about him time after time but would you listen?'

'Please, please,' my Ma was pleading: 'If only for the lad's sake. It is raining and we are both freezing. We can't go back. You wouldn't see us on the streets, not on a night like this. We can sit in a chair. Anything, we can't go back.'

'No, you can't stop here. You made your bed, you lie on it. We told you not to marry him but you always knew better.'

With that she closed the door in our faces. We pair just stood there helpless. There was very little help in Ireland at this time for battered or abused wives. Ma was desperately searching for a solution. We had to seek shelter from somewhere. Suddenly she remembered a friend who might help. The rain was relentless and by now we were both soaked to the skin and shivering as we retraced our footsteps to Irishtown and to where my Ma's friend lived. Her name was Sheila and she had been friends with Ma for as long as I could remember. She was a lovely woman and a great friend to my Ma.

She was really nice when we finally reached her home. She had immediately come to the door as soon as she heard Ma's knocking.

'What's wrong,' she said looking us both up and down. 'Is it his nibs again?'

My Ma silently nodded her head before saying 'Yes, and it is getting worse.'

We were both ushered in and I was taken to the bathroom where I was quickly dried and warmed, put into pajamas and placed under a blanket on the settee where I was soon fast asleep. Hours later I was taken to see some people. I was afterwards placed in the orphanage from which I was to later escape only to be betrayed to the Garda when I arrived at the wrong auntie's home.

But now I was in the Letterfrack Industrial School and along the rows of beds hidden in the darkness I listened to the other boys snoring, their dreaming sounds, the occasional cough or fart. The windows were bare of curtains and through them I could see the light of the moon shining on our small patch of the earth.

Tossing and turning, my thoughts filled with the past and the uncertainties of the future, sleep just will not come. As soon as I started to drift off a boy's coughing brought me back to consciousness. I wondered how many other boys are lying there in the darkness listening to the same sounds. What was going through their minds I could only wonder?

'Fuck this,' I thought to myself: 'I will never get to sleep this night.'

As soon as my thoughts settled the brother known as Chinney emerged from his room and began to scream at the boy.

'Swallow it, swallow it, you bastard. Stop coughing it up. You'll wake everyone up.'

The brother had already done that with his screaming and those he woke up must have been bewildered by his words and temperament. But little did I know they were used to it. This was a regular occurrence.

'If I have to come back in then it will be the end of you,' he cursed. 'Swallow it or else.'

His words were followed by the sound of a slap on the child's head. This particular brother I later discovered was a particularly notorious individual yet he was in charge of the dormitory that was to be my home for the next four years. I tried to imagine how long four years might be by thinking back that far. I had been six years old then and that seemed a lifetime ago. Eventually I fell asleep.

Clap! Clap! Clap! 'Get up, all of you.'

This was a sound that would echo through my life from those mornings when we were woken by Chinney. Afraid of what might happen if I formed friendships with others I had decided I would keep my own company as much as possible.

I hadn't forgotten Redser's betrayal had put me here in the industrial school. The other boys had their problems; And God knows I had my own.

The first week passed me by. Much of it was spent on the scaffolding leaving me even more frightened of heights than before. I was petrified by the Sunday when we went to mass. There were more parishioners in their pews on the day of worship. Sitting opposite the villagers looked very grand in the finery but to compensate we too had suits to wear. The younger girls among the folk sitting opposite would shyly look across at us boys and giggle to themselves. At the end of the service the priest would detail the donations made by each.

'Butcher, one and sixpence, farmer sixpence,' and so on.

If the weather was good we would be taken for a walk along the main road but never through the village. It gave a great sense of freedom if one was picked to go on the walk, even though we had no idea at all in what part of Ireland we were now living. The only clue was that it took a day of travelling to get here.

Sometimes we would walk in a double line which gave the opportunity to chat with whichever companion we found ourselves sharing the walk with. Not everyone was talkative though, some were withdrawn. Perhaps they had problems communicating or were afraid of feeling the hand or boot of one of the brothers.

On Mondays the dreary routine started all over again with clap, clap and more clap, clap until we were each on our feet sharpish and standing beside our beds, a line of obedient little serfs. Then it was church followed by breakfast. The work from the scaffold had come to an end and so I was placed in the school. I found myself in a room on the ground floor facing out towards the front gate and the main road. There were about twenty-five of us in this classroom. The brother in charge seemed younger than were the others.

Occasionally the brothers were changed to suit themselves whilst on occasion, presumably to allow freedom for some, brothers would cover for others whilst attending to their own waifs.

One of these Christian Brothers was known to be a bit of a lunatic. He always carried with him a leather strap that had lead stitched into it. This was about a half inch thick and perhaps sixteen inches long with a grip for the hand carved into it. I often wondered who made these leathers for the brothers. Who was the manufacturer of these lethal weapons that were used on young boys to inflict so much pain and suffering?

When he was using it on a boy the child would be required to hold his hand open and upwards about twelve-inches above the brother's desk. Raising the strap as far back over his shoulder as he could reach this brother would then bring it down with as much force as he could muster. This meant the unfortunate child's hand when struck would slam against the desk top, a technique that resulted in the victim's hand receiving a double injury accompanied by excruciating pain. The searing pain was described correctly as like having grasped a red hot poker. Often, as we were studying he would stride up and down between the rows of desks and for no apparent reason slap the boys on their legs or hands, he just enjoyed doing so. Many a boy ended the day's schooling covered in welts and bruises.

Another punishment was to make a child face the wall. This often happened when the brother thought he had inflicted enough pain and the child had taken as much physical punishment as he could with the leather. Often the boy would be ordered to kneel facing the wall rather than just stand with his back to the class. There was rarely a reason for his doing so, the ordeal was randomly inflicted.

Luckily for me I could read and write by the time I was placed in the school but many of the other lads could not. Sadly they left the school as illiterate as the day they arrived. Their sole purpose in being at Letterfrack was to serve the brothers and the state and not to be educated.

I recall the day I was required to work on a written composition, the theme of which was to be a storm. So far I had penned: 'A tidal wave had come in from the sea and washed away all the stones …' As the brother was passing my desk he paused to peer over my shoulder, to better see what had been so far written.

'Tidal wave! Tidal wave?' he screeched at the top of his voice. 'There's no such thing as a tidal wave, you idiot. Get to the top of the class.'

Tearing my work into strips his eyes bulged with fury as he kept calling me an idiot. He then firmly gripped my wrist so my left hand was held aloft over the desk and beat it until all sensation of feeling left it. I was then forced to my knees, facing the wall, where I was to remain for the rest of the day. It seemed my crime was to use my own imagination and initiative - something that was frowned upon, freedom of thought put the fear of God in them. They wanted unthinking robots. We were not there to be taught or to learn, only to obey their every whim.

There was no one to turn to for comfort or justice and so we had no reason to believe that there was another world out there. The school's regime was for us normal and we had nothing to compare it with. I had committed crime and this was my punishment and I thought it was normal.

Obviously, with the establishment being so isolated and far from our homes we couldn't expect visits. The only form of communication was by post.

I often received comforting letters from my Ma and in many of the letters there was a little money for sweets. I was too smart to tell her what was going on at the school as letters were left open for the brothers to read. Woe betide any child who spoke the truth and in doing so was deemed to have lied. We had reached the stage where we thought the vicious regime was normal for boys who had been badly behaved. Having said that, not all of the children there were delinquents, many were orphans or simply placed there due to family breakdown.

As I was slightly built I was placed in the tailoring shop but the job lasted just about two days. Perhaps it was because I had accidentally stitched my finger causing blood to appear on the cloth. This brought yet another beating before I was sent to the kitchen.

The kitchen was the responsibility of a balding and very corpulent brother who wore glasses and was somewhat portly. Behind his back, we called him Mutton Head. There in the kitchens I would endlessly mop, clean floors and surfaces and peel vegetables. I remember it was about my third day in there when, mopping up the dining room, I thought I heard a whimpering sound coming from an area outside the main door. This was under the stairs where the sweet shop was when it was open. Nervous but curious I eased the door open and peered around the door's jam. There in plain view I could see Mutton Head standing rigid with his back to the wall. Having pulled his cassock back I watched sickened as I saw the reason for the whimpering. A young lad, with the brother's hand on the back of his head, was sucking the Brother's erect penis. I slowly closed the door, horrified and shocked at the spectacle I had witnessed. Although I was sexually unaware at my age, as it was not considered in Ireland to teach sex education in schools and you only learned on the street or by friends, I instinctively knew what was going on was very wrong.

Naturally I thought such practices, like the beatings, might be routine in nature and was sickened by the thought of doing as that boy was made to do.

I didn't of course have anyone to tell what I had seen but I wouldn't have done so anyway. I could well imagine the beating I would have got had I been caught grassing the brother. Frozen with trepidation I continued to mechanically mop the floor and prayed the brother would never come near me. I immediately started to plan my escape from the kitchen job as I hadn't seen this brother work anywhere else at the prison-school. I knew I had to be elsewhere to be safe from his clutches.

As my dining hall place was at the top of the table I started a row with a big lad who sat to my right. Much bigger than I was he had a bit of a mouth on him and was from Limerick. I began to taunt him about his being a wet head which earned me a slap in the face.

That was all I needed.

Grasping the table I flung it and its contents over. As the crashing sound died down a sickening silence descended on the dining room. Everyone was in awe. The poor Limerick lad ran through the doors and into the kitchen with me screaming like a banshee in his wake. I found the lad quivering with fear under one of the kitchen sinks but as I did so Mutton Head caught up with me and lifted me into the air, kicking and screaming my wrath.

Kicking him as hard as I could I screamed my protestations but he wasn't listening. I thought to myself, you won't mess with me, you fucker. I kept on screaming my pent up rage and feared I was changing into some kind of nutter. I had really lost it and was in full hot-blooded rebellion regardless of the consequences.

From here on I was going to fight them and their rotten system, either I would break them or they would break me, there would be no compromise with these evil bastards. Even if they killed me I knew they wouldn't break my spirit.

Hauled from the kitchen by the perspiring cursing Christian Brother I was beaten black and blue. The blows and kicks rained down on me until finally I was dragged back into the dining room, forced to face the wall until everyone else had finished their supper. The repast over, we all went into the other hall as it was raining outside.

At no stage was I ever checked out to see to what extent I had been hurt, I was of little concern to them, compassion was as empty as was their souls. I was no more than a piece of meat in an abattoir. As soon as I had been brought to this place of the damned I ceased to exist as a human being, in my own thoughts too. The soulful part of my life was gone, left behind in Dublin. I did at least achieve my aim, I was sacked forthwith from the kitchen. From tomorrow I would be working on the farm and my days were going to start earlier than did the dawn.

They did and the first light often found me sat on a dairymaid's stool, bucket in front of me relieving the animal of its milk. From time to time the beast would kick the bucket, not literally of course and much of one's labors appeared as a pool of milk. The department head was a lay person: Tall and slim he was the son of the head farmer and had the habit of wearing a coat that made him look like an 18th century gentleman. He didn't carry a leather strap but did carry a big cane stick, useful for slapping his Wellington boots as he did his rounds. We knew that when the milk was spilled a cane across the legs would remind us of our clumsiness and so I did all I could to keep out of the way of the cane.

I quickly became adept at manipulating a cow's teat and could deftly twist and squirt the milk straight into my mouth. This was refreshing though it was body warm, a pleasant enough distraction too. As milking started long before breakfast and we were starving with an hour or so still to go it alleviated my hungriness.

After breakfast it was necessary for us to return to the farm buildings and give them a thorough cleaning. During the summer the cattle would be put out to graze, in the winter confined to the sheds.

It always amazed me how they would walk in a soldier-straight line as they exited or arrived back at the milking sheds. I was now picking up a new career as a farmer. Sure, it was going to be a lot of use to me when I returned to the Irish Republic's capital city, the nearest blade of grass being that at Phoenix Park. The advantage of being with the farm animals was it was rare for one to hurt me and if it did it was unintentional.

Farm work meant long hours of work. Animal husbandry doesn't work to a clock and my labors were taking their toll on me. I was twelve now but exceedingly skinny, puny was perhaps the right word to describe me. There was never a break in the climate for winter or summer there was a cold clamminess about the place.

It was having such an effect on my health I became a frequent visitor to the doctor for whatever remedy she thought most suitable. The doctor was an older woman who lived in the cottage facing the small pond; it was just up the road near to the farm itself. Her surgery was situated along the hall between the classroom and the cloakroom. The thing I remember of her most was the shoes she wore it was as if she had two clubbed feet.

I thought her being a woman she would be more compassionate towards us kids but her impartiality was such that she might just as easily have known what was going on. In fact, as she was the one who dealt with excessive injuries and chose never to enquire as to their cause I could only think of her as being complicit, even if only by turning a blind eye. She would have had to treat boys who had bruised and torn anuses on a regular basis, and I am sure she did not think that these injuries were self-inflected.

The only thing that could be said in her favour was that she was never hurtful towards me or as far as I know the other children. It was however a dereliction of duty for she was the one person who would have been listened to by authority had she expressed concern. She chose not to.

One day I was too ill to be at work and was just moping aimlessly when coming down the stairs from the dormitory I saw the door to the sweet shop was open, there was not a brother to be seen.

Cautiously I crept inside to find myself in an Aladdin's cave of confectionary. Grabbing three bars of Cleves Toffees I quickly shoved them inside my shirt and legged it into the washrooms. Oh my God, this was all my birthdays in one, how I was going to savour them.

Having hidden the bars in the jacks I crept back up to the stairs and into my bed, relishing the thought of having got one over on the brothers. I was still there when after the day's work was over and the lads returned from the fields they asked me where I had been. I told them I was excused work because I was sick.

'Well it's lucky for you, you weren't at the farm today as Titch was screaming your name. He was going berserk and was kicking out at kids in all directions while screaming your name.'

Titch was the brother who had taken over from Big Foot on the farm, Big Foot, a brother who had given me many a good kicking, was not as bad as others. Titch was a skinny little fucker and he clearly thought that beating shit out of a kid made him some sort of equal to Big Foot.

It was a wrong calculation as there was the time when, working at the bog I stood up to him. Only a minute beforehand he had beaten me black and blue.

Today, I hadn't the faintest idea why he had been screaming for me. I did see him later in the evening but he passed without saying a word. I never did get to find out why he had wanted me, maybe that was just as well.

Soon my strength was beginning to return and I was put back into the sheds and again milking the cows. Winter was coming on. There was constant mist, everything was damp and the chill was constantly in the air. When the normal routine had been met the brothers always found extra work for us. Their philosophy seemed to be that the devil makes work for idle hands, but as far as I was concerned the devil's work was already being done by the brothers.

Typically the extra work meant prising rocks out of the muddy fields, then carrying them to an adjacent field where we placed them on a growing pile. We usually did this task in single file and clearly some of the rocks were too heavy or slippery for some of the boys. I was struggling to keep hold of my rock and my right leg was stretched behind me when the lad behind me dropped his boulder straight onto my outstretched leg. My involuntary reaction was to drop my own, luckily on to the ground rather than the lad in front.

The pain from the injury almost caused me to pass out; everyone could see the blood coursing down my leg. The flesh behind my knee had been ripped apart but there didn't appear to be anything broken.

Titch had come running over when he heard my scream and as soon as he had seen what had happened he really laid into the lad who had dropped the stone. Battering him to the ground he was still kicking him as he lay in the mud crying for his mother.

For me and my injury there was no concern at all, he seemed more interested in the opportunity to lay about one of the boys. Whilst this was going on one of the older boys took off his braces and fastened them tightly around my thigh as one would with a tourniquet.

'This might stop the bleeding,' he said to me.

The brother on seeing this small act of compassion then turned his attention on my benefactor. He couldn't get this lad to fall to the ground and the child just stood there and took the beating being administered. His failure to beat the lad to the ground led to the brother's loss of face and his authority took as big a bashing. From that day on two brothers tended their youthful charges. I for my part was allowed to go to the doctor's surgery and was half carried there by two boys delegated to accompany me. To this day I still have the scar despite the best attentions of the school's doctor. I was soon fit enough to be back at work in the milking sheds and carrying out the other farm duties.

Because I was going to be limping for some time Titch dreamed up a job that would keep me in the one place. Handing me a sledgehammer he directed me to two huge granite blocks measuring perhaps ten feet by four.

'I want you to smash these into small pieces,' he said with a smirk. He thought the rocks were bigger than me. Again he was proved wrong. This twelve-year old skinny kid called on strength beyond his years and for weeks the sledgehammer rose and fell monotonously.

The chippings would fly everywhere and my bare legs became pockmarked with the constant barrage of sharp granite pieces. Again, the scars stayed with me for life as did the scars on my heart. Often these wounds would bleed a little too profusely at which time the lady doctor would rub some embrocation on my legs. I might easily have been a chain gang prisoner and yet I was still a child. Perhaps they were harsher on a child because a youngster was denied the strength and spirit to retaliate. If it wasn't me being randomly picked upon and beaten then it was another of the school's kids.

This was for us normal routine. There was no reason for us to believe it was different at any other such establishment. None of us had anything to compare it with and we accepted our lot with bad grace but without a thought that the excesses being carried out would one day horrify the world.

When not fucking around carrying or breaking rocks throughout the winter we were set to work hauling on ropes to remove trees. This was accomplished by tying the rope to the tree about two thirds of the way up. Having done this we would set about undermining its roots with our shovels, spades and picks. We worked hard until each tree's hold on the earth was weakened enough for us to haul it down. A tree's roots are almost as extensive as are its branches. Not surprisingly it could take days just to remove one tree. When the tree was weakened, Titch would line us up very much as depicted in etchings of slaves at work on the pyramids.

Then we in unison would tug steadily on the rope whilst the Christian Brother, stick flailing, would run up and down the line whacking us with the bamboo stick screeching: 'Pull, Pull, and Pull!'

This procedure could go on for hours with the tree as set on holding on to the earth as we were set on removing it. We daren't give up, if we did so then Titch would work himself into a frenzy in the belief that harder strikes and louder screams would achieve what muscle power couldn't.

To this day I have no idea why the farm's tractors were not used to dislodge the trees. But you can't whip and scream at a tractor. We often wished we were as unfeeling.

After each tree had finally been wrenched from the ground we would set about cutting it into pieces using cross-saws. The logs would then be carried up to the brothers' quarters. All of this took up time and again it seemed the brothers were determined to keep us working even when there was no real work to be done.

The industrial school was self-sufficient. Its livestock included cattle, pigs, chickens, and sheep. There was no shortage of fish and of course an abundance of wheat, vegetables and corn. The turf needed for the fires was cut from our own bogs; we were even rented out to local farmers at hay and turf cutting time. Everything on the industrial school's lands was fashioned into the perfect slave plantation. To these local farms I was sent out many a time and always had with me a packed lunch that included an urn of weak tea that would turn to stodge after hours of lying in the urn.

I refuse to believe the local population was unaware of the mistreatment and it was apparent that we were considered to be an economic asset to the locality. One can only suppose our misdemeanors, which accounted for some but not all of us, removed us from presumption of kindliness or compassion. The cattle were treated far better than we were. In the eyes of the pious villagers we were all criminals and thoroughly deserved the ill treatment.

CHAPTER 6

One afternoon I was back from the farm and in the dormitory changing my clothes when Brother Chinney came out of his room.

'What are you doing here boy?' he asked.

'I'm getting changed into some dry clothes.'

'Come down to my room when you're changed.'

I had no idea what he might want of me as having changed I made my way to his room. What does he want I wondered? I went to his room to see a single bed on the right, a wardrobe and dressing table. There was a large window facing out on to the courtyard below. There was a spy-hole carved into the wall and it was clear the brother could see through the spy-hole whilst lying on his bed and as I entered I found him lying on his back on his bed on top of the bedding.

Strangely, his hands were beneath his cassock as he lay there.

'Come, sit on the bed,' he said.

I thought to myself, no fucking way. 'I am okay here,' I said. 'What do you want?'

'It's only a little chat I want with you.' He said

From the way he was stretched out on the bed I could see why he was called Chinney. His chin was unnaturally long and pointed too. I could see his hands moving briskly under his cassock.

'Do you masturbate?' he asked.

Masturbate? What the fuck is that I thought to myself. In fact I was thinking fast and already trying to figure out an escape strategy. Not wishing to appear stupid I told him I did so sometimes.

'Oh,' he said thoughtfully. 'And when you come do you do it a second time?'

I was now thinking what the hell is this nutter talking about. 'Yes, sometimes three times,' I replied thinking this might be the answer he is looking for. In the meantime I couldn't help but notice his hand movements under the cassock are speeding up and he has a silly lopsided grin on his face.

'Sit beside me, boy, sit beside me now.'

I was twelve-years old for goodness sake and by this time I was totally confused and getting really worried. Turning on my heel I blurted out that I had to be off and then legged it through the door. I glanced over my shoulder and could see him chasing after me with what appeared to be a truncheon tenting his priestly smock. My feet were flying as I ran the length of the dormitory. There was no way I was sitting by that fucker I was thinking to myself as I took to my heels. Fleeing down the stairway I fled across the yard and up the steps. Seeing no one about I carried on running by the carpentry and tailoring rooms on my right hand side and without any pre-thought realised I was escaping the industrial school.

Dressed only in short trousers, boots, a shirt, jersey and short jacket I headed up through the gates and took a right turn along the lane in the direction of the church. There was a building on my left and a gate leading into one of the fields where we did our rock carrying. Over the gate I went with bitter memories of my having hurt my leg there as I planned my way around the mountain's side to see if I could find a main road and hoping that I would be heading in the right direction.

I kept on running, gasping for breath and occasionally dropping to a fast walk. I wasn't going as far or as fast as I should, given the mud of the watery bog and the gorse which scratched my legs.

It was soon starting to get dark but I could still see the mountain's shape behind me on my right hand side as it seemed to stretch forever. Soon I came across a river and had to take a time consuming detour to get across it. By this time I was starving and frozen to the marrow.

It was no place to stop. I had to keep going and my thoughts focused on finding a house or barn where I might find shelter. Knowing St. Patrick had banished all the snakes from Ireland seemed to take away the fear of been bitten by one in the long grass and by the time the moon rose I could see a little more clearly. In fact I was impressed at how well I could see in the dark, all the carrots my Ma had given me for dinner no doubt.

After some time I could see a hedge and a brick wall and set my feet towards it and in doing so found I was in luck. I was now on a road that seemed to stretch out in front of me in the distance. It would make the going much easier and enable me to cover greater distances. The thought gave me renewed energy and with feet pounding away I ran with foggy breaths issuing from my mouth as I sucked in air to keep me going.

I had covered less than half a mile when I heard the voice 'Stop, you little bugger.'

Fuck. Unable to see where the voice came from I thought to myself 'It is a banshee or a ghost.'

By this time I was in the middle of the road going like the clappers of hell flat out. You will never catch me I was thinking to myself as my small feet pounded the metaled road. At that point the big copper came leaping out of the hedge ahead of me and I ran straight into his arms. As I did so I was kicking and screaming, my arms and legs flailing.

'Calm down, boyo, calm down.' He was saying as he held me in his grasp. 'It is okay. You're safe and I will take care of you shush, shush calm down now.'

As though to further reassure me he offered me a toffee.

'Now just stand there and don't think of doing any more running'.

Retrieving a big torch from his tunic he switched the beam on and pointed it to the sky. I could see its beam reaching as high as the low clouds as he seemed to twist and turn it to make some type of signal.

'Just be good,' he said. 'We'll soon have you home, and you will be warm and dry in no time.'

After about ten to fifteen minutes I could hear a car approaching and as soon as it got near I could see it was the big estate car that first took me to the school by the brother. By now I was so exhausted and distraught I just collapsed into the car's backseat as the copper joined me.

It would seem he was just dropped off on the road on the off chance he might see me as they would know the best vantage points to hide in.

'You little bastard,' grimaced Friar Tuck from the driver's seat. 'You have had everyone up this night with no one getting any sleep and boyo you will pay dearly for that.'

Dropping the policeman off at the Garda station which was just before the industrial school on the right hand side of the road, we carried on up to the school from where I was dragged from the car and more or less kicked across the yard and up the stairs into the shower room. I was allowed shower following which I was put to bed. I was starving. No surprise about that but what did surprise me was that I hadn't received the beating I had been expecting. Little did I know what punishment was going to be mine for there was no precedence to what I had done, no one had ever just run off on an escape before like that.

On the following morning, after church and upon our return to the yard, I heard Chinney calling me over. Right away I knew I didn't like the mad look on his face and how he was looking at me with his eyes bulging out of their sockets; he looked demented to say the least.

'Run! Run!' he screamed at me over and over again. I had no idea what he meant. 'Run, you little bastard, run, run, run.'

Holding up his cassock with both arms he started to kick my arse as I began to run around the yard.

'Every time you enter the yard you run, you hear me? You run, you little bastard. You will run till you drop and then you will get up and run again' Do you hear me?

And so from that moment on each time I entered the yard I was never allowed to stand nor sit. I had to run all the time when in the yard. This meant there were days when I might have to run for several hours but that wasn't the end of it.

Saturday night was cinema night, a time when we could all gather in the hall to watch a movie. We boys always sat on one side of the hall, the villagers on the other. I believed that our hall was the only source of Cinema in the area for the local people. On the first Saturday after my unsuccessful escape, before the villagers arrived, I was taken up onto the stage. There I had my trousers tugged down and with my arse facing the crowd of lads who were assembled for the film I was made to touch my toes. I was then beaten, receiving a ferocious amount strokes given by Chinney using his special leather. After about four lashes my arse was on fire. All I could hear was his gasping and grunting as he laid into me with his leather. I was then taken to the rear of the hall where the projection room was situated and made to face the wall. The pain was such that my knees threatened to buckle and my sobs were wrenching my body apart.

I could only think that relief from the pain could only come through death. Eerily, the movie commenced after the villagers arrived and settled themselves in. They each passed me by but not a single one of them remarked on my plight. They placidly sat and watched the film from where they could plainly see and hear a child sobbing his heart out. They were unmoved. I am sure the movie moved them more.

Neither then nor now was I looking for forgiveness for my attempted escape. I just thought it remarkable that there were so many who knew of such terrible abuses but never uttered a word. The running rule in the yard carried on for three months and Chinney, when on duty took pleasure in helping me around by taking flying kicks at my arse. I also faced the wall in the cinema for the same three months.

What I had been subjected to was not a deterrent. Hatred was to grow within me for all the brothers. I was more than ever determined that they would never get the better of me no matter what they did to me. It wasn't revenge, it was justice. A justice that would put to right all the wrongs of yesterday and ensure they were never to be repeated.

Some kids went home for Christmas but I never did. Throughout the season of goodwill in Letterfrack the beatings and a myriad of other abuses continued as normal. One winter's evening we boys were in the school's hall playing table tennis, each game's winner getting the chance to stay at the table until he was beaten. I had become very good at this game and had a fast and mean serve. As a consequence I hogged the tables.

One of the Christian Brothers nicknamed Tea, a lanky brother who wore spectacles, would make me give up a table even when I was winning. One night in particular he started screaming at me for winning as often as I did. Taking hold of my arms he dragged me down the hall where there was a turf box measuring I supposed six feet by two. Its contents were used to hold the blocks of turf if the braziers were lit. This night the box was about half full. Shoving me into the box on top of the turf he then ordered some of the other lads to sit on its lid and bang like hell on it. Rarely have I been so frightened, I was convinced I would be smothered and to this day I am unable to stand anything covering my face. This torture was kept up for what I was told was thirty minutes but it seemed longer. This was because my crime was being good at table tennis and so I made the decision not to be good at anything in the future. All it did was provoke jealousy and that brought cruel penalties.

Christmas came and went and was notable only by my having received some money and a card of course, from my Ma and Da, brother and sisters. They sent money whenever they had a little to spare and never missed a card when it was my birthday or Christmas. The money could be spent at the sweet shop where there was a good choice of sweets, crisps and mineral drinks.

The winter was cold and the turf still had to be cut in blocks from the bogs. Off we would go, the small column of hapless waifs and strays, walking two abreast through the farm and up the hill to the bogs. Sometimes I was given the job of cutting, which was easier than was picking and stacking.

I would deftly slice into the sod before throwing the turf chunk on to the bank. The other kids would then carry them using their bare hands to deposit them on little stacks. There were snappy cold breezes up there, perfect for drying them out. One can only picture the grey images of underfed freezing kids, carrying frozen sod-blocks in their bare hands. Some would literally cry out, such was the pain of their chapped raw hands but brother Titch showed no concern towards any of them. He would just keep bellowing at us, urging us to work faster telling us the faster we worked the warmer we would become.

It was a vicious circle. If you had it good as a cutter in the morning you paid the price when during the afternoon you were picking the sods up and carrying them to the stacks. You just gritted your teeth and got on with it, all the time crying inside. At this stage of my life I had finally figured out that prayers went unheard. Those responsible for our religion and welfare were heartless and often sadistic. I began to identify God as being equally unfeeling.

Often several of us were selected to go outside to work on other people's bogs. It was on one such occasion I set out with about ten other boys. Where we were heading wasn't too far away, about a mile in the direction of Kylemore Abbey. Arriving about 8.30 a.m. on, to the best of my recollection, a miserable, bitterly cold day we were to be the stackers, ferrying blocks of frozen turf cut by the locals.

We had been hard at it for about two hours when one of the smaller kids lost his footing, slipped off the bank and into the sodden bog. It was like a cess pit and if it was as cold in the dry air, the frozen state of the water hardly bears thinking about. Titch looked on at the spectacle, quite unmoved as locals ran to the child's aid. One of them jumped in and immediately began to sink as we watched the terrifying drama.

Two of the locals took off their jackets and using them, and one of the staffs, they were able to pull both boy and man from the bog. Luckily they were both unharmed apart from being soaked through and so frozen their teeth were chattering and they were shivering uncontrollably. The kid was as white as a ghost and not surprisingly was in shock. For once we were not left out into the cold but taken back to the school immediately so the group's boys could be showered and given dry clothes.

What would have been the final outcome if the kid had slipped into the mire on our own school bog, as Titch would not have come to his aid and the consequences I could not think about.

CHAPTER 7

It had since been decided that I should go back to working on the farm, milking the cows and doing the other farm chores. These jobs I didn't mind. Certainly I had to rise at first light but there weren't many brothers involved in this work.

The local man in charge of the farm was a large pipe-smoking fat man who wore a hat most of the time. He normally dressed in a brown jacket and a yellow waistcoat and tucked his grey slacks into his wellie boots. It was his son who was mostly present in the mornings. He was the dapper one who loved to whack his stick on the side of his wellies.

Sometimes the milking could be great fun but not when the cow kicked the bucket. One that I was milking seemed to have sores on her teats and could get agitated when being milked. In one week she had kicked the bucket three times. This meant I had to be punished. On two nights I went to bed hungry, my supper having been denied.

We would kneel at our bedsides while Chinney would recite a decade of the rosary. Then we would recite out loud:

'Now I lay me down to sleep I pray to God my soul to keep. If I die before I wake I pray to God my soul to take.'

Pray. Pray. And more Praying, I wished someone would pray for me that first night when I was starving, cold and so lonely. But why did they pray these brothers? Why did they do what they do and then they pray? I could not understand it; it made no sense to me.

I know I was afraid of heights but I was even more afraid of starving to death so on the second night, at about four in the morning, I went to the washroom and slid the window up. I was then able to get out of the window and shin down the building's drainpipe to reach the ground floor. Creeping silently along the outside wall I finally reached a window set in the wall beside the door leading to the dining room. Climbing up I managed to open this window and to then clamber through it before venturing across the dark and deserted dining room. There was a bread press from which I took a loaf. Creeping back the way I had come, taking care to close the window behind me, I worked my way up the drainpipe again and into my bed where I sent half of the loaf of bread down my neck. Hardly surprisingly I had a bout of hiccups which stayed with me for most of the day but I was at least full and would be filled the next night when the other half loaf would follow the first.

Besides nourishing my belly, I had learned that I could get out of the dorm without being seen, and that Brother Chinney did indeed sleep and couldn't hear everything.

On the farm there were many hogs and sows. These were kept in small buildings opposite the cowsheds where the milking was done. There was one morning when for some reason I arrived earlier than usual and thought I had the place to myself.

I was in the cowshed going about my work when I heard one of the pigs squealing in a way I hadn't before heard. Curious, I peered through the window to see what was causing the strange noises. My jaw dropped as I watched the farmer's son exiting the big sow's shed. Running, he jumped over the wall to land in the yard, nearly stumbling as he did so and I could clearly see his erect penis hanging out of his trousers as he fumbled with the front of his trousers. As he recovered his composure he was staring about him and looking guilty as hell before walking off to the back of the yard. What was all that about I found myself wondering? It was much later in life that the penny dropped about what he had being doing in the shed with the sow. And, it was us who were supposed to be bad kids?

One day the head farmer told me the big sow was going to have bohniefs [piglets] and suggested I stay to help him deliver them. We had her in a separate pen to the normal sty and she was lying on a bed of straw. We settled ourselves down in there from late afternoon. The farmer had everything prepared for what could be a long wait and there were as many cups of tea as we wanted. It was a long wait for it was 5am the following day before she started to give birth.

My God, the piglets just kept slipping out of the mother. The farmer would cut the cord as each emerged, dab a little iodine on the piglet's tummy and then place each youngster in a straw-filled box. It was a sight to see when the twelve of them were finally nesting in there. All little pink things and with all their squealing it was bedlam.

'Now, boy,' he said to me 'you have to take their teeth out so they won't bite their mother when she is suckling.'

Producing a pair of pliers he methodically began to pull the teeth one by one. As he did so he put each of the tiny mites to their mother's teats so they could feed.

He told me it had been a grand night and said 'That's more money for the brothers' coffers.'

At that time I did not understand what he meant by that.

By the time the birthing was finished it was gone 8 a.m. and I was given permission to go to my bed in the dorm. Apart from a couple of kids who were sick I had the place to myself. That was until mid-afternoon when Chinney joined me in the washroom as I was freshening up.

'What are you doing here?' he asked me.

I told him about the pig and piglets at which point he came close to me and taking my wrist he pushed my arm up my back, like you hold a partner when dancing, before pulling me on to his knee. Putting his face very close to mine it seemed that he intended to kiss me. Fuck this, I thought to myself.

'You come any closer to me and I will bite your fucking nose off,' I warned him.

The words were hardly out of my mouth when he angrily threw me across the washroom floor. I came to a stop under the sink to find my head had hit something and I was bleeding badly from the cut.

'You little bastard,' he screamed 'I will finish you here, I will finish you for good, you little bastard.'

I was crying, terrified and trying to hold my injured head. My hands were covered in blood and the pain was making me feel sick. It was then that one of the ailing boys that was in the dorm in bed came into the washroom. He must have heard the commotion. Chinney just glared at me and stomped out of the room with his mad eyes bulging out of their sockets.

Grabbing a towel I tried to stem the blood before going down the stairs where I found Friar Tuck standing at the sweet shop. He took one look at me and then it was off to the doctor for her to patch me up. The sweet shop was just below the washroom so the brother manning it must have heard what had gone on and drawn his own conclusions. He didn't mention anything. The brothers always looked after their own.

Four stitches were needed to pull the torn scalp together. My fear of Chinney was now greater than ever and I was worried about what was going to happen next. I would have to be on my guard at all times as there was no one to turn to for help or no one to tell of my fears. A lot of the lads in Letterfrack were orphans or placed there for the most trivial of matters, often temporary problems at home. Often they were sent there because their father and mother had split and were no longer living together. Others were there for missing school and others were petty thieves, sent to keep the company of career thieves and those who were simply born bad. It was a one size fits all societal refuse dump for the unfortunates and miscreants. Out of sight and out of mind, certainly mindless.

The thinking behind the setting up of industrial schools was beyond my comprehension, unless there were ulterior motives, economic or otherwise. The environment could hardly have benefited potentially good and aspiring youngsters. Letterfrack and other industrial schools were exemplary only as a means of educating all youngsters, at the crack of a whip or an oath, to be influenced and educated by society's low-life. Their period of detention would leave them ideally suited to despising the society that had nurtured them, and to react accordingly throughout the rest of their lives. These industrial schools were universities of infamy that corrupted both supervisors and their hapless detainees. Each was a bloodstain of the Republic's escutcheon.

Fights between boys were a daily occurrence and the weaker children, when not beaten or abused by the brothers were battered senseless and ill-treated by the bigger and older boys. Such aggression was channeled or rather turned into entertainment by Br. Tea who decided he would hold a boxing match in the hall. Instructing us to fashion a boxing ring or sorts from four benches he produced a couple of pairs of boxing gloves. Then, with careful deliberation he lined us up along the wall, decided on one of the taller lads and handing him the gloves he ordered him into the ring.

Pulling me out from the row, handing me a pair of gloves he said 'There you go boyo. Let's all have a good laugh will we?' he said with a big grin on his face.

Climbing over one of the benches and into the makeshift arena I was thinking, fuck, I am dead. This moron was going to kill me.

Reasoning that the best form of defense was attack I shot out of my corner towards my opponent and landed a straight right to his chin. Startled by the speed and ferocity of the assault the taller lad lost his footing and landed on his back. I was not sure who was the most surprised, him or me.

'By Jesus', I thought 'I can do for him.'

I was sadly mistaken if I thought Br Tea would be impressed. Stumped at my unexpected triumph he gave my adversary all the time he needed to recover his wits and his confidence. The boy then came at me flailing but ducking under his swinging arms I struck out and smacked him good and proper on the back of his head as he ducked. Again he crumpled to his knees. What was happening gave weight to the maxim: It isn't the size of the dog in the fight, it's the size of the fight in the dog.

Even so I was still frightened out of my wits and all I could think of was that I had to avoid being hit by him because if one of his roundhouses connected he would lay me out. Undeterred by my effectiveness he bounced to his feet and was soon all over me, raining punches and hoping one of them would decide the matter once and for all. From somewhere I couldn't fathom I was keeping up my strength and spirit and didn't fall to any of his punches. Again I struck out and this time caught him on the chin, again he fell to his knees.

At this point Brother Tea decided enough was enough and the fight should end there and now. Taking the other lad's arm and holding it erect he declared him the winner. I had dropped him three times, he hadn't put me down once but he was declared the victor. At least I had learned that strength isn't related to size and that was a valuable lesson that would sustain me through life.

Brother Tea lost interest in boxing having backed a loser and whatever his actions the rest of the boys knew him to be a cheat, even the beaten boy knew that. The brother had lost credibility and been exposed as a cheat, worse, a cheat who loses.

Winters are very cruel on Ireland's western Atlantic coast but there was no allowance made for the harsh weather. We dressed more or less as we did in summer regardless of season. We were issued with heavier socks, a vest and a pullover but still wore shorts and so our legs were often literally blue with the cold. The only fire place was the one in the hall. It wasn't very big so just a few lads were able to gather around it. If you were small then you had very little chance of drawing any heat.

Fights among the lads continued to be a daily occurrence; it was the one anti-social activity that was tolerated by the cruel brothers. One day, outside the church a bigger kid was trashing a much younger and smaller one when he lost his footing. Immediately seizing his advantage the younger kid immediately got on top and straddled the bigger boy's chest. He then began to repeatedly head-butt his tormentor, lunging his forehead into the older lad's face until there was blood everywhere. The younger boy's rage had given him a maniacal fury and his adversary was unconscious by the time the maddened youngster was dragged clear. That younger boy was to later become one of Ireland's most notorious gangland criminals. No doubt such tenure was honed by his experiences at Letterfrack.

Brutality and fear was never far distant. It was a Saturday evening when I accidentally bumped into a bigger kid who was carrying a lot of weight. Despite my protestations that it was an accident he wasn't too pleased and probably saw opportunity for channeling his aggression. I was challenged to a fight in the lower washroom toilets the following morning. All that night I tossed and turned whilst sleep evaded me, I was convinced I was going to be thoroughly trashed the following morning.

Clap! Clap! Clap! Chinney was up to his early morning wake-up routine and we all heard him barking. It was now back to reality for me and I faced a fight with a bully whom I have no chance of beating. I had little alternative but to head towards the washrooms where it was freezing cold and the winter's mist hung over the outside yard like a wet blanket.

Fatty was there waiting for me. I had hardly walked through the door when the blow struck me on the back of my head. I fell to the floor from its force, thinking to myself, I am fucked here. It was then I remembered that bigger is not necessarily stronger. I remembered also the tables being turned when the smaller of the two boys got the upper hand in the churchyard scrap.

Leaping to my feet with the agility of a cat I ran straight at the fat bully and we traded blows. Clearly there wasn't going to be a winner when neither is prepared to give ground. The blows traded between us became fewer and soon, gasping for breath, we paused as we eyed each other up and down. It was he who broke the stalemate.

'Quit?'

'Quit!'

We shook hands on it as he said to me, 'You're some goer for a little fucker' before heading towards the stairs whilst hoping we had not been missed and our disheveled state wouldn't be noticeable.

The rest of the kids were wondering which of us had won and their jaws dropped, you could have cut the silence with a knife as we both walked in as friends. Chinney seemed unaware of the fracas, which was a relief. He was too absorbed in one of the school's newer kids and I was thinking to myself, Lord, help him.

The longest road is the one that leads nowhere I was thinking, and out here in one of the most depopulated areas of western Ireland in the nineteen sixties truly is best called nowhere. I persevered and took each day as it came. Did any child ever pay a higher price for being too trusting in his friends and such a minor infraction as entering a social club for pennies? I felt sometimes the wretchedness would never end.

We were into February and there was little of the daylight as dawn seemed to go straight into dusk and those longest nights were unending. I had got my arm caught up in a thorn bush. One of the thorns had become bedded in my skin bringing with it signs of infection. Taken to the doctor I learned that a poultice was to be applied. Boiling bread in a pot she applied the still heat-sizzling pasta to my arm. Fucking hell the searing pain was nigh unbearable. How can this be helping I asked myself. She was worse than the fucking brothers.

'Keep this on,' she said as she wrapped a bandage around it. 'Come and see me tomorrow.'

It was small compensation that I got the rest of the day off. I would rather have worked the farm. So there I was, wandering around the yard aimlessly when Chinney spotted me. Calling me over he asked me what I was doing there and I explained to him what had happened.

'Go up to the dormitory,' he said 'I will be up there shortly.'

When I got to the dormitory I found it unusually empty. There was invariably at least one ailing child in bed.

Walking the hall's length to where the brothers' quarters were I stood outside Chinney's room door. Brother Tea's room was on the opposite side of the corridor. It was while I was standing there that I noticed for the first time there were windows over each of the doors and both were open. Although they were quite small I was convinced I could get through either of them. I keep this revelation to myself; it might have some future use.

After a while Chinney appeared, took out a bunch of keys from his cassock, inserted a key into the door's lock and pushed it open.

'In you go, lad.'

Here we go again. This fucker just doesn't give up I thought as he lay on his bed and on this occasion on his side facing me. He lit a cigarette and drew on it as he coolly looked me up and down. The cigarettes were Sweet Afton in their familiar yellow packet. Smiling he took another drag and then asked me if I would like one. To be honest I could kill for one but smelling a rat I told him I would not.

'What? You don't smoke? Little rats from Dublin start at about seven years old. Take one,' he added as he offered the opened packet. 'I am just being friendly.'

'No thanks, I don't smoke.'

'I see you are back on the farm. How are you getting on there?'

'I like it fine,' I told him. 'I love the openness of it all and I am learning lots of things.'

'Good, good, It is what you are here for,' he said still smiling as he pressed the cigarette butt into the ashtray that is already brimming with cigarette ends.

'Have you been masturbating recently?'

'No!'

God, I thought to myself, not again?

Chinney said looking at me thoughtfully. 'Good. You know, if you ever got married your future wife will know you have been masturbating. She will know just by looking at your Mickey [penis]. Would you like me to look at your Mickey [penis] so I can tell you if she is going to know?'

'No, I don't think so,' I answered defiantly.

'You are never going to learn are you?'

'Yes, I am learning,' I retorted. 'I am learning not to come up to your room on my own ever again.'

I paused and then added 'Brother. I do not like this and I am very afraid of what is happening. Can I please go now and I will not say anything to anyone? I have not spoken a word about the other times so please, please, can I go now?'

'You will stay till I tell you to go,' he told me and with that he placed his right hand under his cassock and started fiddling around as if trying to locate something. I was rooted to the spot and afraid I would get a battering or worse. As my mind raced, he started moving his hand up and down but kept it under his cassock. Again he was wearing that stupid lopsided grin on his leering face. His chin was protruding and the effect was exaggerated as he hadn't yet shaved. With his black hair he looked as evil as Satan himself.

'Come boy, come closer to me,' he murmured whilst his hands continue doing ninety to the dozen under his cassock.

'I am okay here, sir.'

'Come, boy. Lie with me here.'

It was getting time to leg it again but I was conscious of the bitterly cold weather out there. Perishing cold and unprotected one wouldn't last long on the windswept moors of the Atlantic facing county. He then let out a long sigh and both he and his hand relax as he closed his eyes whilst I wondered what next?

His eyes opened for several moments and I couldn't help but notice how piercing blue they were and they shone brightly. 'Go now, boy, and not a word to anyone. Do you hear me? Not a word!'

Leaving the room I felt a strong sense of relief that he hadn't at least physically abused me but I couldn't help wondering how long my luck would hold. How long before he goes too far and rapes me. With my skinny frame I would be no match for his physical strength.

As I descended the stairs in silence I noticed the sweet shop door was open and so I dawdled a bit and listened carefully. After several minutes Friar Tuck emerged, walked into the yard lit a cigarette. I noticed he had left the shop door open. Sneaking inside I grabbed the first thing I could lay my hands on, bars of chocolate. Withdrawing quietly and moving as quietly as I could I made my way down the corridor, past the doctor's surgery and then to the downstairs jacks. As soon as I closed the cubicle door behind me I wolfed down the contents of the wrappers. Such was the mess around my mouth I put my head under the tap to wash away the evidence.

I had learned a couple of things that day. One was that the windows were left open over the brothers' room doors, and two that Friar Tuck seemed to leave the shop door open every other afternoon, especially when he went out to the yard for a smoke.

A plan was formulating in my mind about my next escape. It would not be as foolhardy as the previous unplanned flight. Next time I would be prepared. Staying here could only be worse for me now that I was aware what Chinney and the kitchen cook were up to with the younger kids. But who would believe me?

Next morning I went to the doctor to have the poultice removed. As she pulled it off out came this long string of gunk, loads of it.

'You will be fine now,' she said, 'We extracted the poison just in time so lucky for you. You could have lost the power of your right arm so you have got to be more careful in future.'

Even after a long day in the fields or the bog it was sometimes difficult to get off to sleep. I often found myself drifting into dreams or should I say thoughts of past times that were already growing more distant. Thinking of the past stopped it all disappearing and I had to stay connected with my past, my Ma and Da, brother, sisters and of course Dublin. I could still remember making my Holy Communion in Ringsend Church. This is where my Ma hails from and if you were from Ringsend you were called a Raytowner. This expression derived from the stingray, a lovely fish to eat and I find it as palatable today as I did then.

Getting ready for your Holy Communion was a big occasion. You used to go to confession on a regular basis but you could not take communion at mass because you had not made it as yet. I remember one day there were a lot of boys in the queue for the confession box as we had all come from school to do a trial run.

'Bless me father. I have sinned,' one would say.

He would then ask you to list your sins but what sins does a seven year old have? I told lies twice, father: I stole a biscuit from my sister and suchlike. But they always asked did you have any bad thoughts or deeds? At seven I don't think so.

On the day of my Holy Communion there were about three kids in front of me when I started to feel like I wanted to piss! Shit will they ever hurry up, what's keeping them in there?

By this stage I so wanted a pee that I was nearly doubled up with bladder cramps. Into the confession box I trotted and pulling out my Mickey [Penis] I could almost hear the hissing as in a vain attempt to minimize a puddle I sprayed the booth. By the time the priest pulled the panel back and gave me his blessing I was kneeling in my own puddle of urine.

'Bless me, my father, I have sinned.'

'Yes, my son. And do tell me what those sins are.'

'I am kneeling in a pool of piss in here.'

'You're what?' he bellowed.

'Kneeling in piss, father. Someone has pissed in your box.'

The small door promptly opened as he exited the confessional box and coming around to where I was kneeling he reached in and dragged me out.

'Boy! Why have you done this?'

'No, no,' I tell him earnestly.

I knew the kid who had gone before me was well out of sight and justice by now. By this time a small crowd of older people had begun to gather.

I heard a voice saying 'Oh, the poor lad: He has gone and wet his self.'

The priest was looking for the teacher. He just wanted me off his hands but it wasn't so easy for me. I had started to cry as my pants bore silent witness to my sin. My front was wet and the teacher cannot but see that I was the culprit. Why don't they put toilets in churches? Maybe priests don't piss or shite. It wasn't long before a cleaning lady approached with her bucket and mop. Dabbing me dry she mopped out the confessional box too.

There had been a similar occasion at Letterfrack. I had woken very early and had no idea of the time but I could feel the front of my nightshirt was sopping warm wet. The mattress too was moist and I knew right then I had pissed my own bed. I couldn't be certain it wasn't a dream but I was cute enough to do whatever was necessary to avoid Chinney knowing of my fall from grace.

Silently creeping to the bathroom I rang out the nightshirt. Then, returning to the dormitory I quietly stripped the sheets from the bed and exchanged them for dry ones from the cupboard. Climbing back into bed I waited for the brother's handclapping, which I knew was imminent. All had gone well, he never did find out. I relished my escape because I could well imagine the joy of Chinney had he discovered I had pissed the bed. Making the most of it the punishment would have included me running around the yard, holding the sheeting up with the air flowing behind me. This was a favorite form of chastisement but it didn't have the desired effect. All it did was humiliate and exhaust the unfortunate bed wetter. One can only wonder at the mentality of the people who dreamed such punishments up. One could suppose them to be far greater sinners than were we 'inmates.'

It might be presumed some of the Christian Brothers were kindly and those who were not were in the minority. The difficulty was in identifying them. As a body they kept themselves to themselves and they stuck together in a form of herd self-protectionism. All had good reason for not drawing attention to themselves. It was all for one and one for all.

One day we were sowing spuds and each of us were on bare knees and constantly prodding a small stick into the soil in the ploughed furrows. Dropping the seeds in we then pulled the soft earth over them, patted to firm and moved on to the next seedlings. Everything was done by hand, everything except the ploughing but I swear before God that if they could find a way to harness a child to a plough they would have done so, even a team of us.

We could at least talk between ourselves, even banter when we were working the fields. I hadn't made friends as such but there were a few boys I chatted to. The lad working with me that day was a fellow Dubliner. He was a tall lad from the district of Driminagh who looked a lot older than his fourteen years. He was chatting away about some old person who lived near him at home. She was by his account a woman who, despite having six children, was perfectly gorgeous. So much so, he said, you could eat chips out of her knickers. Yes, even without the salt and vinegar.

He wouldn't shut up about her, all the time repeating 'She was made for love. You could smell the sex off her.'

'Did you ever ride her?' I asked him.

I had no idea what the expression actually meant but had heard it often said.

'No, not yet,' he replied but added that as soon as he was released he would make a play for her.

'I can see her now,' he added. 'Lying with her legs up in the air and me jumping her.'

'Jesus,' I thought. 'Is that how you do it, you jump on her?'

Maybe that was why they have big diddies, to break our fall? Fuck! I would like to do that sometime.

'Move along, you bastards, move along or you will never get these rows finished today.'

I never heard any more about jumping on women, instead we got thousands of seeds of another kind planted during that balmy spring day. It wasn't in fact a bad day as days go in Connemara. We worked hard until nightfall and then as always, two abreast we wended our way back to Letterfrack Industrial School. As we progressed Titch kept on wielding his stick, striking out at the younger kids. He just couldn't help himself; he was programmed to inflict pain on the weakest in society.

Few of us could forget the expression on his face when two of his small charges broke ranks and made off into the adjacent fields. For some reason he was on his own that day and couldn't run after them as had he done so it would have meant abandoning us.

All he could do was scream 'come back, you little bastards,' at their retreating forms.

We all started to cheer the small rebels by shouting encouragement to them 'Keep going, lads. Get away!'

As we jumped up and down in excitement, Titch ran up and down the row of boys, lashing out with his cane. Soon the youngsters disappeared into the bogs. Maybe they would get away I thought to myself. Hopefully they would find somewhere they could shelter from the cold night air before the darkness of night really closed in. Although it was spring the temperatures still plummeted at night to below freezing and the small lakes dotted throughout the bogs were mostly frozen. I was not alone in praying for their safety, not that I was overly keen on God at the moment.

The stick-waving brother moved us all along at a faster pace than we were used to and clearly he couldn't wait to do whatever was necessary to get the young escapees back again. He certainly had some explaining to do and it must have been humiliating to tell the other brothers he had lost two of his charges.

Survivor

Our yard had a buzz about it and by this time the entire school knew of the escape. Bets were being taken as to the length of time they would remain free. As a former absconder myself I knew what they would be up against and was under no illusions as to their chances of beating the system.

After a little time we were quietened down by the brothers whilst in the distance we could hear cars scouring the lanes, others were coming up the gravel driveways leading to the school itself.

Ushered into the dining hall it was difficult to ignore the buzz of excitement and by 5.30 p.m. we were back in the yard. By now it was fully dark and extremely cold, which conjured up thoughts of the distressing situation the two boys might now find themselves in. It was possible to die through exposure in the bogs on a cold night without shelter and especially if wet. We stood around in groups, wondering what had become of the two youngsters, debating whether they would survive the night.

Normally at this time we would be directed to the hall, especially with it being so cold. This was never done for our benefit but for the brothers who were not too keen on the cold. Had they been able to leave us unsupervised in the open they would of course have done so.

It must have been a little after seven o'clock when two cars pulled up outside the school. The doors opened and Titch and Mutton Head emerged, the former having a broad beam on his face. Stretching to get a better view of what was happening we could see Titch pulling the two hapless waifs from the car. The poor mites were filthy dirty from their time in the bog; their hair was disheveled as it might be when they had just awoken. Both of the boys were weeping copiously.

Marching them towards the carpenter's shop Titch stood the two of them up against the wall. He then took up a big water hose and satisfied he had the pair just where he wanted them he turned the jet of water on them. With a smug grin he then began to hose the two lads down. By this time the temperatures had dropped to well below freezing and not surprisingly the two youngsters were screaming and clutching their arms around themselves on vain for protection. Standing close and watching the spectacle with interest were about five of the school's brothers and two men from the village.

Not a one of them cried out 'Enough.' Shameful.

As he hosed the two boys down Titch was screaming 'Bastards, bastards! I will kill you even if it kills me, you bastards.'

We could only look on, sickened, whilst hoping that the boys would recover from the treatment being meted out to them. The screams of those two small boys were still ringing in our ears as we mournfully went to our beds that awful night. We checked and they were not in the dormitory so we had no idea what had happened to them. It was rumored they had been forced to sleep naked on the floor but that was hearsay. The next morning the two of them were seen running around the yard as we made our way to mass at the church. Perhaps God was there? They were the first to have gone on the run since I had absconded and the Brothers were dealing with them just as severely as they had dealt with me. Their ordeal never deterred me from running away again. In fact all it did was convince me I was right to plan my escape from this hellish place.

CHAPTER 8

IF THERE WAS ANYTHING GOOD to say about routine it was the rarity of landmark events which meant time passed quickly. The days quickly became weeks and with the spring and greener grass, the flowers and the leaves turning the green countryside even greener there was the smell of change mixed with hope in the air.

The brothers tended to leave me to my own devices and as I went about my tasks on the farm I felt comfortable in my own company. There was little change to everyday habits but one day we were told it was time to slaughter a pig. We five chosen to be included in the process gathered a little nervously under the arch of the farmyard's gate. As we did so the sow was taken out of her pen pulled by the rope tied to her neck. Guided to her destiny with fate she was pulled into position under a block and tackle.

We boys held her steady while the brother placing the stun gun's muzzle to her forehead pulled the trigger. There was a loud ear shattering bang. The sow began to kick, slumped and went into unconscious shaking and trembling. The rope around her neck was quickly untied and deftly her rear legs strapped to the block and tackle's harness. At this point we were told to haul and haul we did until the creature was swinging in the cold spring air of the farmyard.

As soon as she was fully aloft the brother placed some buckets under her head before taking a knife and slicing the animal's neck from ear to ear. In a torrent the blood spurted and poured straight into the buckets. This was to be used to make black puddings we were told. After a little while the flow slowed to a trickle.

At this point the brother again took up his knife and expertly placing it at the dead sow's throat ran it down its belly until it was opened to its midriff. As he did so we watched the sow's entrails slop out on to a square of tarpaulin that had been placed to catch them. Without any sign of squeamishness the brother put his hands into the animal's belly up to his armpits and retrieved its entrails, its heart, liver, spleen and suchlike. These organs were placed in a separate bucket.

Water had been boiled ready for our next task. We boys were each handed a knife with the instruction that we shave the carcass of its hair. We were of course very nervous about being involved in this as we were after all still children. City kids were unlikely to have seen a pig, let alone slaughtered one.

We scraped and scraped until the skin was absent of hair and the carcass was left steaming in the morning air. We were at least being taught how to be butchers and farmers. It was better than learning nothing at all.

It was about this time I became increasingly skeptical about religion and questioned whether it being constantly pushed down our throats was the right way of going about convincing us of the sublime faith. I became more and more distant from the commonly held beliefs. I had little choice but to follow these rituals but my inner thoughts were now repelled by this utter crap we were being force fed with.

We were as orchestrated as the farm animals were, a boy farm to be seeded and harvested. It was beyond my comprehension how the brothers and others who abuse kids, often sexually, could take Holy Communion each day. Could it be me who was wrong?

Was there something I had failed to grasp? Perhaps they could sin at will as long as they begged for forgiveness each day, the confessional being the get out of gaol card. Little wonder I was confused but I had my own philosophy. If you did not sin then you didn't need the protection of the church. This seemed to settle these vexed matters better for me. Accordingly I would just chant the mantras but doing so without giving them any meaning.

Sunday morning mass was the event at which all villagers were present and would find the saintly priest reading out the names of those locals who

had made donations to the church. It would go something like this Mr. ******
the local ****** one shilling and six pence, Mr. ******** the local******** one
shilling and so on. It was a great way of embarrassing locals into shelling out
as much as they could. I bet God was happy with the results which found their
way into the collection tray. It caused me to wonder how he could ever spend
all the money collected each day in all churches around the world whilst we
were being starved here.

I was further perplexed by the penny required for the black babies' boxes.
These were scattered about everywhere, the industrial school included. Surely
the great church could give to them that which was collected each day in their
churches? But then I was just an undernourished innocent twelve-year old kid
and all of this was just a mystery of faith. It seemed the intention was to keep
it a mystery. And so proceeded the institutionalising of us youngsters, all those
who had gone this way before and all who would follow. It was the perfect
partnership, church and state.

We were never allowed into the village on our own but were marched
to its outskirts before taking a left then out of the main gate avoiding its
main thoroughfare. We always trooped two abreast. Because of this we never
learned much about the village or its small population. We had little idea of its
true size, of how it functioned or who made up its key figures.

Although we too were part of the community there was an ambiguity in
the relationships, an apartheid of sorts. Certainly many of the villagers passed
among us but we never struck up friendships or got to know them or their
purpose, their faith or their backgrounds. We were seen as part of the community but apart from it. We were lesser beings, different. There was no attempt
to mingle with us or to get to know us at all. We were non-persons, a ghostly
column of coming and going, a presence that was virtually invisible. We were
the elephant in the room

The local farmer who was also in charge of our farm had two daughters
whom we would see from time to time. There were put to work cooking and
cleaning in the big house and would come to mass each Sunday and other
holy days. They were often seen at the movies on Saturday nights. This caused
me some confusion. I had always been taught girls would have boyfriends and

Saturday nights would be the one occasion that might be set aside for their boyfriends.

Their isolation was perhaps a reason why so many country girls from counties like ours would eventually try their luck elsewhere, in cities like London or New York. There surely they would find contentment, work and husbands. I decided I would go to London or New York when I was older. Little did I realise that my internment at Letterfrack would make it difficult to travel. I was now a confirmed criminal.

The preparations for the summer holidays were by now under way. This was a time when some of the lads would learn if they were to be allowed home for a holiday. I dismissed as fanciful my own chances having been labelled an escapee. I was left behind with about forty other kids for the summer. It was no holiday for us, everything carried on with a brutal and tedious normality.

We were taken swimming on some of the more pleasantly warm days to an inlet about a ten minute walk away. Again we would sally forth in our little two abreast rows. Turning left we would head off in the direction of Clifden. Climbing over a fence we would then walk the short distance to this small rock-covered cove. From there we were allowed to jump or dive into the sea and to enjoy ourselves. We sported playfully and the memories of doing so enriched my life as little else could. There was such joy in experiencing the freedom of the sea, to imagine for golden moments I was as free as a sea mammal.

This was so different to an occasion that confronted me when I was younger. I had been walking along the banks of a Dublin canal when a group of lads had taken hold of me and fully clothed I was thrown into its murky waters. In a negative sense that cruel experience also remained with me, it was the sense of utter and helpless devastation.

I had submerged with my eyes and mouth open and recall seeing fish swimming before emerging thrashing about and spluttering. From the middle of the canal I somehow managed to doggy paddle to the canal banks. The bullies thought it was a great fun and could hardly contain themselves on seeing my bedraggled state. What they didn't know was I had been born with The Caul. This meant or so I was told I would never drown so up their arses, the dopey fuckers. I had pulled myself out of the canal and soaking wet had made my miserable way home. I can still visualise the stares I attracted as I wended my way to my home at Railway Terrace.

Ma was furious when she set eyes on me and saw the state I was in. As soon as she realised what had happened her temper softened, thanking the Lord I had been born with a Caul. A Caul was a form of skin membrane that sometimes covers a baby's face when born. She had deposited mine in a matchbox in the hospital but it had gone missing. She always swore that a nurse had robbed it to sell to a sailor. Cauls were much sought after by sea going people. The important thing to me wasn't in possessing it; it was my knowing I had been born with one, which meant my never having a fear of water. In truth it might not be more than an old wife's tale. Enough to say that swimming in the cove I was as content as might be a seal.

There was one day when using the cove we saw quite clearly a shark's distinctive fin and there was no doubt in our minds as to the menace that might suggest. The brother looking after us told us not to concern ourselves. He said it was a basking shark and common to these waters. We could also see seals enjoying their environment but for us there was nothing quite like leaping or diving off the rocks into those wonderful in-rushing waters of the Atlantic Ocean. Alternatively we would be taken for long walks in the countryside, but wherever we were destined it always led through the main gates and a turn left. There must have been a reason for it but it remained a mystery to me.

So perhaps the holidays weren't so bad after all but there is of course no place quite like home, no matter how humble it is. I missed my home, my Ma and my brother and sisters desperately. I did receive letters and money from my Ma on a regular basis so I was always able to buy sweets.

The warmer weather brought another bonus, we could play football in the yard. I wasn't too bad at soccer and so was picked often. It wasn't a sport we could volunteer for, each of the team's squads were selected on merit by one of the brothers. Luckily for me, the brother who usually arranged the games had taken a liking to me and so I got a game each time one was played.

There was one time I recall when I had come very close to scoring but on the point of taking the shot I was roughly bowled over by one of the bigger players. The brother lit up, he was screaming mad and gave the boy a really good kicking before making him stand facing the wall for what was left of the match. I was also awarded two penalties. The brother explained that the foul was so bad it merited both attempts. I didn't let him down. I scored each time which pulled us ahead by two goals.

Although this brother showed kindness to me he never ever tried to molest me. He was something of a nutter and I was glad to be on his good side. I wouldn't have wanted to receive a beating from him as he was always very severe.

On other days we would go off to the Gaelic field to play Gaelic football but this game held no interest for me. Hurling was another of the school's favorite sports but this again wasn't my kettle of fish. Soccer suited me just fine.

The work allocated during the summer consisted mostly of working in the fields. There we would pick potatoes by hand and carry them in baskets to a trailer and then empty our baskets into it. At such time as it was full the cart would be towed away by the tractor to the storage shed. Once the fields were harvested the farmer's son would use the same tractor to plough the field for whatever crop was intended for the following season.

Throughout the months following a few of us would be taken to the spud shed. There we would get on to our knees and taking each spud check it for quality, the good ones being placed behind us. This was called turning the spud and my strongest impression of this activity was the rancid smell of the storage shed and the darkness too. By the time the day's work was over your hands were blackened and stank to high heaven. It often entered my mind that we could catch the potato blight disease that had led to the famine that so ravaged Ireland a century earlier. Luckily we never did so we were not compelled to emigrate. I was far enough from my home as it was. One would think that being so involved in the dirty side of the potato industry would put one off the things for life, but it never did.

There was neither radio nor television at Letterfrack, nor did we ever set eyes on a newspaper so never had the slightest idea of what was going on in the outside world. Our county was extremely remote. As a form of exile it must have suited the Christian Brothers perfectly for they were far from prying eyes. I received letters from home but they were of family matters, all trivial. I did know that I was the only one to bring shame on the family, the only sibling to get into trouble during my younger years. It was thought I was always in turmoil and looking for whatever I could get up to next. Being the eldest I also was the one who witnessed all of the trouble and strife that went on between my Ma and Da.

I did in truth have two older half-brothers but they had been born out of wedlock and one I thought was my uncle. I never discovered he was my brother until I was sixteen. The other brother had been taken away by the nuns. He was to spend the first sixteen years of his life as an orphan of the Irish state. He spent all of his childhood years in industrial schools similar to the one I was incarcerated in at Letterfrack. I never did learn why one brother led a very comfortable childhood as a charge on his grandmother whilst the other undoubtedly must have suffered terribly as a consequence of being left to rot in the notorious industrial schools. But, these matters were beyond not only my understanding but beyond my influence.

Nevertheless, both brothers blamed me for their dysfunctional childhoods and they were unmoved by my protestations that I had not even been born until years after they were. There needed to be blame apportioned and I was the one it was directed at. Later on in years the older of the two often took advantage of my easy-going nature, arriving without notice on the presumption that I would give him whatever money he needed. Needless to say we became estranged, which probably saved me much money. The other was equally demanding and must have thought I was his surrogate mother, expecting me to keep and feed him. To some there are advantages to being disadvantaged and they are cute enough to work it out for themselves.

The industrial schools set-up was a barely disguised system to make use of the nation's disadvantaged boys and girls on an industrial scale, a revolving doors method that was in truth nothing other than state-approved indentured slavery. By contrast our troubles under the British might seem minor for pain feels sharper when inflicted by those of one's own kind. This in a nation of conviction-led Catholics brings no credit at all to the Republic of Ireland. There were few of its troubadours singing about their self-inflicted troubled times. No one was singing The Fields of Letterfrack.

This system to my knowledge was perfectly acceptable to the nation's judiciary, the apparatus of state including the Garda. All were making money from the miseries inflicted upon the nation's orphans. They were not only deprived of their parents, they were deprived of their statehood, their self-respect and their good name. Even those like me, placed there for such crimes as petty stealing, had far more stolen from them by those who had no excuse. To my mind they have no god either. Their status in the community was also a carefully contrived illusion.

There is much sentimentality about Ireland and it is universally regarded with affection, the birthplace of great writers, poets, playwrights, of men of understanding and literature. It seems not to have occurred to anyone to ask why it is the one European country that leads the rest in emigration. In Ireland there is apartheid with a difference, it is less well defined than skin color but it is just as prevalent and the scars are as great.

Ireland has been and still is a divided country firmly in the hands of ruling elite that abuses its power as do many Third World countries. It cultivates its carefully manicured image which is out of kilter with reality. Ireland will never share the comparatively prosperous contentment of its fellow European nations and their peoples as long as its affairs are controlled by a self-serving incompetent few whose positions are based not on merit but kissing the right backsides. Ireland is the ultimate bugger you mentality. It is a parody of the Red Flag anthem, 'The working class can kiss my ass, I've got the boss's job at last'.

Then again, who am I to offer such insight, a lowly little gurrier like me? A child who had to be abused daily, worked for profit, used as an industrial unit year after year and for what? Being involved in what was little more than a mischievous prank. This had set on its tragic course an overzealous police force, a cold-hearted sanctimonious judiciary, and a pack of wolves in Christian sheep's clothing.

Did this make Ireland a safer place; did it add anything at all to its standing and its reputation? No, only to the wealth of a tiny few whose shame stains the walls of their palatial homes. One day, unless they are already departed this earth their own Letterfrack's will open gates to welcome them into their next world. My one overriding concern is that their callousness does not rot my soul as some of the potatoes I examine are putrefying. If that should happen then they would take the credit for spotting a bad one earlier.

This self-protective elite are manufacturers of bitterness and anti-social behavior, their mills turn out damaged goods. In that respect only the term industrial school has significance. Whatever anti-social attitudes may arise from the bitterness of our childhood experiences they must pale into insignificance when set against the crimes of their tormentors. Victor Hugo's *Les Miserable* was an account of tyrannical state abuse in France; it reared its ugliest of heads in Ireland too.

CHAPTER 9

Everyone had now returned to the industrial school from their summer holidays and all was quiet and subdued. The kids who had the good fortune to be able to go home had since been relieved of all the new clothes and shoes they had returned in. Policy was that you only wear Letterfrack school clothing. Parents had spent a great deal of money to proudly clothe their offspring so that they might make the right impression upon their return to internment. These clothes were promptly destroyed, such Christian charity. The clothing could have been sent to good charities like St Vincent De Paul who would have made very good use of it but no, the clothing was used as rags for cleaning purposes throughout the school.

It was harvesting time and there was the hay to be cut. We would file out to the fields. Instructed to stoop over so our hands and arms were outstretched towards the ground we formed up as a human hay bailer. We would then be stretched out in a single line stretching across the breadth of the field. Upon command we would all bend over and start collecting the hay by raking forward with our hands and creating a big wheel of hay that we pushed forward.

This work was unmerciful as you could spend up to four hours at a time bent over relentlessly moving forward whilst raking the hay. When we got sufficient amounts gathered some of us would be given pitchforks and we would then make the hay into haystacks. That was the one part I liked and always hoped I would be given the opportunity to build the hay stacks. We would spend all day in the fields and would feed on a lunch of bread and tea. We would only be allowed about a half an hour to collect our bread and tea.

If you were not at the head of the queue then your break would be used up in the queue. The brothers were very strict on time keeping, especially Titch. I cannot recall ever being given water at any stage of the working day even though it could be very hot in the fields.

The hay stacks would grow on a daily basis until they began to take on the enormity of castles. Only then would the hay be collected before being stacked on a tractor and trailer to be taken to the silage pit. It was also stored in a big shed set aside for feeding the cattle over the winter months.

Some of us would be picked to go to the silage pit to trample the hay; I was always picked for this job. This was a big round crater about fifteen feet in diameter. The hay would be put in and molasses added by one of the brothers. We kids would then trample around in circles as we stamped the mixture into the ground. The smell of the hay and molasses mixing was nauseating and it would be sticky under our feet. We would walk in these treadmill-like circles for hours and days on end, trampling the hay until the pit got filled to near the top after which there would be more treading down to do. Constantly stooping it was grueling and exhausting work. There was only half an hour set aside for a break each day. Far better a southern states plantation.

But at least the livestock would have good feeding from the results of our sweat shop labours. Likely they were thought more of than us kids for they had a bought and sold price, we never did and we were expendable. No wonder boys died there and buried in still secret locations. Certainly the cattle in the fields looked well cared for. They were certainly sufficiently well-bred and husbanded for the purposes of breeding. Farmers from miles around would bring their cows to be serviced by our big strapping bulls; it was an awesome sight for a city kid to see.

Soon the days were becoming shorter in length as the late summer turned into autumn and leaves began to float to the ground, winter's warm coat for the tree roots. Dreading another winter in the fields I was trying to maybe get into a job in the tailors or carpenters shop but to no avail. There was no opportunity for applying for a particular posting; we all just got on with whatever we were instructed to get on with. So the fields and the farm and the bog too it was to be regardless of my feelings.

Each year one of the brothers would commission a play for Christmas and he would select a group of boys he thought were suitable for the required roles. This year I was picked to take the part of a Garda officer in the play. Surprisingly I was over the moon at hearing this. I spent much time studying my part and other parts too and found this very fulfilling.

We would go to the hall in the afternoon to study and do the rehearsals. At least and for once we were treated as children and not slaves to the brothers' unique system of education. I really liked this acting thing and had done my best to learn every word and move. By this time I desperately wanted to be the best actor in the school, it would make me feel wanted and respected, twin joys never before experienced.

Coming up to the week before our big performance we were studying twice daily and this was followed by a dress rehearsal. One of the kids had been having some difficulty in remembering his lines and faltered a couple of times during the rehearsal. The brother in charge of the drama class, and who up to this part of the preparation had been open and helpful, went stark raving mad. He just lost it. Dragging the then hysterical kid from the stage he took his leather out from under his tunic and started to belt the shit out of the youngster every which way he could.

Bang. Whip. Over the head, across his face and all over the child's body everywhere he could hit using all the force he could muster. When he was finished and breathing heavy from his belt-wielding exertions the poor kid looked like he had been in the ring with a heavyweight boxer for the full twelve rounds. He was bruised black and blue all over and weeping uncontrollably and pitifully.

Such an unexpected irrational outburst of madness frightened me and the other children to the core. It was made worse because we had looked upon this brother as a normal person trying to help the kids where he could. It was the sheer unexpectedness and uncontrolled madness with which he vented his fury at the youngster we found so disquieting. Alas, this brother was as mad and bad as was Chinney, Titch and the others. Each of them was branded with the same madness.

I still cannot understand why there was never an inspectorate, a solitary official appointed to ensure the wellbeing of the youngsters in the charge of the state. The Christian Brotherhood had literally been handed a license to act with the utmost licentiousness, to even murder at will. They took full advantage of their omnipotence

Needless to say the kid recovered somewhat but it was certain the mental scars would remain for the rest of the mite's life. If it was consolation he was at least allowed to keep his part in the Christmas play. Suffer little children, come unto me indeed. We suffered and we came, and then we suffered again and again.

On the night of the opening the villagers respectfully and expectantly trooped in, taking up their seats on the right of the hall just as if it was a Saturday night picture show. It was apartheid at its best and most institutionalized. Everything went well in the first half of the play and we had a break in which we were given lemonade and cakes that had been donated by the villagers. The second half went very well too and we received a standing ovation. The play ran to about an hour, when finished we were all so excited everything had gone so well on the night. I was hardly likely to be the one who wondered at what might have been the horrifying consequences had a major mistake been made by any of the kid cast. Would that brother have gone mad in front of the serried rows of villagers? I don't think so!

It was a great night and I couldn't wait until next year to play another part if I was privileged to be picked. I was cock o' the walk for weeks after the play. It seemed once again I had found a role in life worth dreaming for.

CHAPTER 10

As THE YEAR PROGRESSED AND events surrounding Christmas and New Year became a distant memory nothing changed by way of routine. Up in the still dark wintry mornings, the hoar frost upon the trees, vapor rising from our nostrils as we wended our way to wherever we were destined. The morning began of course with the church service for nothing stood in the way of it. As Easter approached there were also the Stations of the Cross to attend.

Each night we would have the Rosary even if it was cut short but certainly a decade had to be chanted out loudly in reply to the brother leading the reading. Religion was pumped into us at every opportunity, before and after meals, before bed and after awakening, in and after church at any chance that could be construed as a time of prayer. The prayers might well have been 'Dear God! Save the bog and all the fucking turf we can cut from it with the help of our slave kids.'

Abuse by those in authority was often devious and imaginative, physical and mental, sexual and threatening. It was inflicted in many ways and pumping religion relentlessly into children, especially when they are lonely and vulnerable, was abuse of a different kind but abuse all the same. Theirs was a god who battered down on you, you never voluntarily offered supplication. I could never see how ramming religion down your throat without your approval could result in you embracing it and so the more I was subjected to religion the more I learned to hate it as a false god.

At Easter we never received any eggs of any kind, we ate religion and it ate us. We did get a long walk outside the school grounds on the Sunday. This was so refreshing and I always felt exhilarated after such walks. But this feeling of wellbeing was never to last long. The cold slap of reality hung menacingly over each day's routines.

It was so when on a bleak Monday soaked in mist and drizzle I found myself cutting the turf again, tossing the sods up the bank. If I had a weak throw the sod would come bouncing back down on my head. This resulted in my once missing my step whereupon I slipped into the mire and was soaked through to my skin.

Brother Titch thought this great fun and was howling with laughter at the sight of me looking so pitiful. Dripping from head to toe with what looked like shite I was freezing and crying uncontrollably. A large sack appeared from somewhere and it was handed to me. Rubbing myself vigorously I was able to somewhat dry myself off but my clothes were still wet and my boots soaked, there wasn't of course any way by which they could be dried.

Titch for the rest of the day was in a great mood as a consequence of my discomfort. I refused to give in to his joy and continued to work as best I could, feigning enthusiasm and bravado. Nothing would have pleased him more than to see me distraught and in obvious discomfort. Boy was I hurting inside and frozen to the marrow throughout the rest of the afternoon.

I presumed that after returning to the dorm, changing my soaking clothes and taking a shower for which I would receive a beating, I would feel and look better. It was a thought that heartened the ever optimistic me.

That evening my meal was wolfed down being far hungrier than normal. I could see some of the older boys looking at me in awe after hearing what had happened and how I had coped so stoically. This helped me to get over the episode and I was glad to be in such good health afterwards. It also taught me that being heroic resulted in better results for oneself, something I would relate well to throughout my life. Whenever I was under pressure it was better to be brave rather than be an 'undecided' sort of person.

And so in life such things are learned without realising one is being taught lessons that help to make you a better or worse person in life. The mind takes experiences good and bad and after reasoning stores them until they are needed whether you like it or not.

The years I spent at Letterfrack Industrial School were to scar me for life. The constant uncertainties and the removal of the natural progression of decision making, a rite of passage for all youth passed me by under a welter of blows. As a result I was rarely able to hold a job or relationship down.

On the job part I was to end up self-employed and remained as such for the rest of my life. On the relationship part of life I was always looking over my shoulder for ghosts that might have never existed. They were however branded on my psyche to shape my character and personality. Not surprisingly I found it difficult if not impossible to place my trust in people and a deceit, no matter how small, was to open scars time after time.

This was something as a kid I found hard to comprehend, the meaning of trust or love. Each time I learned to respect and even like a Christian brother the weakness would be seen as a failing whereupon it was something to be taken advantage of. These two were learning experiences for each time I was betrayed my naivety was curbed and I learned to see them for the predators they were. So in life I would always try to put up a hard and strong front even if in my mind I was feeling weak and overwhelmed.

Things would have been so much better if Irish governments and the religious orders that held a malignant influence over them had done things differently. What an opportunity missed and to what advantage? Here was the golden opportunity to turn around the fortunes of the country's abandoned and desolate young people, to turn them into the greatest assets any country could wish for.

They, the government and the religious orders, had such a wonderful opportunity to take these children and to then educate them to the highest standards. Instead they chose an ungodly course through which they squandered so many lives with their foul cruelties, their physical and sexual torture and unrelenting abuse. Paradise lost through predatory self-gratification.

Even though I lived through this appalling system in all its unvarnished wickedness to this day I still cannot understand why this was hidden under the cloak of convention. Why were they blind to the damage they were doing? Why couldn't one person see what was being inflicted upon thousands of vulnerable boys and girls over so many years that for them could be truly described as god-forsaken?

To the perverted and corrupt government and the religious orders, the so-called pillars of society, Ireland must have seemed heaven come early. Here was a pilgrim's end for the debauched and the shameless. Perhaps they were depraved enough to either resent the notion of an afterlife at which amends must be made, or they saw earth as a place to make one's own version of heaven. No doubt they were under the impression they would be given the all clear on their deathbed simply by confessing their sins. Why not? It is what they are taught and what they believe. Theirs will be a clean slate on entering the Kingdom of Heaven.

Given reflection it seems this is still the problem in our potentially great country. The haves and the have nots still live the life of the great divide that is hell-bound to continue in all its talent-sucking rapaciousness into whatever the future holds for it.

Can they see what is right under their noses or does the stink put them off? It is here in Ireland that our wonderful lyricists, our poets, dramatists and television agents need to focus, the home-grown whistleblowers.

They could so easily repair the damage and broken lives, restore Ireland's reputation. The ground has already been laid for them by Victorian philanthropists such as the founders of the Salvation Army, the National Society for the Protection of Children, scores of societies and foundations who then faced down that nation's abusers. Those here in Ireland who inherit their wisdom and sensitivities have the blueprint.

But back to Letterfrack Industrial School. Here we were again getting ready for summer holidays. It seemed I might be allowed home as it had been some time since I did a runner. I hadn't done one of those for quite some time and to the brothers I might have appeared to be a reformed character. I was hoping I could go home to see my family for a couple of weeks. Their coming to see me was out of the question as my family didn't have a car and public transport was nonexistent.

It would take one day to get here and a second to return home, an impossible task for any parents in the 1960's.

The only person who ever visited the industrial school was a former inmate. I recalled his arrival in a red mini car which he parked outside the tailor's shop. We boys were all in awe of him. He was a big lad and dressed so well. We had only fleeting glances at him before the guards came to remove him from the school's grounds. It seemed the car had been stolen in Dublin, not good but equally ironic his reason for the visit. He was there to demand payment for sexual services rendered unto the brothers during his incarceration.

This focused our minds and there was much gossip between the boys as to who could drive a car and who could not. I was out of it. I was far too young to drive and in fact I had never given the matter a moment's thought. The rest of the kids fantasized that they were great drivers and were able to hot wire any car. Doing the rounds were many fantastic stories, no doubt dreamed up or exaggerated about lucky escapes, hair-raising chases, of how the Garda could never keep up with them. There was a reason for their ineptness of course, the culshies, as country people were nicknamed in Dublin, were experienced only in driving tractors and horse driven carts.

Closer and closer crept the beckoning summer holidays. Having set my hopes on going home I reached the stage where I was presuming I would be allowed to. Had I learned it was to be otherwise I would have been totally gutted? Then, on the Saturday afternoon Friar Tuck assembled us in the yard where we were set in single rows. Having settled us he took out several sheets of paper from beneath his cassock. Holding them up and peering at the wording he began to call out names of boys, instructing those who heard their name being called to move to the front and form a single line.

This was the roll call of the boys who were to be allowed home for a holiday, the moment of truth. Confused and upset we had no idea if the names being called were those who were to be allowed home or were to stay. Such a cruelty was typical of the brothers; they never missed an opportunity to discomfit us. Why did they hate us so much? Was it a reflection of the hate they must have felt for themselves. Caught up in institutionalized horror were they victims too, like prison guards who become inured to suffering or see it as a perk of the job?

I heard my name ringing through the air and joined several others in the line. I was extremely apprehensive as from where I was I couldn't see a single orphan. They of course had no homes to go to so this could mean I was going home. It took about an hour to call all the names and sort out the lines. It was then that Chinney came out of the door behind us and going to the front of the lines proceeded to announce those in the first two lines were going home to see their families.

We were each required to acknowledge we were being well looked after and were most gracious to the brothers for their care and support. We would of course have said yes to anything at this stage. In reality we thought the life we lived there was normal and would see no reason in discussing our lives with others. Anyway, such was the constant humiliation that we were disinclined to discuss it with anyone, the shame being too great and God alone knows what the repercussions might be. We all knew God could be deaf to the needs of children. He left others to do that, and made them accountable. I thought that was how it worked.

And so the Christian Brothers were safe. Years of experience had taught them they were safe and anyway, who would ever place the word of a child higher than that of a Christian Brother?

I was exhilarated. It was three weeks to release and I could hardly sleep with excitement. Running constantly through my mind were the thoughts of what I would do when back in Dublin. I couldn't remember ever being so elated. Those days and nights were interminably long.

In the meantime there were trees to be dragged down and it was rumored that we were going to drain the large pond. It was more than a rumor for soon we were gathered on the bank of the mere near the doctor's house. It was about 9.30 in the morning, a glorious summer's day as I recall.

Two of the brothers emerged from the farm doorway; they were wearing their green thigh-high waders and soon joined our group. At the pond end was a sluice gate and they positioned themselves on either side of it. As they turned the ratcheted handle the pond waters began to escape to then rush down the hill in a torrent. It was an awesome spectacle and the stench was rancid.

It took several hours to drain and when it had done so the drained basin was filled with eels and fish flopping about in their distress. I had never before set eyes on eels that size, I think it was the first time I had seen an eel.

One of the boys said: 'They are conger eels. They can kill and eat you so keep well away from them.'

Another said they were electric eels and the shock could easily kill you. My God, I was thinking to myself, maybe they want us electrocuted and eaten to spare the expense of sending us on our holidays. Naturally I kept well clear of the creatures.

It was at this point that the two brothers waded in through the mud and silt and began to throw the fish and eels to the banks where they would end up in barrels put aside for the purpose, each of them having been filled with water. Our job then was to get into the drained pond and generally clean it of waste material, weeds, assorted junk and detritus. This was to take three days of back-breaking work, there was no opportunity to stand and stare as onlookers. Uppermost in my mind the passing of the days and with the passing of each I was increasingly excited at my imminent though temporary liberation.

After the pond had refilled, which took about four days, it was quickly re-stocked and it was a sheer joy to see the wildlife sporting about having been freed from their restrictive containers. Their colors shimmered as they leaped and thrashed about in their natural environment. They seemed to be expressing a thanksgiving.

Other creatures were not as fortunate for some of the sheep were to be slaughtered. The farmer had explained to us how the best way to drift into slumber when sleep wouldn't come easily was to picture sheep, to imagine them leaping over fences and count them as they did so. On this occasion he took one of them from its pen and quickly strapping its feet together placed it on its side. Then, taking a large knife from his belt and holding the sheep's head up in one hand he slit the animal's throat from ear to ear. Then, kicking a bucket under the writhing beast he held it in such a way for the blood to drain into the bucket. Near satisfied that there wasn't much blood remaining he held the carcass up by its hind legs to allow the last strings of coagulating blood to ooze into the bucket.

Laying the dead sheep on its back and untying the foot strap he slit the belly open as had been done to the sow. Quickly placing his hands inside its still warm carcass he roughly jerked its entrails out to allow them to dry on the ground. The organs were separated and placed in another bucket. He then laid the sheep on its back and untying the rope that bound the feet he proceeded to slit the belly open. These he explained would end up as sausage skins.

'Jesus,' thought I. 'These were going to be the skins of our fucking sausages?'

When the carcass had been thoroughly cleaned he then slit the skin at the top of the animal's feet and folding it over simply snapped each of the legs. Then, making his hand into a small fist he began to skin the unfortunate animal. Calling me over he showed me what to do and so I experienced the strangest of sensations as I felt my knuckles slowly slide down between the skin and the flesh.

When the skinning was completed the remains were placed on a wooden block and cleaved into portions. These were no doubt destined for the brother's kitchen where his daughters would be preparing the brothers' meals. It was an amazing experience for a thirteen-year old child to see the workings of a farm and the slaughter of animals that you had hitherto seen only in picture books.

To discover that a sheep could be so easily skinned by hand was quite a revelation to say the least. So I took comfort from the fact that the learning experiences such as these would be assets in the future.

Other than that the school has caused me to regard authority as a threat, to never trust authority. From there on I would never trust or believe anything, at least view with cynicism and suspicion anything uttered by those who preach goodness and gods, or claim integrity. This was not an inherited wickedness or anything in my genes. I was sure a kindlier childhood environment would never have stained my thoughts or my soul.

When we left the farm that day we went to the yard to wait for the call to supper. There I was pulled aside by brother Tea.

'I want a word with you' he said.

I didn't like the sound of that and I was very much on edge. My conduct had been exemplary, what could he possibly want with me?

I was beginning to tremble when he smirked 'You are going home to your hovel for your holiday's boy. You just remember this. This is your home for some time yet so you be very, very careful with what you say. Things could get a lot worse for you.'

'I know, brother, sir,' I said quietly. 'I am really happy here and I am looking forward to coming back.'

'Good, that is what I wanted to hear from you. Now you run along for your supper is very nearly ready now.'

At the time I didn't really pick up on the implied threat or even grasp the full meaning of his words. From a distance and given greater experience of life I realised its significance. It was their turn to be apprehensive as to what this little whistleblower might say when back in Dublin.

I have wondered since if there were stories about the industrial schools already seeping through the porous surfaces of society, if such stories were ever acted on. Back then I was interested only in my own survival.

It was July in 1965. The Saturday on which we were to leave came around quickly enough. Those of us lucky to be going home were up at the crack of dawn. We were each given a little bag with a change of clothing some shirts, underpants and socks to take home with us. We were excited knowing we had an early start as it was going to be a long journey.

The roadway at the top of the yard was filled with much hollering and good humored banter as the bus reversed into the driveway. Bawled into a line by Chinney we boarded the bus quietly for the brother was far from pleased at our obvious happiness. There wouldn't be much exuberance in the bus either as both Brother Chinney and Brother Titch were to accompany us all the way to Dublin.

Other kids went to other parts of the country, places like Limerick and Cork but most of the kids were from Dublin. Taking my seat at the rear of the bus I could hardly disguise my excitement.

'Here we go, here we go,' I was chanting quietly to myself as the bus's engine kicked into life and the driver put it in gear.

The much looked forward to moment had finally arrived as the bus heaved and jerked slowly towards the school gates, turned right and trundled along the main road. It was a long road of many tight bends but it was soon to pass Kylemore Abbey. The edifice looked almost Wagnerian in its solitude, sharply silhouetted and glistening against the lake and landscape.

I have since learned that it is a boarding school for better off girls and is run by a nun's order, but I don't think they would be abusing the little rich girls?.

I did wonder had they an inkling of what was going on just down the road from their impressive castle in its manicured grounds. Not that it mattered; they were quite innocently unaware of our plight and living conditions. Perhaps that is just as well. It is said that ignorance is bliss. I should imagine it is for knowing certainly wasn't.

The bus was fully occupied. The brothers having the front seats were smoking heavily whilst we sat in subdued silence. Things could still go wrong we supposed. Or, the apprehension had been replaced by another emotion, the wonderment at what it might be like after such a long time to return to once familiar roads, locality and home. We had been told to keep our noise down, there was to be no fooling around so each of us sat quietly gazing out of the vehicle's windows. Each with our own thoughts as we watched the passing countryside. Perhaps we savored the welcome we were expecting?

As we entered Galway City we could clearly observe more people in one eyeful than we had seen during the previous year. They were strolling about in their short sleeved tops and the girls in short skirts. Some of the older boys were expressing themselves in colorful ways: 'Oh boy, Look at that one,' was commonly heard along with sharp intakes of breath and whistles from pursed lips. Isn't it grand to rejoin the real world? It is perhaps nature's balm that under the most trying circumstances we adapt to our new environment, even a threatening one, and forget the joys of freedom.

We arrived at Galway Station in good time which left just half an hour before we would continue our journey home. Some boys dashed for the toilets, others among us waited patiently whilst taking everything in. As we were all grouped together and in the care of the two bothers I suppose we were seen as an ordinary school outing party.

But to be sure the railway station's staff would know who we were. This much was obvious as the ticket master kept a very wary eye on our group. So he might for weren't we convicted felons, criminals on leave?

Soon the steam engine pulling its string of carriages squealed and hissed its way into the station and with a squealing of brakes jarred to a halt.

'Take care you lot,' we were told by one of the brothers 'There's a gap between the platform and the doors.'

Like meek rabbits being herded from pen to pen we boys quietly climbed aboard. The rebelliousness I had felt when leaving the castle at the beginning of my sentence had long evaporated. That had since been beaten out of me. We were instructed to be on our best behavior. After all it wouldn't do for other passengers, the sanctimonious, to feel threatened by a little horseplay by youngsters.

No doubt they would be thinking quietly to themselves how outrageous it was that such lowlife were being allowed out on holidays. The horsewhip would be far better for them and thus civilized order might be better maintained and the citizens might sleep more peacefully in their beds.

Clackety-clack, clackety-clack, the train picked up speed and the floor beneath our feet was beginning to sway as the miles to Dublin became fewer by the minute. Clackety-clack, clackety-clack as excitement built inside and many a bottom lip was chewed and a nose wiped on a sleeve.

At some point a few of the kids began to sing: 'Were off to Dublin in the green, in the green, were off to Dublin in the green where the helmets glisten in the sun.'

This infuriated Chinney who bellowed: 'Shut your mouths and keep the cackle down or you will be going back to where you have just come from.'

Again quiet reflection resumed as the train rushed past clackety-clack, clackety-clack all manner of wonderful sights. There were trees in the fields and the man made rustic walls that reminded us of what was said to be now our real home at Letterfrack Industrial School. It made me wonder if we were passing similar 'schools', a gulag chain of them?

As we passed we were startled by some of these strange looking buildings behind the stone walls. We couldn't help but wonder what lay beyond them, what remained hidden from passing society. How many had passed our own institution comfortable in the knowledge that it being in Ireland all was well with the world.

Occasionally we would hear the train's whistle wailing and as often the platform of a railway station would rush by. Some of us were playing cards; everyone was quiet and reflective, pondering the fickleness of fate perhaps. Knowing the natural high spirited nature of boys as a species I suppose we were oddly quiet to onlookers. That is if they noticed and could be dragged away from their own worlds. Of course other boyish groups would not be supervised by these two notorious brothers, and only we could know of the baseness that their notoriety was set upon.

The entire journey to Dublin took up nearly six hours of travelling time and passed off without incident. Neither I nor they would be able to think of the journey as long or short for to us it was timeless. We were travelling forward but we were travelling back in time, between the mysteries of life with time being suspended during the train journey between Galway and Dublin. Ours was a vacuum, a nether world and a re-birth.

With much whistle blowing and the screech of tortured metal against metal the train entered and jerked to a halt as it hit the buffers at Kings Bridge Station. Instructed to stand we were addressed by Brother Chinney.

'You must be back here on Saturday week at half past eight in the morning sharp. You must be on your best behavior at all times. You are, remember, still under the control of the Irish state and must behave as such. This means no trouble of any sort under any circumstances. Do you all hear this?'

'Yes, brother!' we replied in unison.

'Off you go then and remember eight thirty on that morning, sharp.'

He bit the word 'sharp' off like he was snapping a bone in his teeth. Nothing changed his sour demeanor unless it was brightened by a child's discomfit. I had much to remember him by.

The train having finally come to a stop I reached for the door handle. I had no idea what the welcome if any was going to be. Who will come to meet me, will it be my Ma or my Da? Will they be together or on their own?

Our file was separated from the rest of the alighting passengers and we walked up to the platform's exit from where I could see a group of people obviously awaiting arrivals. I thought to myself that some of them look very much as parents look, impatiently and anxiously scanning the faces of the individuals, couples and groups of passengers now approaching them. Then there were names being called out and much waving of hands in the air, reminding me of the pictures you see of soldiers returning from wars. Fuck the brothers, I think as breathless I realised this is not a dream I have woken from. I am home in Dublin.

I was running headlong down the platform towards the group of waiting people. The other boys were too and the parents were shouting and screaming, waving to them and encouraging them to come more quickly. From the mixed unidentifiable mass of faces emerged that of my Ma. There she was, her face lit up by excitement and anticipation. I had no idea how I would have reacted to my father's presence.

'Ma, Maaaaaaaaaaaaa,' I screamed with joy and like a silly Billy the tears started to gush uncontrollably. Although I am thirteen-years of age I was in a state of total self-destruction, losing control of myself as weeping with joy I fell into her arms and we embraced.

'Hush, hush, child,' she murmured. 'You're home now. Everything is alright.'

I couldn't see her tears through my own, nor could I feel her sobs for I was sobbing too. Engulfed by extremes of emotions of joy I collapsed into her embraces. They were emotions of a kind I never ever want to experience again, not in this life or the next. There is only so much joy the human spirit can endure. I had reached my limits in my Ma's welcome.

CHAPTER 11

It was one of those enchanting days when Dublin spreads out before your eyes, a beautiful city that embraces the River Liffey as it flows into the Irish Sea. Strolling along Victoria Quays, holding my mother's hand, was sheer bliss as we made our way home to North Great Georges Street situated to the north of the inner city. Our route would take us along the quays and over Capel Street Bridge into Capel Street. There throughout its length were dotted shops and cafes and a constant stream of passers-by.

I wondered if my face still looked tear-stained as I gripped my Ma's hand even more tightly. Turning right into Jervis Street and then to Moore Street we passed through the stalls set out by the fruit and vegetable market traders, sidestepping people as we did so but hanging on to each other for dear life. Though it was now well into the afternoon they were still in full voice and again I heard the cries:

'Bag of your best pinks here now, or fresh cabbage here. Just take a look at the shape and size of these bananas.'

Perhaps the vendor herself believed the nutrient value of her goods would put all of life's ailments to rest. Ma stopped and bought some fruit before carrying on dipping in and out of the strollers, the gawpers and the buyers until we reached Parnell Street. From there it was only a few minute's walk past the Rotunda Hospital and Ambassador Cinema and then we approached the Town and Muck where all of my troubles had found their genesis.

By the time we crossed O'Connell Street, the scene of such savage conflict that would lead to liberation from occupation it might be wondered if for some at least it wasn't frying pan, fire. Is that what they meant when the officers commanding Britain's firing squads yell fire?

Finally we reached our tenement, the place I knew as home. Nothing had changed, not from what I could see. It was very much as I had left it and clearly the change was in me, and how profound that was.

'I have made you a coddle,' my Ma said gently as she set about doing what mothers do second best, prepare food in the kitchen. A coddle is a Dublin stew. It is made by taking the household's biggest pot and into it goes the lot: potatoes, sausages, bacon slices, onions, white or brown soup mixes. It was a staple diet, especially for drunken husbands who returning from their revelry on a Saturday night found it easy to heat up and get down. The coddle was archetypically Dublin and of course the quest was to get as bladdered through drink as was possible.

Pulling a rickety chair up to the small table my spoon was poised to mill the coddle.

'Look,' my Ma said 'I have also got a batch loaf for you; it is straight from the bakery and still warm.'

I think it was her heart's gift for she knew well how I loved the batch loaf, in particular what was called its heel. The end was normally cut thicker than were the inner slices.

Ma explained the kids were all playing outside and by now I had learned that my Da was at work. He was back to being a coal delivery driver and Ma told me he wanted a word or two with me.

'You know your older brother,' she said, not so much a question as an affirmative.

I do of course.

'Well,' she said 'He is no longer living here with us. There were a few difficulties with him. He has gone off to England. He has joined the British Army.'

'Good,' I piped up as Ma placed the plate in front of me.

I was starving and could have eaten a cow between two bread vans. The news was exciting for me. Now he would be able to travel the world with the services, taking in all the sights and different cultures and lifestyles. It occurred to me that this might be a smart career move for me too. It certainly was food for thought as I wolfed down the food necessary for keeping body and soul together. Letterfrack at that moment seemed a long way away but not half as far away as it should have been. Here in the comfort and security of my own home its stark terrors were more clearly defined than ever before. Today it was as though I have woken from a bad dream for home was just as I remembered it and Ma's cooking at its best.

'Yes, good for him' said I between gulps before venturing outside to see what was going on if anything.

I hadn't been sitting on the tenement steps for very long when a girl approached.

'Hi, what are you doing here?'

'Just dossing,' I said.

'Maybe you would like to go for a walk? Would you like to go for a walk? What is your name?'

I told her my name as I noticed she was wearing a short skirt and couldn't but help but look at her plump thighs and then her diddies. Her ample bosom seemed to be trying to escape from her bodice-like top as taking my hand we set off to goodness knows where.

As we followed our feet my companion chattered non-stop about all kinds of shite that is going straight into one of my ears and out of the other without stopping. I would not be telling her I have come home from Letterfrack. Anticipating leading questions I had already hit on an idea. I would say I had been living near Cork with my uncle. In fact I did have an uncle who lived in Fermoy in the County of Cork so it was only half of a lie.

My new found friend thought I was delightful to which I could only ask myself if the girl was stark raving mad. She hung on to me very much as my Ma had done and I felt the stares of people as we passed by. By now I was feeling a little edgy and couldn't figure out why we were attracting so much attention. Nothing perturbed her as we completed our walk. I thought she was a little put out when I disappeared indoors. She clearly liked my company although it was her who had done all the running, the walking and the talking.

The reason for the interest in me was revealed when full of curiosity about the attention I attracted I asked my Ma.

'Son,' she says: 'You have the most wonderful tan. You are so brown from the country sun, it is as though you have been on holiday. That is why they are looking at you.'

My coloring was something I had never given a moment's thought to but after this explanation I took more notice of the complexions of others. It brought into sharp focus the white often grey pallor and beaten demeanor of my fellow Dubliners, the affects after decades following liberation from the occupier's yoke. Often silently these Dubliners shuffled about their business as they wandered from street to street, out of the grey, the grey being consumed by the grey, a people fog.

Da never came home before time was called at the public house he favored, later than that if he could get a 'lock in.' Today, the day of the return of the Prodigal Son he was not to be moved one iota from his ritual. It was past midnight before I set eyes on him and in some ways was sorry I had. He was happy enough and his vocal chords were well oiled as making his way up the dark tenement stairway he sang his harmless ballads.

'How's my wayward little boy?' he said as he peered at me. He was rocking slightly to and fro carefully picking his words as a man might warily find his way through a minefield.

'Are the bastards treating you well, son?'

'Pausing for effect he went on 'because if they are not I will be ringing their fucking necks so I will. I will fucking kill them, all of them,' he slurred as he slumped to the table's edge.

At that moment I knew that disagreeable that Letterfrack was, this was not the alternative I needed. I couldn't exchange that for this. The memories came flooding back, the shared bedroom and the night pissing. Now I no longer wet the bed and can even get through the night without the need to piss in the piss bucket. How strange it is to share a bed I think to myself, aware of my younger brother's presence besides me as I drift off into a sleep.

Life goes on; I woke in the night to hear my father using the bucket. Pshhhhhhhhh and then, 'Fuck!' as he made his way back and on his way to his bed flopped in a chair. His bed was separated from mine only by a curtain room divider.

Early next morning I could hear my Da washing in the sink. He cleared his nose into the sink before getting dressed properly and heading off to work. I wondered how he would survive Letterfrack. My thoughts moderated with time. Granted he was always in work, always earning and reliable. If it meant he was equally reliable at drinking and getting drunk, and gambling too, then such was our herd instinct society there was little chance or encouragement to do otherwise. It was life, Dublin life.

The family were awake at this time and there were comforting sounds and odors drifting in from the kitchen. This morning the breakfast will be piping hot tea, batch bread and dripping. I loved the dripping, especially when it is brown for I can then taste the juices of the meat that goes into the making of it.

My sisters and brother weren't going to school, it was their holidays too and they were quickly out of the house to do as other children do. Theirs was something of a different world for me. I had changed although like them I was still a child. Perhaps it was because I had seen the raw sewage of humanity and it had colored different hues to theirs.

I was still feeling a little strange being back home. I was also keeping a wary eye out for the girl I met yesterday, hoping that I didn't bump into her. When I did emerge from our tenement home my feet took me along Parnell Street and into Gardiner Street. There was a chance I would meet Redser there as maybe he was back home too. I did notice a lot of men grouped around street corners as I went on my way and wondered what that was all about. There was definitely an undercurrent. I can feel it and then I hear a word that is new to me:

'Scab!'

I could see groups of men running towards two lorries heading our way. The clusters of poorly dressed men, the lines of life drawn prematurely on their faces, were rushing madly towards them.

They were calling out 'Scab, Scab.'

The lorries were being driven down Summer Hill towards Parnell Street and they were loaded with what appeared to be bags of cement. I watched startled and if anything mesmerized. As if in slow motion I saw the lorries pull to a halt, their drivers' in fear of putting men beneath their wheels and them clambering over the bonnets and grasping at the vehicles' doors.

All the time they are shouting, 'Scabs,' and 'Northern Ireland bastards, robbing our fucking jobs.'

The drivers were roughly hauled from their cabs, which was probably for the best as within moments both of the lorries were torched and flaming furiously.

There wasn't a Garda to be seen and not a sight of a fire engine either. I listened for the sounds of their imminent arrival but I heard nothing at all except for the rough voices. This was the tapestry of our times and our country. There was perpetual unrest, a simmering resentment at the misfortunes of life. Men born with aspiration found themselves being seen as expendable. Such outbursts as these represented the fabric tearing at the edges. Their lives when born were celebrated yet they leave the earth unfulfilled.

I left the mayhem behind me. I was motivated to go on my peaceful way by Brother Chinney's departing words about keeping out of trouble. My nose was clean so far. I wanted it to stay that way. The feeling of liberation as I walked where I wanted was a sensation I was still coming to terms with. Although I was aimless I was free. Perhaps one has to lose one's freedom to experience the intoxicating consciousness of freedom, just to cross the road and gaze into a shop window or to decide on a whim to take one road rather than another.

I didn't bump into any of my mates on that first day of liberation day but no matter, I was content enough to be home and to at least be patrolling their everyday environment. Those thoughts alone made me feel a part of real community again. I was no longer an outcast, an exile to be used and abused, my everything decided on by others who were more remote than would be foreign occupiers. If I felt alienated at Letterfrack and indeed some sections of the ruling class it could only be because our lives were being run by aliens.

The weather was kind. It was one of those balmy summer days when no matter how difficult one's life may be, no matter how dark the future, hope springs in the human breast. Dublin was the loveliest of cities. It was compact so you could walk from one end to another in no time at all and without feeling betrayed by tiredness. It didn't matter that I had little money. Where was the need? I could enjoy so much that money cannot buy?

You cannot go out and purchase the keys to your cell doors. You cannot lean across the counter and say, 'A nice sunny day please,' or tell the assistant you would like a portion of euphoria. These are beyond price, they are a gift denied to only those who either cannot see them or take them for granted. I saw and experienced them. Not once did I take them for granted.

And so this day I followed my feet to Stephens Green, along Grafton Street and followed a route that took in Dame Street, Halfpenny Bridge, which was called so as it was at one time a toll bridge that strands the river Liffey. I wondered how it got built, this lovely bridge all done in iron and timber.

By the time my small feet had negotiated Jervis, Talbot and George's Streets it was time for me to take my seat on the tenement steps, this time with a bottle of lemonade. Wasn't life grand indeed?

'Well, the fucking dead arose and appeared too many.'

Surprised I turned on hearing the half familiar voice to find Redser standing there as bold and brassy as ever.

'Jaysus,' I retorted: 'You frightened the fucking life out of me. Just watching the world go by. How the fuck are you, you little shite?'

He told me he was fine and presumed right as he mentioned my being home from Letterfrack and on holiday. I told him I would be here for the next two weeks.

'Me too,' he muttered darkly: 'From Dangein. The fuckers only give us ten days though, but it is grand anyway. Are you doing anything later?'

I told him I had nothing planned as yet to which he replied that he had a little job in mind, if I was interested.

'Shite,' I was thinking, 'what kind of a little job?' I asked him what he had in mind.

'Well, we have the keys of an old boy's car and we're thinking of going up to Southside, smash a window and get our hands on some goodies. It is all the rage now. You just get close to a big fucking window, throw a brick through it and Bob's yer uncle, it's called smash and grab.'

'No I don't think so. Maybe me Ma is going to take us to the Brue to play some games and hang out. She says it'll do me good to be seen with better people.'

'No way' I thought to myself, 'no way was I going to get into that fucking mess again.'

'Go and ask my bollix, you little shite then, and don't come calling to me when you need some friends' said Redser.

With that parting shot he lit a fag and puffed smoke rings into the air defiantly. As he did so I turned on my heel and went up to our room. There, mother said she had the dinner just about ready. We were going to have eggs and spuds and then added that she has saved some of the batch loaf especially as she knew I loved dipping it into my egg. Music to my ears I thought to myself.

After dinner Ma did take us to the Brue. It was only a tenement but far better than ours and when one crossed the road to it one crossed a social dividing line. There she spoke to the manager about my attending during the evenings for a little while. He thought it would be a good idea.

The Brue was a boys club run by yet another religious order of which there were many. The theory was that only street children leading disorganized lives got themselves into trouble. The devil was notorious for making work for idle hands.

They provided the club to get the kids off the streets and offered inducements like table tennis, rings, board games and card games to keep us amused. The rest of the boys were friendly towards me and there was a courtesy about them which was a little different from much of what I have had to get used to.

I settled in very nicely and was made to feel like one of them from the word go. I was quick to make friends and was asked if I wanted to be the fourth player in a game called don. It was something along the lines of bridge but this version was for the lowlife, the criminals and those on the edges of society.

One evening while awaiting my turn to play rings I overheard a group of about four older boys talking about some lady. They were going on about her Mary being black and hairy and just like steel wool.

They caught me listening and one of them said 'are you ok young one?'
'I was wondering what a Mary was'. I replied
They all started to smile.
'Have you never heard of a Mary before?'
'No' said I.
'Well it's a Mary McGee. And this one had a big black one with hair as thick as steel wool'.
'Oh' I said 'but what is it?'
'A Mary McGee is what girls have between their legs' they all said in unison and start laughing.

These events, the strolling and the club, provided me with the space I desperately needed following the misfortune. On the Saturday Da told me he was taking me out to buy me some new clothes after which he would be taking us to the races. Finding myself in Guiney's again I was quickly fitted out with some new trousers, shirts topped up by socks. Then, with the parcel tucked under my arm we set out by bus to Leopardstown and the races. Again it was the loveliest of days and everywhere there were crowds of nicely dressed people milling about. Up on their little wooden platforms the guys in their brown coats were shouting out the odds, taking the bets, offering advice and taking the offered notes.

My Da joined the queue in front of one of these fellows and handing over some money took the tickets in return. Then, making our way to the stands we found what was the best spot for watching the horses break free from the boxes. There in the stands were no end of 'old ones' dressed to the nines, all wearing their funny hats. It seemed to me that the older blokes didn't look much better in their top hats and striped trousers but it set them apart from those like my Da, some wearing flat caps whilst others are bare-headed. To the blokes in the brown coats they were all the same as was the money that changed hands. In this respect there was no class distinction in money. It goes from the rich man's hand to the pauper's and back again, but the latter would normally have to count not only his change but make sure all his fingers were still there too.

'They're off!' I heard the piercing shout which lifted everyone up off their seats, the ones who were sitting that is. There was a stampede towards the front so everyone can get a better sight of the horses as they pick up speed and race neck and neck along the course route. I nearly went head over bollix in the rush forward but Da held on to my arm tightly. Everyone was hollering and screaming their numbers, as if the horses could hear and take note of their wishes. Maybe their remarks were aimed at the riders: 'Come on number whatever, you dopey eejit. Come on, get your whip out, you dosser!'

Soon the horses were hurtling along at breakneck speed and into the last furlong. At this point the crowd were in a frenzy of excitement.

Even my Da was screaming 'Get up there, get up there, you lazy fucking nag.'

With the first three across the line there was a roar of disbelief. There was confusion as to how the closely run race ended. At the finishing post with hardly a nose between them there were three horses. The general clamor was dominated by the constant exclamations demanding who the fuck won.

'Quiet now,' said the steward disapprovingly. 'This has been a photo finish; just have a little patience if you will.'

Everyone was edgy, stepping from one foot to the other, biting their bottom lips and clearly agitated. Then the near silence was broken by a roar. The outsider placed 16/1 had won the race.

'Jaysus be damned. I've got the fucking winner,' said my Da 'And I went and put the fucking bet on each way. But no worries, boyo, we are in the money.'

There were a lot of sad faces in evidence and endless tickets ripped to shreds and thrown contemptuously to the muddy foot-marked grass. Dad on the other hand had a big self-congratulatory smirk on his face as he queued for his winnings. There was no reason to wonder why he was so elated.

After alighting from the bus he was straight into the pub leaving me with the parcel under my arm and a ten bob note in my pocket.

'How did you get on?' asked Ma when I entered the flat and placing a kettle on the hob took my parcel from me to examine its contents.

'I think he won,' I told her, not quite sure what it had all been about but knowing Da had left Leopardstown with more money than he had arrived with. 'He's in Cusack's bar getting drunk I think.'

'Oh well, easy come, easy go,' she replied, probably thinking 'a fool and his money are soon parted' or words to that effect.

Immediately following dinner I went across to the Brue for a game of cards and after having my best night ever arranged to meet four of the others for a trip out to the Bray the following day. Later that night I, and the rest of the tenement, could hear the old feller making his faltering way slowly up the tenement steps.

He was singing his head off and on this occasion it was his favorite, the policeman's song. It was either that or a recital of *The boy stood on the burning deck.*' He had not the slightest concern for those who were disturbed by his drunken entry. Many of the neighbors were afraid of him and could be forgiven for thinking discretion was the better part of valor.

After a lot of failed attempts to remember the words or the order in which the song should be sung, the chorus being provided by my Ma's nagging, he was finally edged towards the bed upon which he fell and was soon snoring loudly. He was the only one of the family who snored and so there would be precious little sleep for the rest of us, especially as the silence between snores was broken by his breaking wind. Next morning I asked me Da how he got on at the pub and if he had a great time.

He told me he had but told me too 'that fucker Lugs Brannigan was outside with the Black Maria and was going to rush the place if we wouldn't all piss off home as it was way past closing time and we were all still in there.'

Was this the right time to ask him for a loan? I was hoping he had forgotten the ten shillings he had given me the day earlier. 'Da,' I said: 'I am off to Bray with some of the boys from the Brue. I need the train fare and some spending money.'

'Wait and see, son,' he said 'I'll just see if your Ma has left any money in my trouser pockets. She's worse than a pickpocket when she gets busy.'

'Here,' he said as he hands me two half crowns.

I have to admit that when he had some money he was free with it. This went to the core of my Ma's problems with him for he buys all and sundry drinks at the pub.

'Mind how you go with those Nancy boys,' he said. 'You keep your back to the walls, they're all tossers.'

I told him they were fine and the only difference between us was that they spoke a little different. I hesitated to say they spoke better. That might in his eyes have marked me out to be a Nancy boy too. So it was that I went off in the direction of Westland Row where we were to board our train. The weather being so fine it was not surprisingly the train was full to standing room only as it rushed through the Irish countryside towards the little seaside town of Bray. It was a favorite haunt for families who like to spend their free time gazing out at the sea or strolling the streets and waterfront.

For me and the others it was the amusement arcades and I, because I still had the ten bob note, was not short of spending money. I was not a gambler as such but it was fun trying my luck on the slot machines, rising to challenges or testing my skill. The machines were usually cleverer than I was though.

It was while we were in one of the bigger centers that on a whim I decided to move my ten bob note from one pocket to the other. Unknown to me a girl was watching as I did so. After trying several games without any luck we stood idly around wondering what to do with ourselves for the rest of the day. The first I noticed her was when she approached, introduced herself with a 'hi' and asked me if I was new to the town.

She was a good looking girl with deep auburn hair reaching down in waves to her shoulders. She was wearing a pink top, a short white skirt and a pair of light white flat-heeled shoes. 'Jesus,' I thought to myself 'Isn't she so beautiful? What Christmas tree did she fall off?'

I was wondering what on earth she could want and was soon to find out.

'Where are you all going?' she asked.

We told her we were going up to the head for a stroll. That was the usual thing people did when on a day trip to Bray. Walk up to Bray Head.

'Can I come with you?'

We five boys looked at each other with raised eyebrows. Then, without hesitation other than our expressions we told her we would love to share her company. And so off we went with the girl tagging along beside us chatting away amicably. The questions between us flew as we learned a little about each other. She was older than any of us, at a guess nineteen or maybe twenty-years old and she had an inner city accent.

As we walked along side by side I could feel a warm glow from the closeness of her. On occasion she pulled a little ahead and I got the perfect view of her shapely long legs and her tight little bum swathed in the cotton fabric of her skirt. A sailor might have described it as two eggs in a sweat rag but for all of that, a delight to the eye.

After a while we paused to give our legs a break and chose rocks to sit on, the grass being moist even in the fine weather. The girl sat a little in front but facing me. Her long legs seemed to stretch out endlessly in front of her. I noticed her diddies were not well developed but a nice handful I was thinking to myself.

We chatted together for a while before setting off once more on our stroll. I couldn't believe my luck that such a beautiful girl was taking an interest in me. We hadn't gone far when she discreetly took my hand and stretching a little whispered in my ear 'Shall we pair off for a little?'

Again, I couldn't believe this was happening to me. I was under no illusions, I was not the best looking in the group and a couple of the others would I thought be more appealing to the girl. My only asset was my tan but that was about all.

I agreed of course and turning around to the lads I told them we were taking a break, we two would catch up with them a little later at the bottom.

There was the expected looks between themselves and a snigger or two but they were amused and no doubt wondering how I managed it. They wished us both a good walk.

I was on cloud nine as I strolled along with my little 'film star'. I was quite sure that other blokes with their girls must be turning and envying me. Inside my pocket there was a packet of fags and retrieving them I offered her one. I couldn't help but notice how long her slender fingers were as she thanked me and took one of the cigarettes. Her nails were painted a bright pink. I had never seen that color on nails before.

Happily puffing away it was at her suggestion that we made our way to a nice little cove we could see off to our left. It was a shaded area with ferns waving gently in the light summer's breeze. Here there was privacy from prying eyes and not once did it occur to me to question the happily unfolding events.

Lying closely together on the grass I was resting on my elbow and absorbing her beautiful contours whilst reflecting on how softly she spoke not to mention the magic of her eyes. She was breathing softly and I was getting what might be thought of as a mild orgasm just by being in her company. I had of course been close to girls before but never as beautiful and as affectionate as this one. I was experiencing sensations that were quite new to me and my heart was skipping a beat or two as we lay beside each other and talked. The sun was warm on my back and was dappling her face affectionately, just as I would like to do.

'Would you like to ride me?'

She came right to the point didn't she? Ride her? Jesus! How the fuck am I going to ride her in a place like this and right out of the blue like that. I had never heard the expression foreplay. What could I do? Dumbly I nodded and thought I would say yes and just go with the flow as you do.

They say it is as easy as riding a bike so I can ride a bike too, problem solved. With luck she won't realise I have never ridden a girl before.

'I would love to.'

I couldn't help but wonder if she detected the near stammer in my voice as I wondered where the hell we go from this point. As I lay there bemused she repositioned herself slightly and edging her skirt upwards I could see her white knickers were clearly in view. Oh, there was no happier bunny than me but she has noticed I am uncertain and acting somewhat awkwardly.

'Have you done this before?' she asked.

'Yes!'

'Spoofer! She laughed. 'Tell me what you do next then.'

Fuck, I think to myself. What do you do next? She knew the right questions to ask didn't she, surely there were better ways to lose one's cherry than under these circumstances.

'I come over, you turn around and I stick my Mickey up the softest bit of you,' I whispered to her.

'Up where,' she asked suggestively and I could see the slight seductive controlled smile edging her lip. She examined my features with what I thought was amused affection. Shite! Should I say, up your arse? Oh what do I do? Help!

'Well, maybe I have not done this before,' I conceded.

Okay,' she whispered alluringly. 'I can teach you but the lesson in lovemaking will cost you.'

'I am not sure what you mean, cost me?' At this stage my Mickey is brittle hard and throbbing, a state of near ecstasy she can't be unaware of.

'It will be ten bob and I will show you,' she murmured quietly, positioning herself as though it is already a done deal.

'Come here,' she said 'Give me your hand.'

Taking it she guided it into the top of her knickers and I found a little slice of paradise as I fondled the clutch of pubic hairs and the moistness between her thighs. By this stage she was having a good moan so had clearly discovered paradise too. But there was a price to be paid if the gates were to be entered. Taking my hand out of her knickers she told me it would be ten bob if I wanted it to go any further.

'I don't have ten bob.'

'Yes you do,' she replied 'It is in the right hand pocket of your trousers. I saw you put it in there when you were in the arcade.'

Would you fucking well believe it? This wasn't love at all. All she wanted was the ten fucking bob in my pocket. It sure rained on my parade and I was so deflated that my Mickey became deflated just as quickly. By now she had seen the disappointment written large on my face and was set on trying to save the situation from collapsing as quickly as my Mickey had. Moving over she kissed me gently on my lips. I was dumbfounded by the changing events but I did at least respond, it was the nicest of sensations as her lips gently brushed my own. Is paradise beckoning again?

Tugging expertly at my trouser zip she reached in and recovered my flaccid Mickey saying: 'Oh, it is one of those is it?'

With that she began to rub some life into it with her right hand whilst with her left she produced from somewhere a paper tissue. Talk about coming prepared! Placing my hand back inside her knickers I did a little exploring and this time it was me that is doing the grunting and the moaning. The pace quickened and oblivious to whatever else might be happening in Bray that day I responded to the occasion with urges that were well beyond my control.

Horrified, she was up on her feet and squealing that I have got my spunk all over her brand new skirt.

'You should have told me you were coming,' she said, her voice was high with indignation.

How the fuck was I to know I was coming. I had never done this before. It was far more than my virginity that I lost that eventful day but perhaps it was another of life's lessons learned. Why should the ride be always so bumpy I thought?

Picture me, lying there abashed with my Mickey again flaccid, dripping the after cum as she swung her handbag, a blow that caught me on the side of my head before storming off up the hill. As she did so the rest of the world returned to sharp focus. What should have been a deathly silence was interrupted by an almighty roar, a cheer had erupted accompanied by much hand clapping. Looking upwards to the skyline over the small cliff's edging I could clearly make out the silhouettes of the boys from the Brue enthusiastically giving me a round of applause for my performance.

'We saw it all and heard it all,' they were chortling: 'Wait until we tell everyone back at the Brue.'

I suppose it went without saying that I dejectedly sat on my own during the long train journey home to Dublin and I never again set foot in the boys club.

But all in all I was not too put out by this episode I had learned a few things especially about the fairer sex. You need money for this sort of girl. For them it's all that they are about. I had also learned how to wank so not a bad investment in time and I had held on to my ten shilling note.

The rest of the week's holiday passed without any major upsets and Saturday came around all too quickly. The light at the end of the tunnel had been less bright with the passing of each day. On the day of departure I was up at 7am for we had to be at the train station an hour and a half later. Ma was to accompany me. This was in more ways than one the reverse of the walk we had taken two weeks earlier. My mood was not good.

The weather was fair and as we made our way along Moore Street. The stall holders were all in high spirits. Their stalls were bending under the weight off produce ready for the busiest day of the week. It was too early for customers, many would be still in their beds.

I was downhearted at leaving home again but knew there was no choice but to make the most of it. If I kept my head down I might well be home again for a week at Christmas.

As we drew nearer to the station we chanced upon others who were returning with us. Oddly enough they were all in the company of their mothers, there wasn't a father in sight. I suppose it must be concluded that it would be collaborating in the betrayal. I could see that point of view. Otherwise the father's role in life was to work, if they had a job. For many their life purpose was to breed children, which is not the same as rearing them.

Brothers Chinney, Titch and Friar Tuck were on the station platform awaiting our arrival. There we were separated from our mothers. The younger ones were crying and I must confess I was wiping away the odd tear.

'Don't worry,' son,' Ma said reassuringly. It is only time and even kings cannot stop time from passing.' Her comment was wise and was to stay with me for the rest of my life. Such is the power of words spoken in thought and compassion. What neither of us knew was that it would be another long two years before we set eyes on each other again.

CHAPTER 12

WE WERE PLACED INTO OUR usual lines and head counted and learned there were three kids missing. As we stepped aboard Brother Chinney went to the Garda on duty at the station. There he reported the names of the kids who had failed to turn up. The train was delayed by thirty-minutes to give them a chance but it eventually pulled out of the station without them. Those boys were never again seen in Letterfrack but word was that they had been caught and were sent to Dangein to see out their time.

The atmosphere on the train was somewhat subdued for the return journey. Anyone who had fags was in the train's lavatory with the windows open as they smoked their brains out. I had a twenty packet of Players and was definitely going to smoke every one of them even if smoke was to come out of my ears.

Clackety-clack, clackety-clack the train sped on its way to Galway City flying past fields and low lying hills. In our carriage there was just the haze caused by cigarette smoke. Titch was furious at our relaxed attitudes but being on a crowded train there wasn't a lot he could do about it.

On arriving in Dublin two weeks earlier we had been dressed to look typically like a group of school kids with our neat hair and clothes. On the return journey we were a motley crew of all types of dress and hair styles. There were crew cuts, shaven heads, boys wearing kaftans and hipsters. There were all the colors of the rainbow in the shirts now being worn. Ours was more like a group of youngsters going on a rave but that was before raves were invented.

Jerking along at its best speed our train was rocking from side to side and it wasn't long before I began to feel a bit unwell.

One of the kids gave me a pint of milk he had in his bag, courtesy of his Ma.

'Here,' he said. 'Take this. It will put a lining on your stomach, settle it.'

I had never before suffered with travel sickness but then I had never travelled so far as this before, just the one earlier trip to Letterfrack. After drinking the milk I seemed a lot better so had another fag. Fuck, these things are rotten I thought to myself but it's the thing to do as it is supposed to make a man out of you. And so you keep on puffing like a little dragon?

Reaching Galway Station we all trooped off with dejected expressions. As we left the station and headed for the bus we could see a number of Americans standing about with their suitcases. It was obvious they were yanks as they looked so different in their manner, dress and posture.

One of the men turned to one of the women in their party: 'Look Muriel. It's them scallywags we heard so much about. Thank God we're finished in Salthill. Could you imagine that lot in our hotel?'

'Kept awake all night no doubt,' the lady replied sourly.

With that, one of the older kids released a huge fart and ran towards the bus laughing manically. No doubt the yanks were impressed with his anus tricks. On the bus we were again head counted as it pulled away on the road that led to Letterfrack Industrial School. In the bog and so it was but we were from Dublin in the green.

Sitting at the rear of the bus I was still working my way through my fag packet and where I was sitting there were steps leading down to a back door. After a while I began to feel sick again and this time I couldn't keep it down and spontaneously vomited all over the place. I was as sick as a dog and felt sure I was going to die. The dregs of my stomach were self-evident and by now all down the steps and I could see carrots in it even though I had not eaten carrots recently.

Wiping my mouth on my sleeve I had to travel in the back of the bus with my mouth stinking and the smell around me making me dry retch. Those boys who had been sitting near me had wisely moved forward along the bus and I was made to feel like a leper for the rest of the journey.

On arriving at the school the instruction was to go and fetch a bucket with some cloths and to then clean the bus. That was followed by a good slapping. Welcome back to Letterfrack I thought to myself. At least having my own bed in some respects was better than sharing with my brother but I still had a feeling of emptiness, I missed the comfort of his body heat.

For some reason I couldn't fathom out the two weeks at home in Dublin had changed me. I now seemed to be a different person, I felt much stronger and was looking taller after my break, and I had matured a little. Was it my chance meeting with the girl in Bray. Perhaps it takes very little time to turn a young boy into a young man. I was now more thoughtful. The brothers seemed to sense the change in me and never again did Chinney invite me into his room.

After the usual ritual of rising early for Sunday mass and all the religious palaver stuff that went with it things got back to normal.

When home on my holidays I never went to mass and when I got out of this place I would only do so at marriages or deaths, otherwise the church had lost this lamb by default.

Ordered back to the farm, I was working hard each day and all seemed to be going fine as the summer drew to its end. By then the nights were drawing in and there was a distinct chill in the air which penetrated the thin clothing we habitually wore.

We were back to hauling rocks from one muddy field to the next, stacking up the big rock piles before carrying them over to a field boundary and there making a wall. Thankfully I was not required to use the sledgehammer as others were. Breaking the rocks up was the hardest work imaginable. It was grueling and extremely cold work. Titch clearly took delight in our miseries and would run up and down the line as we carried the rocks.

As he did so, like a slave-driver he would scream 'Come on, you lazy fucking bastards. Move yourselves won't you?'

As he bawled he would whack our legs with his cane stick. It wasn't long before the hatred for him began to fester and grow stronger in my mind. I yearned, I dreamed and I fantasized about wrenching the cane from his grasp and giving him a taste of his own medicine. The only thing that stopped me was the recollection of what had happened to a kid who had done just that. All I could do was grit my teeth and hope that he would miss me with his mad swipes.

We were back in the hall during the evenings and Brother Tea was still the one in charge of this particular duty. He continued to glower at me with an incomprehensible look of pure hatred just as he had that night I had kept winning my table tennis games.

'Come with me, you,' he commanded as he pointed at me.

It was obvious from his expression he was in a blistering mad mood. Following him from the hall towards the main building I picked up a large rock and held it behind my back. There was an inward fury at the injustice I was facing and the dark thoughts coursing through my head were that I had had enough of you, you fucking head case.

He swept through to one of the school's classrooms with me following behind. There were by now beads of sweat on his brow and he was licking his lips, probably salivating as he gripped the leather tightly in his hands. This was the strap that we all knew was laced with coins so as to cause further damage and hurt. Was it my attitude that infuriated him? Did he sense I was a better and a stronger person than he was and this was his way of showing who was boss?

'Unfasten your trousers and drop them and bend over that desk.'

Producing the rock so he could now see it I replied 'You try this and I will split you open you fucking sick pervert.'

No sooner were my defiant words uttered than he let out an almost girlish scream and brought the strap crashing down on my head. From there on he tirelessly belabored me. There wasn't a part of my body that didn't feel the agonizing bloodletting blows. As he struck at me wildly he was panting and constantly changing stance, making sure the slashes and blows would reach every part of my body.

'You will never ever answer me back or try the likes of this again,' he screamed.

His voice was getting hoarse with his exertions. Over and over again he brought the strap down or swung it across my head, my body and legs. By this time I thought he had lost all sense of sanity. The devil had taken over him and whatever the consequences, if any, he was now out to kill me. Holding me with one hand the blows rained down from the strap in the other. Afterwards, I was surprised he hadn't continued to beat me until life left me that night. And for what, he was driven by a sadistic bloodlust that could only be assuaged on a helpless thirteen-year old boy.

I was never brought to the doctor and spent over two weeks in bed recovering from the beating. This resulted in me nearly starving as I would only get food when one of the brothers remembered to bring a tray, this was not very often. They wanted to keep me alive, just. To this day I don't know if it was deliberate or designed to make my misery and hurt worse.

Instead of this episode making me more fearful of the brothers it had the opposite effect. By now I had decided they would have to kill me before I would succumb to any more of this battering. When I was better and back at work I considered again it was the time to get out of here. I now feared for my life and I had a real fear that if I failed to escape I would never be leaving the bogs but would remain in them in an unmarked grave. The brothers, as was later shown, were not above murder. I now knew the right direction to head in. I had memorized the route from the time we had gone to Dublin and back.

The first survival trick was to arrange a cache of sweets for sustenance on the road. I would buy these from the shop, bought with the money my Ma sent to me. My plan was to take sufficient food and sweets with me on my next escape. By doing so I would be able to stay out of sight in the fields for as long as possible, to travel further before having to approach houses for food.

My escape was arranged for an afternoon during which I had been sent back to the dormitory, the pretext being stomach cramps. I had remembered the window above Chinney's door and decided to get into his room to rob whatever I could that might help me during my escape bid.

There was no one else sick and so I had the dormitory all to myself. I knew that all the brothers were out at work or busy elsewhere. Creeping silently along the corridors outside the brothers' rooms I paused occasionally to listen for the slightest sound. Satisfying myself that each of their rooms were empty I then lifted myself up to the ledge above Chinney's room door. As expected it too was empty and so I climbed through the window atop the door and dropped quietly into his room.

My heart was racing and the fear of being caught was so real for I knew they would kill me if they were to find me in one of their rooms. I sensed then but know now that there would have been the most casual of enquiries. It would be presumed I had successfully escaped and just disappeared somewhere into the glens and bogs. The region was too vast to be searched, the resources too few and the will nonexistent. I would not have been the first or the last child to meet such an end. Why not? We were society's rejects and had no value whatsoever. The bogs stretch out for mile after secluded mile. They made the perfect hiding place for the disposal of one's sins.

Quickly rummaging about in his drawers I found cartons of Sweet Afton cigarettes and took three packets. I hadn't the slightest idea why I took just the three packets but it is what I did. I also took a box of matches and then climbed back through the window leaving everything just as I had found it.

Creeping back along the dormitory to my bed I hid the matches and fags under my mattress. I was just about ready to make my departure when I heard voices in the wash room. Shit, I thought, I'd better get into bed quickly. Quickly undressing I slid under the blankets and holding my breath listened carefully. I couldn't hear voices but what I could hear was this strange sound like cloth rubbing against cloth. Then I heard Brother Mutton Head from the kitchen say:

'Good, good! That was very good lad and you are in for a big roast dinner this weekend. Now just lick it all off and we can get back to the kitchen.'

Shite thought I, he's got some kid out there and they're doing something they shouldn't be doing. Putting my head under the covers I was hoping that if he looked into the dorm he would not see me in the bed.

After a while all was silent again and creeping silently out to the washroom I found it all clear. There wasn't a soul to be seen or heard. I could hear all the lads coming back from the fields and knew I couldn't take off now. I would not be able to get far at this time of day and would soon be caught.

Making my way silently back to my bed I decided to bluff it out if I was questioned about any missing fags. As luck would have it, and I needed some of that, Chinney didn't seem to realise there were packets missing. The next morning I feigned sickness again.

Leaving it until I knew everyone had gone to their work I slipped from my bed and putting on as many clothes as I could I slipped out of the dormitory and down the stairs. Fuck! What was that? I could hear noise coming from the bottom of the stairs. Holding my breath I stopped before peeping around the banister. Peering down I could see Brother Friar Tuck standing in the main doorway. He was smoking a cigarette, his other hand was behind his back.

It was clear that this escape route was out of the question. His presence meant I either had to remain where I was and wait for him to move or cut through the other dormitory. I was not familiar with the other hall and wasn't sure I could get out through its far end. I thought it better to wait to see if the brother would move.

As soon as he finished his cigarette he tossed the butt out ahead of him and turning brusquely went back into the tuck shop. Here was my opportunity. Silently descending the flight of stairs and along the corridor I went quietly past the doctor's surgery and into the cloakroom. There I retrieved the food parcel I had stashed there.

This left the yard to be crossed and the only way to do that was to stuff everything up my jumper and walk casually across the yard as if it were perfectly natural that I should be there.

My route would take me across the yard and past the hall, to its far end and then I needed to take a left along the lane. At that point I would clamber over a roadside wall and into the obscurity of the field. My plan was to stay as close to the main road as possible. By this strategy I wouldn't get stuck in any bogs or lakes and so would make better time.

I could also listen out for cars coming along the road and be able to use the walls as cover. This time I was determined to get away, I was under no illusions as to the severity, even life-threatening beatings I could expect if I were to be caught on this second occasion. I was unlikely to forget the beatings and other punishments I had been on the receiving end of last time I had gone on the run.

I made it safe and unseen to the field from where I would start my solitary journey. Putting my best foot forward and squaring my chin determinedly I set out walking due east. After about half an hour's walking I heard the sound of a car in the distance. Ducking down behind the wall I waited for it to pass. Holding my breath I could hear its approach and then, after it had passed the spot where I was hiding, the sound of its engine being absorbed by distance. I was hoping I would be able to give myself five or even six hours head start before the brothers realised I had again gone on the run. This would mean I would be so far away they would be confused as to the direction I would have gone in or the distance covered. I was hoping I would be a very small needle in a very big haystack. My plan was to reach Galway, board a train and from there go to Dublin by hiding in the train's lavatory.

Rewarding myself with a cigarette I took deep drags but paced myself. I had no intention of making myself unwell. I hadn't had a cigarette for some time. It tasted good and I felt much better for it. Shortly after resuming walking I met what might easily be my nemesis. I was confronted by a biggish lake.

As it stretched under the road and which for a little way became a causeway I had to get my choice right. Walking around the lake would add considerably to the time I was taking but the distance gained between me and Letterfrack would be not that much greater for the hour or so it would take to get round it. Worse, it would make me a highly visible fugitive as much of its banks were in the open and clearly visible from the road.

I had little choice but to climb over the wall and sprint as fast as my legs would carry me until I reached the lake's far side. If a vehicle was to approach during my headlong flight it was the end of another bid for freedom. I would be seen and even if it was not a threatening situation the car would be sure to stop and question me, a small boy out in the wild country roads as darkness is beginning to descend. I presumed that in such a rural location everyone would know everyone anyway.

Off I went like the clappers of hell, head down, my legs going like pistons with my heart pounding and my lungs sucking in air. The wind was ringing in my ears as I reached the far side of the water's edge. I had just shinned over the stone wall when I heard a car's approach. Crouching down out of sight behind the wall I was holding my breath so I could better read the sound of the car's progress. Wonderful, like the earlier vehicle it drove on past, laboring a little as it approached the gently incline. From where I found myself I could see a small house, perhaps a smallholding off to my right. If anyone was looking out of the window or working in the front I would be clearly in view. I decided to take a chance, cross the road and make my way along the far side of that wall. It would shield me from the house.

With a run at the wall I again shinned over it but my plans were dashed when on reaching the far side of the road realised my route was blocked by a mass of overgrowth and wild shrubbery.

I had little choice but to quickly retrace my steps, use the wall as a camouflaged backdrop and just take my chances. At a half run whilst keeping my head down I covered some distance but as far as my feet would carry me the house remained in view. If I was close enough to see it then they were close enough to see me. It seemed an eternity before its outline was lost in the distance behind me.

Only then did I feel safer but I was in desperate need of a rest and a cigarette. By this time my thoughts were all over the place. Maybe I hadn't put enough thought into this. Uppermost in my mind was the reasoning that I simply could not afford to be caught and returned. I was sure that death perhaps, certainly serious injury would be my lot if those brothers could get their hands and their boots on me. I had no choice but to put as much distance as possible between me and them.

Pacing myself I continued on my way by following the line of the roadside wall which to me seemed a far better idea than trying to go across country. The only potential danger was my coming across a cottage or farm, they are naturally close to the country roads and this road was unlikely to be an exception. There seemed to be many lakes scattered along the road's route, which wasn't helping matters at all.

Darkness fell quickly and from every direction I could hear the sounds of nocturnal creatures. Some of the noises were to me quite strange and caused my hair stand on end. There was many a cold shiver that ran down my spine, many a heart-stopping moment as the night closed in. Taking the philosophical view, I comforted myself with the thought that the creatures were more likely to be afraid of me, and what I couldn't see wouldn't hurt me. I was determined not to stop but to carry on through the night. Distance covered was more important than was rest. I knew the greater the distance the more difficult it was for the brothers' net to work.

The brothers would by now be aware that I had disappeared and I could well imagine the hue and cry. They would already be getting excited at the thought of the punishment they would inflict on me upon my return. But, I was not going to be returned. They would be disappointed.

It was very late into the night when I stumbled across a large farm. The dogs were barking before I could see the buildings but I decided to keep going. I was pinning my hopes on the farmer thinking it was only a wild animal causing them to kick up such a fuss. In truth I must have resembled a wild animal. Had he let them loose I would have shit my trousers because I am terrified of large dogs. I kept going until the sound of the barking faded into the distance behind me. Eventually I came across a little copse that looked safe and decided it was time to take a breather and have a smoke. With a little bit of luck I would sleep for a little while.

As I lay there on my back, pulling the occasional draw from my cigarette, I could see the sky's dark bowl above my head. The stars were shining and twinkling so brightly and a sense of euphoric tranquility washed over me. Feeling drowsy I thought not to fight it and soon fell into an oblivion in which there was no fear, I was a not a fugitive in fear of his life and there were no brothers. Most of all, there were no brothers.

I have no idea what time it was when I woke with a start. Where am I was my first thought, where the fuck am I? Was this a dream, a nightmare? I was so cold I was shaking uncontrollably and I was so wet through with the dew I might easily have been thought to have fallen in a river. As I saw the sun rising I had the sense to know that if I got to my feet and started briskly walking the passage of time would dry my clothes out. Lighting a fag I headed to where I hoped was due east.

Doubts were beginning to set in. Had I blundered? I was soaked through and my clothes were like rags. How on earth would I make myself presentable to board the train at Galway Station? Regardless and determined I set off at a jog. Before long wisps of steam were rising from me, which made me chuckle. Now I was the steam-kid and I might become the cowboy I wanted to be. In my imagination I was Gene Autry, the cowboy screen legend and I was sure going to make it to that town yonder.

On I jogged through the fields and for as far as the eye could see it was open land. My idea to travel overland keeping to the road without actually using it seemed to be working. It wasn't long before my clothes were beginning to dry and it was time to take another breather and treat myself to a few sweets. The gobstoppers were keeping my mouth moist but were doing little to tone down my hunger. I also needed something to drink and keeping an eye out for a stream it wasn't long before in this boggy terrain I come across a clear running one.

Dropping to my knees I lapped up the water as a dog does for this was no time for convention. Having satisfied my thirst I set off again. The hours passed and it was late afternoon when I chanced upon a large building I thought might be a church. I carried on past it, I had no desire to throw my need for charity on religious people, they would be as sure to hand me over to the brothers as would the Garda themselves although with comforting platitudes no doubt, strangely absent when the strap was torturing a child's flesh.

Although I was aware of a lot of cars using the road I was not too much bothered by them. It was over twenty-four hours since I made my escape and I must have covered a great distance. I was in no doubt as to the state the brothers might be in. The children are usually captured and returned within a few hours.

By the time nightfall came I was exhausted and my pockets empty of sweets. I hacked on regardless. The more country miles I could put between me and Letterfrack the greater the chances of escape. The ground beneath my feet was getting harder and the boggier ground was behind me in the distance. Could the reason be that I was getting closer to Galway City I am thinking to myself? The thought spurred me on.

I was jogging along in the darkness when I ran straight into the barbed wire fence and tumbled over and further into the entanglement. The pain was piercingly sharp and came from multiple places. The barbs had ripped my clothing and had torn my skin. The small wounds were bleeding. I was badly winded too, as much by the unexpectedness of it. I could feel the blood seeping through my jumper and putting my hands down my legs I could feel the blood there also.

Clambering to my feet I hadn't the faintest idea what to do. In my juvenile mind there was a real possibility of my bleeding to death out there in the wilderness. Was the brothers' job to be done for them by this misfortune? Had I only seen the fence in time? Trying to stem the blood by licking and drying my hands was clearly not going to work. I needed to find a stream and clean myself up properly. From here on there would be no more running in the darkness for me. The prudent way was to travel more carefully, accidents like that only slowed progress up anyway.

I had never known such hunger and the need for food was now giving me cramps. I was nauseous with need and sucking on the last of a couple of sweets I discovered in an inner pocket. The priority now was to look for a safe place where I might catch some sleep. Within half an hour I came across a small stone bridge crossing the main road. Ducking under it I realised it made the ideal shelter, I had tonight a roof of sorts over my head. This is where I was going to spend my night, curled up in a little ball. Perhaps the cover would keep me free of the dew.

Sleep wouldn't come easily. I was sore from the torn skin and it seemed to be a lot colder than it was during the previous night. Looking back I realise this was on account of my extreme hungriness and exhaustion. I was trying to keep my mind from wandering as my thoughts were driving me nuts.

Might I die out here; will someone one day come across my body or skeleton in a little hollow and wonder who I was and what I was doing there? What if a wild dog comes along and finds me here? The night before I was tired but tonight I am completely drained. The night before I was exhilarated from the adventure but this evening I was lonely and becoming very frightened. I think I must have sensed circumstances were beginning to dictate the outcome.

I must have drifted into sleep because I was awakened by the sound of a tractor or a truck crossing the bridge just feet over my head. A few small pieces of earth dislodged by its passage showered down on me. Waiting for the sound to disappear I then crept out of my shelter. I was bursting for a piss and with my back to the road I took my Mickey out, the relief as the stream flowed endlessly. The sun was coming up. I could feel its warmth and best of all my clothes were dry. A lesson learned; don't sleep out in the open.

The hunger in me seemed to have eased and hoping it didn't return I once again set my feet in what I hope is the direction of Galway. It was later in the morning that I came to my first village and this presented problems. How do I get round or through it without drawing attention to myself? I was crouching behind a wall figuring out my next move when I heard someone shouting: 'Hey, boy!'

Shite, I was thinking. I have been spotted.

The caller can only mean me and with that three rozzers came hurtling towards me, their long black gabardine coats flapping like batwings as they closed the distance between us. They looked like the avengers of death.

'Hey, boy. Don't move. Stay right where you are.'

Fuck this I thought to myself. I didn't get this far to be caught and off I went as fast as my legs would carry me. I hadn't got very far, maybe a hundred yards during which I could hear them closing in on me. The grunting and panting was just over my shoulder when I was thrown to the ground as a result of the police officer's rugby tackle. Exhausted and winded I was no match for the burly policeman whose weight and strength pinned me to the ground whilst the other two closed in. As they pulled me to my feet the one who had rugby tackled me dusted his tunic off.

'Are you okay, lad?'

'I am fine, you big waster.'

The response from his open hand sent me once again crashing to the ground. I am dead now I was thinking to myself as I was roughly dragged to my feet and more or less dragged to the roadside. Clearly in view is the police car all liveried up with Garda on its sides. They must have seen me from the road. Well I was well and truly fucked up now because there is no way I was going to escape the clutches of these three fuckers. They were talking about me as if I'm not there.

'Little bollix! Did you see the state of him trying to make a run for it? He looks like a little knacker.'

'He probably is one. We'll have to get him back to Letterfrack now.'

'How old are you, son?'

'Thirteen, it will be my birthday soon.'

'Well we just spoiled it,' he said with a low laugh. The inside of the police car was stinking with the overpowering smell of wet gabardine and heavy police uniforms and farts.

'So you are thirteen years old and planning on walking across Ireland? I like confidence even when it is misplaced.' The other policemen snorted their approval at their colleagues' wit.

'He covered some distance, maybe twenty miles or more. I don't remember any others making it this far.'

The other one muttered that he had no recollection of a kid getting so far either.

'I wouldn't want to be in his shoes when he gets back,' grinned the driver. 'They will give him a good tanning for sure.'

I was just sitting there, almost hidden between the two Garda while I was listening to this drivel. As the car swept up the road past the abbey I knew it wouldn't be long now before I was in for the beating of my life, literally. As the police car turned into the graveled driveway of the school it followed the lane passing the hall and pulled to a stop outside the tailoring shop. I was thinking to myself, these rozzers have been here to this exact spot before.

Brothers Chinney and Tea were waiting expectantly on our arrival. It was as though they were expecting us although I hadn't heard anything being said on the car's radio. It crossed my mind that there might be some way of divine thought crossing the miles, something that was yet beyond my understanding.

Jerking the car door's handle the door flew open and Chinney reaching in grabbed me by the scruff of my neck. As he pulled me out he hurled me to the ground. He did so with such violence I thought my back must be broken.

As he did so the policemen climbed back in their car and without a backward glance spun the car around, sped down the driveway and turning through the gates disappeared from view. Their duty done, Chinney's was just beginning.

Before their car was out of sight Chinney had become demented and with his swinging boots was kicking out at me. I was rolling about the driveway trying to avoid his boots hitting me. Curling into a ball I was covering my head and my face as the soles and tips of his boots thudded into me.

'You bastard, you fucking little bastard,' he was screaming as seemingly he was trying to hit me with every limb he had. 'You are done for now. After all we have done for you this is how you show your fucking gratitude, you little bastard. All that and all you can do is turn around and run away again. Well, I am telling you, this is the last time because I am going to break your fucking legs, see how far you can run then, you little bastard!'

At some stage Friar Tuck came running over: 'that's enough now, that is quite enough.'

Taking me by my hand he led me across the yard towards the cloakroom. There he took a towel and wetting it under the tap he began to wipe away the blood and the tears from my face. 'It's okay, lad,' he said. 'We'll soon get you fixed up; now hush your sobbing, hush, hush.'

The brother then took me to the showers where I stripped off and stepped into the shower, while he went off to get towels and some clean clothes for me. I was shivering with fear and pain. I was totally drained. I felt near to death. After that I was put to bed and he suggested I get to sleep and we will see how you are tomorrow.

I dropped off immediately and awoke the next morning to Brother Chinney's hand clapping. When I rose from my bed everyone was staring at me in awe but nobody was saying anything. It was an uncomfortable feeling. I felt like some kind of freak. I just carried on as normal. Getting washed and dressed I could see my face was very badly bruised and there were big lumps on my head. There were bare patches where clumps of hair had been wrenched from my head. I imagined that this happened during the frenzied attack by Chinney on me when I was brought back.

As normal I went for breakfast with all the other lads and I could feel everyone was talking about me in whispers and there was many a furtive glance in my direction. After the breakfast was wolfed down we went to the yard. I was standing at the door leading to the yard wondering if I had to run around the yard when Brother Chinney came out behind me.

'Now, my lad,' he says, 'Run! Every time you come into the yard you run. You run as if your life depended on it because it does. Do you know what I mean? Your life depends on you running. Do you hear me, boy? Do you hear me, you little shite?'

So off I went again, ever the lonely runner but I didn't care as my freedom was not your world, it was the freedom in my head and in my imagination. They all saw me running around the yard. If I seemed to do so enthusiastically it was because inside my head I was running as fast and as far away from this dreadful place as I could. I was no longer with them. I was tearing across the fields and bogs reaching out for Galway City and my home city. I was constantly in a faraway place in the back of my mind where my dreams were mine and mine alone. They could not take them away from me.

I never ran in the school's yard. I ran for me and I ran for freedom, the freedom of the hillsides, the road and avenues of home.

I was never taken to the doctor to be seen for my injuries. Nature and time was to be my only healer. So as on the earlier occasion, every time I entered the yard I had to run. This would go on again for months but for reasons I could not fathom the first beating was not as expected followed up by others.

This happy state of affairs was not to last. There came the morning when I was called out of the classroom by Brother Chinney. Again there was no reason for me to be picked on. I had kept my head down and dutifully done everything that was required of me. There didn't need to be a reason for a beating, they were carried out randomly, on a whim or with some forethought. Clearly the brothers relished the occasions.

I was then taken over to the hall by the brother and made to drop my pants and bend over. Methodically he began to beat me across my bare buttocks with his leather. Holding my breath I prayed I would be able to withstand the ordeal without sobbing or crying out in pain. I bit my bottom lip and squeezed my knuckles together. Each stinging strike was like red hot metal tearing into my flesh. I was sure I could beat the bastard and imagined us as being in a fight, his intention to make me scream, my intention to not do so.

The strokes must have been tiring his arm as he swung the leather over his shoulder as to cause the maximum hurt. I could hear him panting and swearing under his breath as he belabored me. After a while the pain was so excruciating animal like whimpers turned into screams as I begged for forgiveness, screaming for my Ma and begging his forgiveness. I was pleading, sobbing my heart out, and crying for him to stop. I couldn't take any more.

When he finally did stop all I could do was lie on my side and scream my pain and my cries echoed through the hall. As I did so he just stood with a sly smirk on his face, obviously excited by the effect his beating had on me.

'You be prepared to receive this type of punishment anytime I feel like giving it to you. You little bastard! I will stop your running. You will run no more. Do you hear me?' He screamed.

'Yes. Yes brother.' Oh God the pain was unbearable! 'Yes brother Sir I hear you, I will never run again. Please brother. Please brother!'

After that beating it took me three days before I could walk let alone run. When in the hall I had to face the wall at all times. I was not allowed to mingle with the other boys, or to play table tennis or any other game.

I was running around the yard one day when Brother Chinney called me over and told me I needed a change of trousers. He beckoned me to follow him. Taking me to the clothes room he gave me a pair of pants that looked like gophers. They were wide at the top and tapered into drain pipes at the bottom. I seemed to recall a bigger lad coming back from his holidays with them, part of a suit that had been hand made for him; they were grey in color with stripes running through them.

When I pulled them on I looked like a circus clown for they were swimming on me. But this was what Chinney wished me to wear and wear them I must. Whatever it took he was determined to break my spirit and so I did whatever was demanded of me as I had come to fear being beaten. There was no respite in my sleep either for my dreams was of being beaten, or of my running, always running.

I wore those pants for about a month until Brother Friar Tuck was in charge of the yard and one day he called me over.

'Who gave you them pants to wear?' he asked as his eyes challenged my own.

I told him. Shaking his head he told me to go to the tailors and to tell them I needed to have a proper fitting pair of pants. This I did and felt so relieved that all the laughing and sniping from the other lads would from there on cease. It was one thing to be forced to run around the yard but to do so looking like a clown was just too humiliating.

My happiness was not long lived as the very next day Brother Chinney was on duty and it didn't take him long to spot my change of trousers.

'Come here, you,' he yelled. 'Where did you get the trousers from?'

I told him that one of the brothers had told me to get them from the tailor's shop to which he replied that I had better go back to the shop and exchange them for the ones I had taken to them. On arriving there the brother in charge said they had since been cut into cleaning rags.

I told Brother Chinney what the brother in the shop had said and the words were barely out of my mouth when his boot swung up and the toecap of it plunged unexpectedly into my stomach. I fell to the ground reeling and holding myself in the most terrifying pain. I had no idea anything could have hurt so much. I was sick, retching, throwing up and gasping for air. I was so badly hurt I thought I was about to die. As he grinned at what he had done I was contorted in agony, rolling around the ground clutching myself and being sick. It was like I was drowning, the sensations were beyond all my previous experiences, I was drowning in pain.

'Get up. Get up you little bastard,' Chinney screamed at me 'Get up and get fucking running.'

I couldn't get up. I was vomiting and in the most terrible pain. He went hysterical, screaming and swearing that I should do what I was told. Other than gasp gulps of air and hold myself I was helpless, I couldn't even stand let alone walk or run. With a look of utter contempt he turned on his heel and left me writhing in my misery.

I had very little idea of how long it was before I could finally stagger to my feet and for what remained of the day I could only limp around the yard holding my guts. All the time I was praying he wouldn't return and make me run. I couldn't take any running and nor could I take another beating.

That night I found it so difficult to get to sleep as every time I tried to drop off I felt like I was not going to wake up; I still had this sensation of drowning. The days were just running into one endless time capsule as I tramped around the yard. The feelings of desperation and loneliness were getting so bad I no longer knew how to handle it. I felt I might be losing my mind.

How long more was I going to have to run? When would they think I had been punished enough? When would this stop? Would it ever? I know running away was not allowed but what was to be done? Was there no one to stop and figure why we ran? Did I have to stay and be abused on a daily basis; is it not built into the human psyche to escape and to run when it was a matter of survival? I had no idea but I do know that my life was being changed beyond all repair in this hell hole.

I was not invited to take part in the Christmas play that year. I was to attend it facing the wall in the hall; my running was to be extended well into February. This was the longest period of punishment running in the school's history so I was led to believe. I was been called 'The Runner' by the other kids.

I overheard some of them saying to a new kid one day 'see yer man over there he's the runner the lunatic runner'

If the Brothers thought this would deter me from running away again they were wrong. I was forever looking for opportunity and as soon as it presented itself I would be away again, haring across the countryside to nowhere in the full knowledge that escape was impossible but attempting to was not Being beating regularly didn't seem to work, not in my case. It only made me more determined to be rebellious and as often as I had a chance I would do wrong if I could. Each time I did it was payback time for the system I was enduring.

When the running finally ceased I again kept myself to myself. I didn't feel close to any of the other kids. All I wanted to do was do my time on my own. Feeling that being a loner was better than being caught up in the problems of others my decision to be an outsider was to help me get through this very troubled period in my life.

CHAPTER 13

DIGGING UP THE TURF AGAIN this year was horrendous and there were cuts, scrapes and bruises all over my body. The slightly less arduous job of actually cutting the turf was denied to me as it was thought it might give me opportunity for fleeing again. It was no problem for me; I just gritted my teeth and got on with it. The clock was always ticking away in my mind and I knew that the day would inevitability arrive when they could hold me no longer unless they buried me in the bog as they probably had others.

The work on the farm was hard. It was cold and wet work, which the body never really adapted to. As a consequence my heart still goes out to children whose situation requires them to work in similar cold and wet environments.

Later I was put back on the early morning milking duties. This work meant more or less around the clock animal husbanding. The cattle needed to be brought in from the fields and then the need to milk them dry. Then there were the buildings, not just the cowsheds to be cleaned. By the time you had done all this it was afternoon and the process had to be repeated. There wasn't a break as such. Between morning and afternoon milking we would be given other chores to keep us occupied. The farmer's view was that time wasted was time lost. It seemed that his son took his father's advice to heart for he never missed an opportunity to whack us with his boot-slapping stick. We were beaten because he liked the power or rather the chance to abuse his power because he could. There didn't have to be a reason, you were beaten as a deterrent not as a punishment. It was as casually administered as taking a biscuit from a jar.

At the school itself the policy of child beating was that it be carried out by one brother but occasionally there were two brothers present. This was when a major beating was being carried out. I could only presume this was because there needed to be a witness, hardly a hostile one, if the effects of the beating were so severe as to warrant medical or outside intervention.

The beatings inflicted on me continued and I could expect them to occur twice each week. My behavior, which was invariably good, had no bearing on the matter. All I could think of was, fuck those bastards. I will do whatever I can to fuck them up behind their backs.

The days were rolling by from one to the other and the harsh routine of each day's work was broken only be the Friday meal when you received on your plate what was supposed to be fish. Other than that there was just the thought that each small ritual milestone heralded another seven days of backbreaking soul-destroying work. The dairy herd needed constant attention and being the bad boys we were not allowed the luxury of a break, thus the work was to be our lives as long as we were at Letterfrack.

We learned that pissing on our hands brought some relief when they became blistered. Yes, even milking cattle teats causes blisters when it is done twice a day seven days a week. Children's hands aren't really strong enough for that kind of work in which there is never a period for recovery.

As time went by and the weather seemed to improve in harmony with the days growing longer. Then there came the day when I was called up to see the head brother. Shite, I thought. What have I done now? I had learned that it wasn't necessary for me to do anything at all to merit a beating or a command that I appear before the brother's head.

Would I be sent to Dangein Industrial School? That place had an appalling reputation and it was said to be far worse than was Letterfrack. I found out later on in life, there was no school worse than Letterfrack, not even Dangein.

As I stood outside the brother's door I was petrified at the thought of what might await me once called in. The fifteen minutes I did wait seemed to last an eternity. These brothers were entirely devoid of compassion or conscience. They would be well aware of the trepidation on youngsters' faces as they awaited their summons. The opportunity for inflicting suffering offered the prospect of pushing the boundaries. I had only once been into his office and I had horrific recall of the beating he had inflicted on me. To them a beating was an outlet, a self-indulgence to break the monotony of their own lives.

Once I was called I entered to find him sitting behind his desk whilst I stood respectfully before it with my hands behind my back. From the comfort of his large leather seat he peered over his glasses at me.

'You seem to be something of an abnormality.' he said.

That makes two of us I thought to myself.

'You're fourteen are you not?'

I nodded my head; my birthday had just passed, not that they would notice.

He went on 'You are a loner and I have thought up a job for you that will leave you to your own devices. You will have my trust in you to do and say only what you are told. You will work with the farmer who will train you in sheep husbandry. Do you understand?'

I was unsure of what he wanted from me but liked the idea of working on my own devices.

Nodding my head I said in a low voice 'Yes.'

He looked at me with what he thought must be a benign manner: 'You will of course have long days and you will work solely in the confines of this school's boundaries, to which you must adhere to at all cost. If you have any problems, or if at any time you feel the urge to run away, then you must come and see me. We shall iron out any problems that you may have. Do you understand?'

Again I nodded and replied in the affirmative. He looked thoughtfully for a long minute as though he himself was wondering if there might be something further to add.

'You mustn't let me down, boy.'

I was in a state of bewilderment as I left his office and couldn't figure out why I had been transferred to such a preferential job that carried with it the opportunity for escape but trust to counter it. Little did I then realise that the work was not preferential. I had at least done what I hoped was my last milking session and as I snuggled down into my bed I could only wonder what the next day might bring.

I got a bit of a lie-in as usually I was up and on my way long before Brother Chinney arrived to clap his hands and wake everyone and get them on their feet beside their beds. Then, after the usual morning routine and with my lunch tucked under my arm I made my way to the farmyard. The rest of the boys were on a short break and wondering what I was doing arriving a little late with my lunch pack.

The farmer was there of course as was his son. I hoped that I would not be working on my own with him. I could never trust him. My mind was eased; he was put in charge of the others who would be doing the milking.

The farmer was a man probably in his early fifties, roughly dressed as farmers are, a rotund almost caricature of a figure with a huge gut and spindly legs. Constantly smoking his pipe it was as much a part of him as was one of his limbs. There were two dogs with him, both collies one of which was old and white. It was called Driver whilst its companion was black with white patches. I guessed it to be about 12 months old so like me it was still growing and learning. For some reason this dog was called Swim.

Setting off with the dogs ambling beside us, they occasionally ran ahead or paused to take in their surroundings. I had guessed right. Swim like me was in training to be a shepherd. Striking out across the pastures and up the Diamond mountain's side we could see Letterfrack Industrial School set out in the valley just as though it was a model in an architect's office.

As we made our way to the pastures where the sheep were grazing my work was explained to me. My job was to keep the sheep within the boundaries of the lines. These were clearly defined by the fences but these were not always in evidence on our territory. There had been some cost cutting and the fences had not been properly maintained if they had been placed in position in the first place. This meant the sheep could wander at will and cover miles in a day's grazing. My job was to track the wanderers down and bring them back. Given the size of the territory this was an almost impossible undertaking. My day would start at 8.00 a.m. and finish at either the fall of darkness or teatime, whichever came first.

Without a watch I wouldn't know when it was near tea time I told him. His reply was that I should keep my ears open for the noise from the playground as this would indicate the time I could leave. Otherwise I would soon get used to keeping the time in my head. During the first two days he would stay with me so I could get used to herding the sheep and instructing the dogs.

By now with some apprehension I was looking forward to a solitary lifestyle when I would have the day all to myself. It was a steep learning curve and I was confused as trying to get to grips with instructing the dogs with different whistle sounds and tones didn't come easily. For some reason the dogs didn't respond to me as they did the farmer. This meant I had to do their job for them, running around and bringing in the stragglers, keeping the rest together and this was far from easy. I must have made a real sight, a half-starved skinny kid dressed in shorts and Wellington boots, stick in hand running around in circles screaming at dumb sheep that peered at me with blank disinterest, it must be said with very little initial success.

I soon learned to say things like 'Driver away out', 'Come in now'. It was all gibberish to me and my Dublin accent was so far removed from the farmer's that I must have seemed to the dogs to be speaking in a foreign language. I persevered and after a few days I was managing to exert some kind of control over the sheepdogs. The sheep were the biggest problem; they did have minds of their own and exercised their independence of thought with enthusiasm. I was soon to learn that this is the way of the beasts, the dumb looks are deceptive and they can be as clever as we are and I had to live with it.

By the following Monday I was judged to be proficient and at last I was on my own up there in the hills, just me, the two dogs and of course the sheep. Each morning proud as could be I would set off with the dogs with a spring in my step. When out on the mountain the farmer was happy enough to let me get on with it and just occasionally he would turn up seemingly from nowhere. This didn't cause me a problem. I was happy enough being a shepherd boy.

Each day was different so it was far from being a boring occupation. The sheep saw to it that I was kept busy and at the end of the day it could be hard work grouping them together before driving them back to their pens. I have no idea how many miles I traipsed each day but there must have been many of them.

One day when heading in a westward direction I could see in the far distance what appeared to be a group of people but it could as easily have been cattle, they were that far away. I could see they weren't sheep. With the dogs in tow I allowed my curiosity to pull me in the direction of the strange sight and drawing closer could see it was a small group of men.

As the distance between us became less they paused in their tracks and looking at me seemed to wait until I closed with them. I had no idea who they were and they looked so out of place up there in the hills. I was thinking, shite. Have I messed up? Are they something to do with the brothers because if they are I am in deep shit because I am now off my territory and without an excuse?

They were in fact land surveyors, two of them being from Dublin. As I approached it was evident that they were both curious and friendly and as soon as we drew close enough to speak one of them greeted me and asked what a lad like me was doing out there in the wilderness and not dressed properly for the weather conditions. The dogs clustered around my ankles so I felt a little in control of the situation.

'I am a shepherd,' I told them. 'I am looking for some strays. You wouldn't happen to have seen them?'

One of them chuckled and asked if I was from the school, nodding his head in the direction of Letterfrack as he did so. I told them I was from the school but that I was also a shepherd. I was proud of the position and the trust.

'Good lad. You're from Dublin?' As he spoke he indicated his companion standing nearest to him. 'So is he, we both are and so you are too judging from your accent.'

He went on to explain that they were making land surveys and then asked if there was anything they might do for me. I cheekily asked them if they had any fags. The way they then looked at each other I thought they were going to report me to the brothers but to my amazement and delight they each took a pack of cigarettes from their pockets. As casual as ever they took several cigarettes from each and handed me a bundle of them. They also handed me a pack of matches.

'Keep them dry and safe, lad. And you had better be getting back otherwise they will be looking for you.'

Grinning and with the first of the cigarettes between my lips I waved them goodbye and turned on my heel. The small event in a routine day was a memory to be cherished but I didn't push my luck. I saw them working in the distance on several further occasions but never again approached them. I knew the brothers didn't want us talking to outsiders. I valued my job and had no interest in putting it at risk.

I often thought that maybe the reason the head brother had given me the job was based on shrewdness. From where I worked I could see far into the distance and the landscape might easily have been the earth's edge. It was a constant reminder of the remoteness of the area and the impossibility of traversing it unseen. The distance was its own a prison wall and as such its own deterrent. Perhaps he had another reason. Was there somewhere in his dark soul a respect for my stoicism? I shall never know but I was grateful for the freedom the job brought with it.

Being away from the school each day meant I had no idea what was going on down there. I relied on the church services for opportunity to find out what if anything was happening. There was nothing for me to concern myself with. Nothing had changed; there were the usual beatings and abuses being carried out including sexual molestation. There were boys who for reasons of survival were happy to act as concubines and others more reluctant. We looked on them as a form of beating and if such behavior could be avoided then we did so, there wasn't any views held on the matter. They were in fact similar for the brothers obviously took pleasure in inflicting pain and humiliation, sexual or otherwise.

Nothing was going to change every child's nightmare and I couldn't have been happier being where I was up in the hills and well away from it. I weathered the harsh conditions well. It occasionally rained at which times I could hardly see from one hill to another but then the sheep were less likely to wander so there was compensation of sorts. The winds blew cold at the beginning and end of each day but I learned to minimize the chill. Either that or I simply acclimatized to it. There was nothing with which I could make comparisons.

It was during one of the summer mornings and it appeared there was hardly more than me and the wildlife present when my ear caught a whimpering sound. I was heading for the bogs at the time and increased my step so better to see where the sounds of distress were coming from. It wasn't long before I came across a small dog trapped in a barbed wire fence. The barbs had entangled in its hair and trying to extricate itself it had only made matters worse and in places its flesh was torn. I thought I recognized it as the doctor's small terrier and to me it looked like it was in a bad way.

Gently and cautiously so as to not hurt it further I untangled him from the wire but then was caught in a further predicament. It was late in the day. If I were to carry the injured animal back to the farm then it would leave me too little time to return, gather the sheep together and get them to their pens.

I had little choice but to leave the little feller where I had found him, get on with my tasks and take him with us when we descended the hilltop pastures. I went about my business and when it was time to return and pick him up there was no sign of the injured animal. This left me with another predicament. What do I do now? It seemed that I could be in trouble for abandoning the distressed creature.

When I and my little herd poured once again through the farm gates I told the farmer of the drama. I explained also the predicament I was in had I abandoned the sheep to bring the dog to him. He said he would take care of the problem and he would tell the doctor. It occurred to me that I should have carried the mite with me for the day, he wasn't that heavy. Hindsight being a wonderful thing it seemed to me that the dog might have added to its problems by getting lost and even getting into further trouble. Was it now lost for good due to my carelessness?

Before heading off the next morning I was called to the head brother's office. It was the first time I had been there since I was given the shepherd's job. Again I blasphemed and bit my bottom lip as I contemplated my fate. The worst hellhole on earth was to go through the door of a brother's home office, especially the head of the brothers. I wondered if word had got back to him that I had been seen in the company of the surveying team.

Little did I know that the farmer had watched my every move that day? He had been following my settling in process from a distance by using his binoculars. It had been fortunate that my meeting the surveyors had happened only on the one occasion, I hate to imagine the consequences had he told the brothers.

On this occasion I need not have worried too much. He wanted to see me about the matter of the dog: 'Did you have anything to do with the disappearance of the dog,' he enquired of me.

I told him I hadn't and explained how I had come across the dog, found it trapped and badly hurt. On freeing it I didn't think it was capable of moving and planned to bring it down from the hills with me when I returned with the sheep a little later.

Again he appeared thoughtful and then finally said that it was okay, he was going to give me the benefit of the doubt and I should now go off and get on with my work.

On reaching the farm who should I see there but the doctor holding her dog in her arms? The mutt had arrived home during the night and she had since heard the story of my kindness both in freeing her dog and of my intentions. Handing me a big bag of sweets she thanked me for my kindness and for rescuing her dog from the barbed wire trap. The sweets and thanks were well received but again it was a reminder that you ran the risk of being wronged even when you were motivated only by good.

CHAPTER 14

WHEN THE SUMMER HOLIDAYS ARRIVED once more I was under no illusions about whether I would be staying or going home. In a way it helped as there were no expectations to be dashed. I had already made my mind up to make the most of the swimming excursions.

All went much as expected, a carbon copy of earlier holidays and excursions. We all got much out of the visits to the cove where we dived, jumped and otherwise swam to our heart's content. There were country walks to be enjoyed but above all else there were the sheep to be looked after. I was happy enough in my own little world and it was a long time since I had been beaten the shit out of by a brother who just felt like doing so.

Out of sight was out of mind. The physical scars had healed but not the ones left on the heart and mind. Our souls remember the small acts of love and charity, regretfully the soul also remembers the acts of malevolent cruelty. Up there in the hills the time was passing more quickly, perhaps because up there I was a free spirit and a free spirit doesn't recognize time with all of its restrictions and controls. I was glad I didn't have a watch. The farmer had been right, the clock in my head kept perfect time.

Driver and Swim had learned to recognize my accent and we had become a team of three equals. They were a great help to me when we were rounding up the sheep. They responded well, especially to my frequent head pats and stroking. Swim was the most boisterous and free-spirited and could be a nuisance. He knew what it was to get a mouthful but taking all into consideration life was as good as it was ever going to get at Letterfrack. Yes, there were no more beatings and my body clock was ticking away, I was constantly reminding myself that my sentence was coming to an end.

Could any child ever have suffered so much for an antisocial prank? Was ever a bottle of soft drinks valued so much, or a few coins sprinkled on a social cub's floors?

The job meant I could not have taken part in the Christmas play that year but it was a small price to pay for my freedoms. Another advantage was that I actually got the opportunity to watch the play. This year I wouldn't be sobbing against the wall with my back to it.

The days had grown shorter as summer slipped into autumn and by the time nightfall was drawing closer to dinner time the weather had turned. There were the occasional days that were comfortable enough but up there in the exposed hillsides I was beginning to feel the wrath of the Atlantic storms. When the wind turned and came from the north or east I felt the chill despite the shelter. If it rained it came down in stair rods and of course there was only nature's shelter to be had. A tree's hollow or a stone wall behind which I could cower. Then more than ever I thought about it being my last winter here

Down there in the industrial school there was no escape from the constant fear of a brother's unaccountable wrath. Such attacks were quite unpredictable. If they were in any way predictable it was when they were least expected or undeserved. I sometimes wonder if that was part of the strategy of terror, the unexpectedness and their being random. A child would hear his voice being called and the terror would still his heart. He knew he was in for a beating. Why would there be a need for a reason? The purpose was the holistic installation of terror and enforced discipline. It was a constant reminder of the brothers' all-powerfulness. There was purpose behind the arbitrary nature of it.

The only protection was to adopt a low profile and at all times maintain total servility. It was no guarantee you wouldn't be selected for casual cruelties, it merely reduced the chances.

It was sadly a time when it was heartbreaking but a relief when someone's name other than your own was called. We all knew what the unfortunate child was going to be subjected to; we had each felt the blows, heard the uttered oaths as the blows fell. Ours had to be a yes sir, no sir, three bags full, sir option for a hoped for pain-free existence.

Here the natural laws of right and wrong, justice and injustice had been suspended. The brothers were always right whilst we were always wrong. It was why we had been sent there, this included the orphans who had never done wrong to anyone. They lost their mothers and fathers, they lost their freedom, their dignity, and they lost their childhood too. Was ever a title ever so sadly misplaced for this was the last place on earth where one might expect brotherly love?

The infliction of calculated and random terror had the desired effect. No one had absconded since my futile attempt followed by the savage beatings and the months on non-stop running around the yard. This followed by the kick in the guts for no other reason than to inflict torment. The deterrent worked well. The Gardaí could sleep easily in their beds at night. Heaven forbid they might be called upon to track down a distressed child.

I got through that winter and with Christmas and the New Year out of the way the lambing season got into full swing. I could never work out why it started so early because the newborn creatures often arrived when the temperatures were below freezing and the sleet and snow was still piling up against the sheltering walls. Whatever, it was nature in the raw and most of them did survive. It was a wonderful experience to be a part of for I found it easy to empathize with each of the mothers. Their newborn would stagger to their uncertain feet whilst still shaking off the afterbirth and before you knew it they would be celebrating life itself.

What on earth possessed them other than the pure joy as they frolicked among themselves? It seemed as though they had small bedsprings in their feet. But, they are mountain creatures and their instincts were inbred. Did they the lambs give a genesis to the cry of maaaa, maaaaa?

Some of the mother sheep were not much better than were humans, most were happy to stay close and provide suckling and refuge. Others were not so maternal and when the kids were abandoned then it was down to us to bottle feed them. Those mothers were no better than their human counterparts who abandoned their babies outside churches or placed them in baskets at hospital main entrances. Has the human race justification in thinking of itself as superior to the animal kingdom when the opposite seems so often to be the case?

To me the birth event was a beautiful and an amazing sight to see and I would do all in my power to save any unfortunate lamb I found abandoned. Some of these creatures didn't last long, abandoned or just too weak to withstand the weather. In such cases I had to bring the small bodies down with me but I always cradled them respectfully. To me they were even more precious than those that lived for they had suffered the trauma of birth but not the joys of life itself.

Up in those sometimes forbidding hills set behind the school some unknown person from way back had carved out a small cave and fortified its entrance with boulders, For me it was the perfect retreat from the weather, especially when I could disappear into it and enjoy my lunch. I reveled in the security of its walls and my being out of sight. It was very much as if I had disappeared temporarily from all of the earth's troubles.

It was my domain and I would spend many a pleasing half hour in there just dreaming of what used to be. One recurring theme was the day I went with my Ma to the docks to see my Da.

I suppose at the time I would have been about five-years old and we then lived in Railway Terrace. Da was a seaman during our time there and he would be away for long periods of time, for as long as six months. The day arrived when my Ma got a telegram to say he would be home on such and such a day. Naturally Ma was over the moon at hearing the news.

To my vivid recollection she was up before dawn, washed and dressed in best clothes normally used only on a Sunday. I couldn't shut her up as she got me dressed and prepared our breakfast. I don't think I had ever seen her chatter so much. As she was keeping me off school for the occasion I was almost as excited, certainly expectant at seeing my Da again. As soon as our breakfasts were down us we set off. I knew the route well. Into Macken Street then cross over Pearse Street heading in the direction of the River Liffey which separated the city. In no time at all we would pass the gasometer and be at the quays.

As soon as we got there we boarded the small ferry boat that took us across to the far side. It was all a great adventure for me, being helped on and off the boat by the ferryman. The workers who mostly used it were well ahead of us and so we had the boat to ourselves. Off we trotted hand in hand past the goods yard and along the dock walls. It was a long walk but even so I took everything in, the Alexandra dock gates and the wharfs where the bigger ships lay moored.

This is where the disappointment set in for there was no ship bearing the name of my Da's ship. We waited patiently, went to a café then returned to wait a little longer. We must have looked a sight and at some point when dark was closing in we were approached by a dock worker. He chatted to my Ma for a little while and we learned that according to their roster Da's ship wouldn't be docking until next week. Ma just said she was wondering why we were the only ones there as we set off to return home.

This was not as pleasant as our walk to the docks. Ma was ranting and raving about my Da never getting anything right and anyway, he would always go to his mother's house first before showing any interest in his wife and children. This meant Da had to duck under our window ledge as his mother's house was three doors further down our terrace. The recollections of that particular failed excursion somehow stayed with me for the rest of my life and hunched up in my hillside cave with my knees tucked under my chin I thought about every step of that futile journey.

Da did come home the following week. His ship had been to the United States and he had brought lots of presents for us. I remember jackets that could be worn inside out, quite a novelty at the time. Ma got a wonderful music box and yes, he did go to his mother's first.

In fairness to him the fault could be traced back to a clerk at the shipping agent's offices who had sent the telegram. Da had no part in it being sent. We were all victims when Da had no one to meet him when he did arrive, he had wondered why.

Such were my reminiscences that marked the passage of time in the hills overlooking Letterfrack. Easter was now drawing near, the days were longer and the winds were less biting cold. Each morning there continued to be the ritual of going to mass, and then repeat it during the evening, mass, Stations of the Cross and the Rosary. There was no escaping the rites. It was all to ensure we didn't become stray lambs and that we remained true to the one god, but no one had asked our permission first. No one had asked if we wanted to believe in this god, it was taken as gospel that we would follow the religious path chosen for us.

By this time I think I can describe myself as a professional shepherd, certainly as good as shepherds go. I could handle the dogs like an expert and I bet I could win competitions with the both of them. We worked so well together despite the fact that Swim could still be a juvenile delinquent when it suited him. I had never been so contented in my life; I loved my job and the openness of the countrywide. It too seemed to be a free spirit when I was as one with it. It was also a constant reminder of the folly of trying to escape. As far as the eye could see there was just the barren bog and the glowering mountains blocking every escape route? Only now did I realise the futility of my earlier escapades.

Apart from the one time when I met the group of surveyors I never encountered another living soul. The loneliness up there was in sharp contrast to the bustle on the Easter Sunday. It was of course a big day and the locals were all togged out in their best outfits and being nice and polite to each other. One could not deny how beautiful the women look in their fine dresses. The weather was complementary for it was a warm sunny day. This in itself was unusual because my recollections of Easter Sundays are their being damp and miserable.

The big day came and went as one might expect and during the evening we all trooped in to watch a film. It was about a young girl taking communion, quite a sad and thoughtful film for us to see before retiring to our beds. It was also the time when from the Tuesday the only great event to look forward to was the summer holidays. My behavior had been exemplary this year and I wondered if my past sins had been forgotten and if not perhaps they had been forgiven. If they can sin and be let off the hook with a visit to the confessionary and an act of contrition then why cannot I too? Will I be allowed to go home for the summer holiday this year?

Naturally I was on my best behavior when the brothers were around and I had really set my heart on going home. But apart from the daily rituals everything else seems to be very much the caprice of the moment. There was never a hint at who might and might not be going, the anticipation was nerve wracking.

From what I was to later gather there was an organised procedure for doing things the brothers' way. From the moment you arrived the brothers between them discussed which of them would be responsible for you. That you would be induced one way or another to fall into the correct mindset and it would even be decided if there might be opportunity for sex with a newcomer. Whatever, the regime certainly included a physical aspect and an unremitting presumption that your servility might be counted upon. One way or another it was going to happen, it was their goal. If you were to rebel then they would simply hone their skills at persuasion by whatever means they thought necessary. There was an unspoken law that implied full compliance, brothers' and children alike.

Only as the time for your release approached would the abuse lessen for by then they had either achieved their objective or failed. Besides, they did not want fresh memories. The vaguer about times a victim was punished then the better it suited them. They didn't like short memories. They counted on your being so relieved at being freed the abuse that had marked your term would be soon forgotten, eclipsed completely by the experience of being independent. They were anyway guaranteed a constant supply of fresh victims. It stopped them getting bored and new arrivals were always relished.

My daily routine as a shepherd continued and before long June was just a week or so away and we were all holding our breath as to who might and might not be going home, apart from the orphans of course. I often wondered what was in their minds at times like this. Or do I wish to think such thoughts? Perhaps it is best not to.

CHAPTER 15

THE NEWCOMERS HAD NO CHANCE of being selected, there being so many for there had been a steady stream of arrivals. This had narrowed the choices down to us older internees. From the large intake it seemed our country had a big problem with delinquent children. A better solution might have been for the shadowy string-pullers to get around the table and figure out why this was happening, why antisocial behavior was not as big in other European countries. Was it because their societies cared better for their children and that concern was returned by a sense of juvenile responsibility rather than rebelliousness at the afflictions of a dysfunctional society? Are the harshly run prisons in the remote countryside the answer to society's failings? If so, where are the Letterfrack's for the politicians and their lickspittle cronies? The truth of the matter is they simply did not care. The requisite solution was out of sight, out of mind.

There we were, all scrumming about in the school yard awaiting the roll call when the word went round that the head brother had appeared and the names are about to be announced. We all lined up in our usual formation and eagerly awaited the news. Joy upon joy! I discovered that my name was called as having been favored with a home visit. I could hardly contain my excitement and couldn't wait to write to Ma and share my good news. I had just four weeks to kill and it certainly added pleasure to my job as a shepherd. There was a spring in my step that would delight any lamb, jauntiness in my striding about with the dogs and my eyes must have been shining brightly. All I needed to worry about was will any mishap mess things up.

It was a Friday afternoon and not long to go before the day the bus would arrive. I was instructed to be at the head brother's office at seven-thirty the following morning. I was mortified at the news. What on earth could I have done wrong to justify such a visit, especially on a Saturday morning? This was unheard of except in the most compelling cases. Needless to say I hardly slept that very long night.

I was awake long before Brother Chinney began his clapping and one of the first to wash. It was then that I told Chinney I was to report to the head brother's office. He told me he was aware of the fact and told me to run off so I am not late. There was little for me to worry about and no standing outside his office door. The head brother was already outside and a warm smile of welcome was on his face.

'Don't look so terrified, boy. I am off to Galway and you are to accompany me.'

I learn that there was a dog show being held in the city. Perhaps my relationship with my own dogs had marked me out as the most appropriate companion. He was taking the two Red Setters with us. They were already in the back of the car when he invited me to hop in. There was a silence for a while and we were well on the road to Galway before he broke it.

'You will be going home on holidays soon,' he said quietly. 'No doubt you will be taking home good memories of how well you have been treated here and of how good we have all been to you since your last escape. How good I have been to you,' he said as though talking to himself. 'Yes, how good I have been to you and what a good job I acquired for you.'

'Yes, sir,' I conceded in almost a whisper whilst inside my stomach was churning and I was thinking to myself 'Fuck you, you shite, you have never been good to me.'

But this was no time for telling the truth so I held my tongue. This was the approach of my holiday and the year of my release. Nothing must jeopardize either.

We continued to travel in silence and my thoughts were taken up by the wonderful views as the car swept along the country lanes on this lovely weekend morning. As we swept through one village after another I briefly recalled my escape. Having already travelled so far in the car and with Galway yet to be reached the senselessness of my escape came even more sharply into focus.

There were people out and about, shopping, and gossiping, going about their daily business, all of which had passed me by when two years earlier we had passed through the same villages by bus.

We must have been getting closer to Galway for the head brother once again broke his silence. He reminded me that we were going to a dog show and whilst it was clear that I was not a happy lad, though I should be, I must cheer up and be on my best behavior.

'Don't worry, brother,' I said. 'I won't be letting you down.'

Shortly afterwards we drove through some large and ornate open gates and then followed a drive leading up to a large stately home. In fact it was a religious convent and outside were parked a multitude of cars, many lined up on the grass against a backdrop of tents and tables.

Parking the car we got the two dogs out, both of which were put on leads before setting out in the direction of the biggest of the tents. This was where we were to register the dogs. The head brother seemed to know a lot of the people attending and there was much handshaking and conviviality. I might just as well have been invisible as they knew any kid in the company of the brother was an outcast and to be treated as such. The only thing that struck me was that I had no recollection of any other kid accompanying the brother to a dog show.

I wasn't too worried about what people thought about me and was content enough to take in my surroundings as I walked along in the company of the brother. The hours passed with dogs doing all kinds of tricks, following commands and being admired or criticized.

At one stage we went into another tent for tea and sandwiches. These had a funny green thing in them that didn't appeal to me at all. I tried to get around the problem by swallowing it rather than chewing whatever it was. As a consequence I very nearly choked myself.

The brother's Red Setters won two ribbons and he was delighted with this. This was followed by much handshaking and farewells as we loaded the dogs back aboard the car and set off on our return journey to the school.

Before reaching Letterfrack he half turned towards me and said he probably wouldn't have another opportunity to speak to me before I went on holiday. He then impressed upon me the importance of keeping in mind that I was being well looked after. That I must have a good holiday and he promised me that he would keep me in mind for future dog shows. He added that my job as a shepherd was assured if I was well behaved and despite my past bad behavior I was appreciative of the brother's efforts to reform me.

I murmured that I would be happy and under the circumstances I had no trouble with lying to him. Nothing would ever heal the scars of the treatment I had received at the hands of him and his fellow brothers. They were too deep, constantly painful and always humiliating. I was now fifteen and a half years old and not particularly intelligent in an academic way. Nevertheless I did know the difference between right and wrong.

I knew too that ultimately he was responsible for everything that went on at the school and that he more than anyone else should be held to account but that does not seem to happen in Ireland, where no one is held responsible. Today's event had nothing at all to do with my wellbeing – more with his.

I can still picture the looks I was getting from the other boys after we returned. It seemed to them that I had been offering a little more to the head brother than I wished them to know. Even the younger kids were looking at me in a strange sort of way, which I felt very uncomfortable with.

The few remaining weeks passed without incident and on the night preceding the arrival of the bus the anticipation could be felt if not heard in the tossing of bedclothes and the whispers that went from bed to bed. I was awake long before the fucking clapping. Little did I know that I was never again to hear it save in my memory: It was July and 1967 the year.

Like sheep trying to get through a gap in a country wall we pushed and shoved our way up the steps of the bus and as we did so we were slapped about our heads to remind us we must board in an orderly fashion. No singing was allowed and as I looked around the other boys I realised that many of them were about my age and unlikely to be here at Letterfrack for very much longer.

On our arrival at the railway station we seemed less subdued than on the earlier occasion but the brothers didn't seem to mind our unruliness. This seemed so out of character. We all crowded on to the platform and despite our high spirits not one of the brothers raised his voice. It was then I noticed a group of servicemen with their kitbags over their shoulders. It occurred to me the brothers might have been aware of some ex-pupils among them who might confront them if they saw the brothers being abusive towards us.

Boarding the train off we went to Dublin and on this joyful occasion singing *We're all off to Dublin in the Green* over and over again. There was an almost Christmas jollity about it all with everyone looking at us and smiling. Were we once again rejoining the human race, were we no longer society's debris?

I had enough other things to worry about, such as what or who awaited me on my arrival in Dublin. I did know I had a new baby brother and the family had moved out of North Great Georges Street but to where I had no idea at all. On our arrival at Kings Bridge Station I looked but couldn't see my Ma anywhere in the milling crowd. I was quite worried. It was inconceivable that she wouldn't be here to greet me. It was then I heard a call coming from my right:

'Is that you, Frank?'

Looking around I saw my uncle standing there. He was in fact my older half-brother but that was a revelation yet to come.

'Over here,' he shouted. 'Over here!'

Going over to him I greeted him and asked where Ma was. He told me she couldn't make it today, it was better that he meet me and he reminded me she and my family had moved home. 'Look,' he said holding out a bag. 'I bought you some sweets.'

The pair of us set out following the usual route through the Quays but this time we were heading towards O' Connell Street. Curious, I asked him where we had moved to.

All he would say was 'You'll see.'

Pausing he smiled and then said 'It is a brand new house. It is in the countryside and big enough to be a ranch. Come on, we will cross Eden Bridge and catch a bus. It will only take us half an hour.'

As we climbed aboard the bus he asked me if I had ever heard of the Beatles. He told me he was in a band and regularly played at church halls. I explained I had been living in what can best be described as a wilderness and that we never ever heard a radio, watched television or even saw a newspaper. We had been completely isolated from the outside world.

When we finally alighted I could only describe our surroundings as being a building site through which we had quite a walk ahead of us before reaching our new home. As soon as we arrived I spotted Ma waiting for us and beside her a new pram with my new brother in it. Otherwise the house was empty. Da was out at work and I was informed there were prospects of our immigrating to Australia. She let it be known that the idea didn't appeal to her at all.

With a lot of 'hold him tightly' advice I was allowed to hold my little mite of a brother and then shown the bedroom I was to share with my younger brother. The room itself was quite long with two beds, one at each end.

'Look,' Ma said. 'Isn't it wonderful?'

Not entirely unexpectedly Ma had made a delicious coddle for me and I wolfed it down as my 'uncle' left us to ourselves. As he cheerily went on his way he called that he would be picking me up at the weekend to take me to see his band performing.

In the living room there was a television and a fireplace. There was a front and back garden but the downside was there were neither shops nor a pub nearby. They had to catch a bus into town when there was shopping to be done and Da could be counted upon to be on the last bus after the pub had closed. He had changed his watering hole and was now drinking on Eden Quay where he could be found all of any weekend.

During the working week he would leave on the first bus which was called the Dockers bus. He worked near the docks on East Wall doing long distance truck driving which took him all over Ireland.

Of course I knew nobody where we were now living but was quite happy to watch the television during the evenings and to take long walks with my younger brother in the afternoons.

The school holidays were on and most of our conversation was taken up with me impressing upon him the need for him to get a proper education and to never ever get into the wrong company or into trouble of any kind. I remarked that from bitter experience so-called mates had no problem at all leading you into the shite but were happy enough to leave you there if you got stuck in it. I told him he must always put what was best for him first and if ever in any doubt then he must call on me.

I wanted to be the big brother I never had. The two elder half-brothers I did have thought it my duty to put their interests before my own.

The following week, as previously arranged, my 'uncle' arrived and what followed was a two bus ride that took us to my Nan's house in Ringsend. She was overjoyed at seeing me, remarking all the time how I had changed and pressing ten shillings into my hand, she fluttered about me like a mother hen.

Not surprisingly I had little or no idea of the value of money, I wasn't aware of its essential nature for throughout my life I had presumed to be fed and given a bed. It had rarely occurred to me I would need to earn and be independent. I was now approaching my sixteenth birthday and was soon to find out what the real world was all about. My childhood had gone. It had passed me by and I was now near adulthood.

After a chips and eggs supper we pair set off for the night's gig. It was to be in a church hall in the Crumlin district. There were to be three bands that night and my uncle's was to play second with the major band, The Bye Laws, playing last. The hall was packed with kids, boys and girls and it was a memorable night that was to leave a lasting impression on me.

From there on I was to find great solace and enjoyment in music. I never learned to play an instrument but I was an avid purchaser of records and much of my later in life was spent travelling to major gigs.

It was necessary for me to stay at my Nan's that night as there was no public transport but on the Sunday morning we set off on our way back to the new house. I say 'we' but my uncle left me at the bus stop at Eden Quay. My mother must have got tired of hearing about my enthusiasm for the previous night's gig and how everyone was dancing around and whooping things along. It had been a fabulous new experience.

I think it was then I was to make my mind up that I was not going to go back to Letterfrack. I was going to abscond but this time home was to be where the running started. So when it got closer to the day I was to return to Letterfrack I told my Ma I had decided I was not going back to the industrial school in Connemara. I would never tell her how bad it was but I was adamant I was not going back there.

On hearing of my decision Da went ballistic but in the end he said it's on your shoulders, lad. If they catch you it will probably mean more time and that will be down to you. He asked me where I intended to live and how I expected to keep myself. Obviously you cannot stay here he reminded me.

I told him I would find somewhere to live and for him not to concern himself. After some discussion with Ma it was decided I would have to get a job and lie low until I was sixteen. It was Da's beliefs that after that age the brothers could do fuck all to me. I would from Saturday on be on the run for three months. Knowing well the likely consequences of my being returned there was no question about the importance of staying out of their reach.

Saturday, my day of no return arrived and on the Monday I got a job in a factory filling shampoo bottles. It was a long walk to and from work but I was delighted to have the job and my freedom, it was a small price to pay for becoming human. I had been of less value than a farm animal for long enough.

It took about a week for the brothers to turn up. It was on a Monday evening and for once my Da was at home having decided to turn the garden over. He was out in front with the shovel in his hands when the car pulled up outside. Two of the brothers clambered out; one was Chinney and the other a big brute of a man I didn't recognize. I was peeking out through the curtains and could see another brother and two kids in the car's rear seat.

Downstairs I could hear Da remonstrating with them.

'He is not here, you fuckers. Now clear off before I have at you with this shovel.'

With that Chinney tried to come through the front gate but my Da grabbed him and dragging him into the garden and holding him by his throat started to strangle him. It was then that the bigger of the two brothers came to Chinney's rescue and the other brother leapt from the car to join in the brawl. It was Brother Tea, the bastard.

As soon as he had leaped from the car, leaving the vehicle's door open, the two kids inside leaped free and ran off up the road. Da hurled Chinney to the ground and lifting the shovel high above his head as though tempted to bring it down on the head of the hapless brother. As he did so he shouted at the two other brothers.

'Get out of my fucking garden now, you scum. Out now or suffer the consequences.'

With that they left and climbed back into their car. By this time the two youngsters were well out of sight. I often wonder what the outcome would have been if my Da had realised just how badly I had been treated, not just me but the others boys too, especially by those pure-bred evil bastards, Brother Chinney and Brother Tea.

That was the last I was to ever see of them. The Gardaí never came looking for me and so in the end I had successfully escaped. Scarred? Yes, I avoided the last few months there but more than forty years were to pass before I could come to terms with those awful events and for posterity if nothing else to record them.

I kept my job until I reached sixteen years of age. Despite Da's earlier concerns for me, so valiantly expressed during the confrontation with the brothers, we never quite saw eye to eye on a number of issues. There was much more that separated us than bound us together. He loved the drink; a weakness I despised for it can bring so much misery with over indulgence.

I was earning enough to get my own small flat and after some searching found the perfect one on the south Circular Road at just three pounds a week. I was earning three pounds ten shillings per week but I was a loner, the shepherd still and was able to survive on this until things were to change.

In my thoughts was the heartfelt wish to forget Letterfrack, to consider it a void in my life, to make a leap of faith across a chasm that covered a near four year span of a child's life. It was never my intention to even discuss it, for me it never happened. It was a nightmare and nightmares are best forgotten.

I wanted to let go of Letterfrack and move on but it would never take its brother's boot off my neck. Whatever was to confront me later in life the malevolent long-reaching grasp of that awful boys' penitentiary would reach out, tap me on my shoulder and remind me I would always be shackled, a prisoner of my past. Whenever I tried to move on, get a job, move abroad it would hover like an avenging dark angel of misery. I was still being punished whilst the guilty were left free to reach deeper and ever deeper into depravity.

Nothing would be held against our abusers because they were the certified State's abusers. It they were to be condemned then so would the State. They knew, the Garda knew, the officials knew, the civil servants knew and those in public life knew what was going on in the so-called industrial schools. They drew the curtains across and left their consciences on the other side.

Governments come and go but the system is always there, it was never in the interests of The Dail's new faces to lift the lid on the iniquities that might be laid at the doors of the predecessors or their system for they were of the same ilk. In Ireland as elsewhere there is a rotating dictatorship between two parties that ostensibly oppose each other but it is public sparring to keep alive the myth of democracy. In reality they all piss in the same pot after drinking from the same cup. There is but one religious entity and for them there was just denial and of course the whispered words, perhaps, in the confessional box. The only ones in the triangle of death left to speak are the victims for they alone have nothing to hide.

Survivor

Part Two

All names have been changed to protect the guilty.

R. F. Heeney

St Patricks Institution

Historically, since 1850, St. Patrick's Institution was the female prison adjacent to the male facility in Mountjoy. It opened its doors to minors in 1956, where inmates were young boys transferred from the Borstal in Clonmel, Co. Tipperary. The regime in St. Patrick's was similar to that of an adult prison. Prison staff were not trained specifically to deal with children and the services provided were not child oriented. Therefore children spent the majority of their sentence locked in their cells with scant opportunities for healthcare, education or recreation and family visits were screened. This provision was wholly inappropriate for the care or detention of minors. The practice of detaining children in St. Patrick's Institution did not comply with international human rights standards.

In 1985, the *Whitaker Report* stipulated that St. Patrick's Institution was totally inappropriate for detaining children and that it had a "demoralising effect" on them. The report stated that the conditions of detention could lead to "the psychological deterioration of the young offenders. These conditions contravened Article 40(1) of the UN Convention on the Rights of the Child which requires that States treat children in conflict with the law in a manner that facilitates the child's sense of dignity and worth and reinforces the child's respect for human rights. It proposes that a child-orientated juvenile justice system must be cognisant of the fact that, first and foremost, these young people are children.

In the two decades prior to the *Whitaker Report* St. Patrick's Institution treated children a harsh response to the smallest infraction of cruel rules. Woe betide any boy who did not conform to the regime. I was one of them boys.

CHAPTER 16

DUBLIN IRELAND, 1967 Aged 16 Years.

I THOUGHT I COULD HEAR the sound in my head of an old ballad playing, *'As down the glen came Mc Alpine's men …'* that was an illusion. What it really was, was, a shrill ringing in my ears after the clout I had just taken on the side of the head.

'You're going to get this every time I see you,' bellowed Jobo.

Jobo's eyes were bulging out of their sockets like they were on stalks. He was the kind of bloke you would never wish to meet in a dark alley or for that matter anywhere else. This dysfunctional thug was pond life. It was unfortunate for me that this neighbour from hell haunted a house just about three hundred yards from where our family lived in the Cromcastle area of Dublin's Coolock.

The sprawling corporation sink-hole estate was situated precariously on the outskirts of Dublin. Socially dysfunctional, it was similar to what the government, in their lack of wisdom, had built in Ballyfermot and Crumlin. So typical of the council, which epitomises the expression, *a camel is a horse designed by a committee*; the estate was built without services. There were no shops, no schools; it wasn't even on a bus route. The estate was said to be the dumping ground for Dublin's inner city slum trash. Built, this overspill estate was filled with Dublin's poorest people and left to get on with it. You get what you grow so the outcome was perfectly predictable. It was no wonder that these estates became havens of poverty for the families who were placed in them.

Jobo, the nemesis, was part of a large family that had recently returned from England. Rumour had it that they had either been expelled or extradited for carrying out acts of robbery and violence and causing mayhem wherever in the Midlands they lived.

The family epitomised anti-social behaviour. Constantly at war with their neighbours, their idea of a good time was to overturn some poor man's bread van in the middle of our road. This, merely for his asking for monies due to him. Brutes. There was no other way to describe the nest of vipers of which Jobo, in his early twenties, was just an example.

In fact, he was your archetypical Neanderthal brute. A head like a World War One shell casing, no neck, the coffin best suited to him was a telephone box. His jet black hair, which never saw a comb, and in all likelihood was infested, was all asunder and spiky. No one, not even a mother, could love Jobo.

That day he had been waiting at the bus stop for me. I couldn't possibly have foreseen the anger he had towards me, his intended victim. There was nothing I had done to merit the beating. He had just taken against me. Keeping my head and face covered as best I could I endured raining blows to the head. These were accompanied by kicks being aimed at my arse for the ten minutes it took us to reach my garden gate. Only then did the kicking, the slaps and the blows finally cease.

Still bewildered and stunned by the beating, I banged on our front door to have my Ma answer it. On seeing the state I was in, she went into immediate shock. I was barely upright, bedraggled and bloodied with snot and blood mingling with my tears.

'What in the name of God have you done now?' she inquired. 'Your Da is going to go mad when he sees you. Get into the bathroom and clean yourself up.'

There was none of the concern or caring sympathy one might have expected. Nor was there any thought given that a visit to the hospital, or Police Station, might be the right thing to do. I was still snivelling and whining as I scurried quickly down the hall to the bathroom.

I had only been back at my home for a few weeks. It was not looking too promising should I elect to stay at home as I had planned. The only relief was my knowing that several hours would pass, enough to compose myself, before my Da returned. He would be on the last bus coming from town. He would be drunk as usual and without a shadow of a doubt singing and making a thorough nuisance of himself.

Since moving to this estate Da had only being coming home to sleep. In truth he just didn't want to be here and would rather we had stayed at North Great Georges Street. That flat had been closer to his local pub and his circle of drinking buddies.

Each morning, bright and early, Da was up and out on the docker's bus. As reliable as a clockwork mouse he returned home drunk on the last bus every night. One could be certain that by the time he arrived home his dinner, in the oven, was by then slowly being cremated. Did it matter? The meal was more often than not tossed contemptuously into the bin. Such were the delights of my family's suburban life in working class Dublin during the 1960s. Alcoholic fathers were unhappily wed to near destitute mothers who constantly struggled against all odds to raise their kids. Such mothers wearily and not always successfully struggled to make ends meet with the pittance that, by some miracle, found its way into their pocket.

After cleaning up as best I could, I composed myself and then showed myself at the kitchen door to enquire as to what might be for dinner. The kitchen was at the back of the house and measured only six foot by four foot. I was an additional contributor to the weekly allowance that my Ma got from my Da. This warranted a daily lunch pack and dinner. Tonight we had spuds and eggs, a favourite of mine.

'Well, are you going to tell me what all this bother is about now?'

'I would, Ma, if only I knew.'

It was a mystery to me as to what that was all about. I knew Jobo's family was a bunch of fucking nutters. Even the girls were known to be mad and reckless. But I had no idea what I had done to annoy them.

CHAPTER 17

I HAD RETURNED HOME ON holiday from the sentence I had been serving at Saint Joseph's Letterfrack Industrial School a few months earlier. Since my refusal to return had me marked as an absconder things had got steadily worse for me. My Da, for a few weeks, was all for his eldest son being back home. Endlessly repeated in the pub he would tell all and sundry about my great escape and the part he had played in getting me away from the hellhole of a Catholic run children's penitentiary. No doubt the story was from time to time embellished and got better as the more pints were consumed. Other than such routine all seemed well in the Heeney household until one night my Da returned as usual. Equally as usual he was the worse for wear after alighting from the last bus.

It seemed there was a new driver on board. Keen to play by the rules and use the designated bus stops, he had refused to let my father off outside our front door. Instead he took him some distance on to the scheduled bus stop, which resulted in him having to walk several hundred yards.

I could hear Da muttering and cussing as he struggled to get his key into the front door lock. Woe betides anyone crass enough to open the door for him. He had this macho thing that no matter how drunk he was he could open his front door. My Ma had a fire going as it was October and cold. She had some clothes hung out on a clothes horse in front of the fire. It was mostly my Da's stuff but there were some clothes of mine there drying also.

'What are his clothes doing drying out there?' he roared. By the 'his' he of course meant me, his son.

'I need my clothes for work tomorrow,' I told him.

He proceeded to take my few bits of drying clothing off the clothes horse and flung them to the floor.

'Fucking little dosser,' he screamed, 'get yourself a fucking job and then maybe you can get your clothes dried for you.'

'I am working' I thought to myself.

A scuffle then broke out between me and my Da. This resulted in him losing his balance and falling over a small table that was close by. Like a bolt from the blue he realised that I was not a little kid anymore. I had just turned sixteen. All the past memories flashed through my mind, of the beatings and abuse I had suffered at his hands. Pushing him backwards onto the table he fell badly and his left arm at an awkward angle went under him. My God. I can still vividly hear the bone break.

'Jaysus. My arm. The little fucker's broken my arm,' he screamed. 'Be Jaysus I'll swing for you, boyo.' He roared in pain.

I knew this was it. There would be no turning back now.

'You're out of here now, boyo. There is no room in this house for dossers so get out,' he cried holding onto his arm with his face contorted in pain.

Up spoke my Ma, 'Leave the boy now. He didn't mean it. It was only a stupid accident and not his fault.'

I could see the anger in his eyes and knew I should leave. This was no place for me now but where was I going to go? It was very late at night and the busses had stopped. Besides, even if I had the money where would I go?

'Please, it's late at night and the lad can't go anywhere now. Leave it till the morning and I will make sure he goes then,' Ma piped up.

At this point my Da left the room and stumbled his way to the top of the stairs, cursing as he went.

'We'll sort this out in the morning,' my Ma stage whispered to me.

Unsurprisingly, it was to be a sleepless night and it was just about 4.30 a.m. when I heard my Da shuffling about as he got himself ready to leave for work. I kept my head under the bed covers in case he looked in at me but there was little need for concern. I soon realised he had slipped the catch and was on his way to the bus stop where his bus was due any moment. Only then did I fall into a fitful sleep, only to be awoken by my mother pretty soon afterwards or at least it seemed that way.

'Get up now, lad. There will be no peace for you when he gets home this evening, for you or for anyone else.'

I did as I was told and a few minutes later I joined her downstairs in the kitchen. I found Ma standing there with the kettle in her hand.

'You will have to leave this morning, you know that,' she said pouring me a cup of tea.

My thoughts were all adrift and I did not know what I was going to do. How the fuck was I to make it on my own? I had just a few clothes and no money to my name.

'I can give you a loan of £5,' my Ma volunteered. 'It has to be a loan though. I need it as much as you do. I will want it back as soon as you can give it.'

How mothers can always have money tucked away somewhere for when it's needed! Her words were a comfort somehow. It meant at least that I was not going to starve. There was no real goodbye as such. My Ma just quietly closed the hall door behind me and without a second look over my shoulder I went on my way into the Dublin dawn.

My immediate intention was to take the bus to town and maybe get a newspaper to see if any flats were available. As luck would have it, the first telephone number I rang had an empty flat available and I could move in that very day. Before I placed the phone back on the receiver, I had agreed to meet the lady where the telephone box was situated, right outside Cleary's Department Store. Not long afterwards this big black saloon car arrived. There was a man driving it but the lady I had apparently spoken to was sitting in the passenger seat beside him.

'What's your name lad?' she asked, after lowering the window.

'Frank.'

'And tell me, what are you doing looking for a flat at your age and anyway what age are you?'

'Seventeen,' I lied.

I could hear her sucking in her breath. She was an older woman and dressed completely in black. She had this big black handbag and was clutching it in her lap. The driver was a rugged looking man with red hair and I recall him having a country accent. I presumed he might be her caretaker or something but instinctively presumed him not to be her husband.

'The flat is up near Rathmines. Is this okay for you?'

It had never occurred to me to enquire where in the city the flat might be. All I wanted was a roof over my head and it had to be that very day.

'Yes, that's grand.'

At her invitation, I climbed into the car's back seat and not long afterwards we pulled up outside a large five storey house on the South Circular Road. As I was to later discover it was only a couple of doors from the Garda Club - a watering hole for police officers.

'Here we are, Frank,' she said abruptly as opening her car door she stepped outside on to the pavement.

'You may come in with us, Jerry,' she added turning to the driver of the car.

We three approached a large green door that was to lead us into a large hallway. This we passed along and it took us to the rear of the house. Once there, she swung open a brown door that led into a square room. The room was about the same size as the one we used to live in when we were in North Great Georges Street. But that one room was to accommodate a family of seven, this room was for one person and that one person it seemed was going to be me. Looking around I couldn't believe my eyes or my good fortune. It was fully furnished. There was a double bed, a wardrobe and beside it a dressing table. There were also chairs and a couch and in the corner there was a curtain and behind it a cooker and a small work top with a sink. It seemed like heaven to me.

'The rent is three pounds ten shillings a week,' she told me.

To me £3.10s was a fortune and I was thinking fast on my feet.

'I couldn't quite meet that,' I told her earnestly. 'I could manage £3 a week?'

She smiled almost as if she had expected me to suggest that amount and without hesitation agreed that this would be the sum required.

'I will call around every Saturday and you must have the rent ready for me. There will be no excuses. Any of those and you are out on your ear. Is that understood, Frank?' She said.

It seemed the deal was done and I nodded my head in agreement. Sure isn't life great? I now had my very own place that I could call home. My home.

CHAPTER 18

It wasn't too long before I found my way around and sniffed out where the local shops were. The most pressing need was to get a job so I could pay my way in the world. The job I'd had in Coolock was going to be too far for me to travel to now. I had kept that morning's newspaper. I immediately leafed through it until I reached the 'situations vacant' columns. There were numerous job vacancies but disappointingly there wasn't much going for a young lad my age. Then, there was one that caught my eye. 'Messenger Boy Wanted.'

This vacancy was on the other side of town in Stoneybatter, near to the North Circular Road.

Trust me to find the best home in Dublin but five miles from the only vacant job. With a shrug at my mixed fortunes I headed there on shanks' pony with a big grin on my face.

The walk didn't take as long as I had imagined it would, and I soon found myself standing outside a double fronted butchers shop. With a devil may care attitude I sauntered inside where I found a big, round-faced man behind the counter? He was chopping lumps of meat with a big cleaver. Around his neck he wore a white, bloodstained bib and underneath it a blue striped shirt. His head was near bald with just a few tufts of grey hair askew and a big happy grin on his face. He looked over the counter at me, down at me as I was somewhat smaller than he was.

'What can I do for you, son?'
'I'm here about the job.'

'Good! Yes, good,' he replied with an even broader smile. 'Do you have any experience in bicycle deliveries?'

Fuck I'm thinking to myself. I'll have to be quick off the mark here. "Just a little bit,' said I and at the same time hoping he wouldn't ask too many questions.

'Ok then, my lad,' he replied good naturedly.

'The job pays £3.10s a week. If that's okay with you, then the job is yours and its best you are here at eight o'clock sharp tomorrow morning. I will then tell you what you will be doing.'

'Yes that is fine. I accept your offer.'

Thanking him, the relief flooded over me as I set off on the long walk back to what was now my home.

Keeping to the main streets I tried to find the fastest route back to the South Circular Road. By walking at a steady pace it took me about forty five minutes, so all in all it wasn't such a bad journey. As soon as I reached my room, and with the door closed carefully behind me, I had a quick count of what money I had left in my pocket. It was about six shillings. I knew I would have to be very careful with what I spent as it had to last for a full week. I thought the best diet would be spuds and eggs. Over the years, whenever things got tough, I learned that this was the best low maintenance meal you could get into your belly.

Although the house was very big there was no noise as such. It felt as if the whole place was empty and, as night fell, I had visions of ghosts coming in the window. I got my head under the covers to keep them at bay and it wasn't long before I fell into a far deeper sleep than the previous night.

It was six-thirty and still dark when I awoke. Blearily, I was wondering where the hell I was but was quick to realise that this was to be my real home - my domain. Swinging my feet out of the bed, I quickly pulled my clothes on and going to the sink gave myself a cat's lick and a promise. This will keep me going I thought as I pulled a comb through my mousey hair.

Leaving as close to seven as I could I headed out into the murky morning with a quick step into my new beginning. Heading down Camden Street into South Great George's Street I turned left into Dame Street and passing

Dublin Castle and the Children's Court on my left, turned right in the direction of Capel Street Bridge.

With the bridge behind me I headed into Mary's Abbey and cut through the Fruit Market. The market was busy with the hustle and bustle of fruit and vegetable traders. There were horses and carts parked everywhere, all shapes of vans and small delivery trucks parked on paths and on the roads. I knew this would leave me in plenty of time to go up by the Broadstone and reach the butcher's shop in Phisboro. It was good planning. I arrived in good time just as the butcher was unlocking the shop door to let in customers. By then a small queue had formed outside and were waiting patiently for him to arrive.

Spotting me, he smiled: 'A hearty morning to you, lad.'

I respectfully waited until the few customers had gone inside before following them. The butcher immediately set about serving the early risers now forming another line up at the counter. Seeing me standing there and realising I was obviously there to work rather than being a customer, a younger man took me into the back of the shop. He was slightly built with a mop of red hair wearing a blue stripped shirt and again the now familiar long, white, blood stained bib.

'Now lad,' he said quietly, and taking me by the elbow, he led me into what I was to learn was the cold room.

In the cold room were various carcasses hanging from the ceiling on big hooks. To most sixteen year olds they would have been a daunting sight but I was used to seeing the likes of them in Letterfrack.

Turning towards me he said. 'What's your name boy?'

'Frank' I replied.

'We will need you to do deliveries on your bicycle when required and also keep the shop and storage areas clean and tidy. You will also be obliged to give a hand in the cleaning, wrapping and cutting of meats.'

Grand job, I was thinking to myself.

'Right,' he said. 'Let's get you ready to deliver some orders.'

He led me into yet another room. This one had large and very thick wooden tables fixed along one wall. The rest of the room was cluttered with pieces of cardboard and there was plenty of brown and greaseproof paper in evidence. Against one of the walls leaned a messenger bike. It looked very heavy and unwieldy. Black in colour, it had this big wicker basket in the front crate.

'We will go easy on you and give you only ten or so deliveries to start with. It won't help you or us if you get confused with the round. Right now. Here is a list in the order of deliveries to be done. They are numbered 1 to 10 and the parcels will be also numbered 1 to 10. Alright?'

'Yes' replied I as I tried to keep my face from showing too much anxiety at the prospect of doing ten deliveries on my first day.

That was making it easy for me was it?

'Right now, let's get you off, me boy,' said he as he carefully and methodically placed each of the parcels into the wicker basket before pushing the bike out of the side door to the street.

'Hop up now,' he said as he held on to the bike's handlebars.

Mounting the bike to the best of my ability I began to shakily cycle down the street not knowing if I was heading in the right direction or not. There were no mad shouts from behind me so I continued in this direction doing all I could to keep the bicycle moving in a straight line. I was well aware that if I was to wobble any more than I already was doing I would come off the fucking thing and land on my head.

After a few minutes and feeling much more comfortable in the saddle, I pulled over to look at the hand drawn map I had been given to enable me get the lie of the land.

'Well be Jesus; this isn't too bad now' I thought as the map showed the deliveries reasonably close together.

That was followed by several not unexpected mishaps on the round but soon with all the deliveries completed I headed back to the shop feeling very proud of myself. It had taken me about three hours to complete my first day's deliveries. No one said anything to me on entering the shop so I presumed that my timing was alright by them. It was then I was handed a big scrubbing brush and a bucket of piping hot water and told to clean the large wooden tables. They were for chopping the meat on and were caked with blood and bone shavings. But, not to worry, I got on with the scrubbing and rubbing. Sure isn't it a grand life now I was thinking to myself.

I then had a small break for lunch but would have gone without had one of the men not offered me one of his own ham sandwiches. When I told him I wasn't hungry, he must have known it was a white lie. I was to learn that up to twenty deliveries a day were required of me as well as general cleaning and sweeping. I would also have to go up to the abattoir from time to time and bring back a full basket of meat.

And that was some job I can tell you. The fucking bicycle was like a bucking bronco when the basket was full. It took all my time and energy to keep it upright never mind riding it, the damned stupid thing.

When I would get back to my flat in the evenings I would be wrecked after all the cycling and walking but I was happy enough. I had found a second hand book store in the neighbourhood and would buy books to read. These could be brought back to the store where I bought them when read. I could then exchange them for others and get a discount. This way I was able to learn to read properly.

All in all life was grand. There were times when I would receive a few tips from the older customers when making the deliveries, sometimes helpfully taking them inside. They never actually paid me for the meat received. Each customer had a Weekly Book going on with the butcher.

I was just about surviving, which was the main thing. I was keeping myself and on Friday evenings, when I would finish work, the butcher would give me what was called a 'wrap up' to take home with me. Inside would be rashers, sausages, black and white pudding with occasionally sliced ham and chops. Not surprisingly it wasn't long before I became a passable cook.

One morning, during deliveries, I went to a house I had not been to before. It was one of the three storey red brick houses just off the Phibsboro Road beside the football ground. In response to my knocking on the door it was opened by a woman who was tall with streaky blond hair and getting on a bit. I imagined her to be in her forties or thereabouts. She was still dressed in her dressing gown.

As she leaned over to collect her parcel her gown slipped to the side and I could clearly see her breast showing, which was as big as a melon. Being at the age I was I had visions of feeling and sucking it. Could she read my mind? She looked at me in a peculiar way and asked me if I would like to come in for a drink of lemonade but me being the eejit I was I said I would stay at the door if she would bring one out to me. That seemed fine by her and she soon returned with a glass of orange squash that I gulped down.

Had I just come across the proverbial bored housewife? Without experience I could only go on instinct and hearsay but I had this funny and not unpleasant feeling in my innards. I never got a parcel for this house again and maybe it was just as well.

I liked the job as a messenger boy. I got on well with the people who worked at the butchers but soon realised I couldn't make ends meet on the meagre amount of money I had to live on after my bills were paid.

One Sunday I reluctantly caught the bus to Coolock to see my Ma in the hope of having a chat with her about returning home. There must have been something pleasing about my appearance.

'You're looking well considering. Are you managing okay on your own?' she enquired.

'Yes I'm fine and things are going great. I have got this good job as a messenger boy and I love doing it.'

'Well your Da if fine now as the arm wasn't too badly damaged. He came out of it okay. He told them at work it happened on the job so he got off work with sick pay. He's not too bothered about it now.'

'Thank God for that,' I smiled ruefully. 'I was thinking that maybe he was out to skin me for it.'

Ma asked me if I would like some tea, which of course I would. We went through to the kitchen where I took a seat. Watching half interestedly as she boiled the kettle and filled the teapot I waited for my moment. The room was just as dour and grey as it was when I had last seen it. My mother had this top loader washing machine in the corner. The lid would never close properly so it continuously leaked water when it was doing a wash. It had seen better days.

'So, what are you hoping to do with yourself now you are working an' all?'

'I don't know at the moment what I could do but I need a job that gives me more money. By the way where is everyone?'

'Your brother is out with his mates and the girls are also out playing. Your Da is in his office for the afternoon session.'

By his office she meant of course the local public house.

I stayed quietly thinking for a moment before coming out with what was on my mind.

'I wanted to ask you if maybe I could come back home to stay as it's so difficult to live with not enough wages coming in.'

'Now maybe you can see what it's like for me trying to rear you all on a meagre few bob. It will have opened your eyes up to the way of things no doubt.'

'I know, Ma. I know that things are not always rosy in the garden but Jaysus give us a chance will you? I'm only sixteen for Jaysus sake.'

'Well, the only way I can see your Da agreeing to you having a second chance is if you are working and handing up your wages. If you agree to this, then maybe I can persuade him to let you come home.'

She poured the tea as she talked. I thought to myself, maybe she is not being too hard on me as things are hard for her, I know. At least I had the messenger boy's job and she could always have my Friday wrap up from the butchers as she wouldn't waste any of it.

We drank the tea and had a chat about things in general. It seemed the yobos from up the road were causing havoc with all and sundry. They had battered the milkman when he tried to get paid and the Garda were afraid to come to their house to sort them out. But one of my sisters Maureen had become friendly with one of their girls. No doubt she knew what she was getting into, but 'Crabby' as my Da called her, was always a bit of a tomboy.

We chatted about this and that and eventually it was getting near time for me to head off and catch my bus into town. Bidding my Ma good bye, I arranged to come back out the following Sunday to hear if my Da was in agreement with me coming home. I said my good byes and asked for my love to be given to my other siblings.

Walking to the bus stop I could not help but feel regret at not being able to stay at my house. Optimistically I knew that my Da would relent and it would not be long before I got back home. My trip into town was uneventful and I got back to my flat before it got too dark. The book I was reading was still open on my lap when in the hope of sweet dreams I fell asleep that night.

Monday morning I was again up like a lark and off to work. The job gave me great cause for satisfaction. It was absorbing and I loved meeting people and chatting about the weather and just general banter. There was a constant stream of customers to the butcher's shop and deliveries were keeping us all busy. It was great teamwork and a source of pride I think to all of us. It was, in truth, hard going on some days but the week flew for me and Sunday came around quickly.

Strolling down to Eden Quay from my flat, I set out to catch the bus out to Coolock. It was amazing how many people were up and about in their Sunday best. I could only imagine it was because it wasn't raining. It always seemed to rain on Sundays in Ireland. I caught my bus and when I got to my family home I was surprised to see my Da was there but my brothers and sisters were out. It made me feel a little uneasy but as it happened all was fine. In fact my Da had a big welcoming smile on his face as I walked through to the living room where he was sitting.

'What are you up to, son?'

'Just working and keeping out of trouble, Da. Doing my best.' 'Well good on yer, that's the way to get on in life. Your mother was saying that you want to come home. Is this right?'

'Yea, I was wondering if maybe, as I have a job an' all, that you would give me another chance and let me come home?'

As if he hadn't already had a week to think about the proposal, he placed his hand thoughtfully on his chin as though he were Solomon himself. For several moments he stroked the stubble on his chin. I stood there not quite sure what his response was going to be. It was beginning to look like a futile request when he looked up at me.

'Well if you're prepared to help in the house and hand up your wages I don't see why not. But I warn you, if there is any hint of trouble or you don't do what your mother says its curtains for you. Is that understood?'

He always called my Ma my mother. 'Yes, Da, I won't give any trouble I promise.'

Little did I know that I was soon going to be eating my own words?

CHAPTER 19

Darkness descends, they say, in all its shades and forms but there was nothing to hint at what was about to befall me. Just as everything seemed to be perfect events took a hand. As a consequence the next two years or so were to become unendurable. Nothing, absolutely nothing, was to warn me of the coming darkness.

I had only been back at my Ma's for just over a week or so when it started again. I had been catching the 6.30 a.m. bus into town and then walking up to Phisboro to my job. I would get there at about 7.45 a.m. or thereabouts.

Yes, all was going smoothly both at home and at work. All my Ma required of me was £2 and ten shillings. This meant I had a £1 plus the coppers in tips I got from the ladies. Needless to say Ma was delighted with the wrap-up I got from the butcher on Friday. I had told her that I was only earning £3 so she thought I had just ten shillings to clothe myself with.

Arriving home on the bus about 5.30 p.m. on a Monday evening I was just about to alight when I spotted Jobo's mutton head at the bus stop. As this was the terminus I had no choice but to get off.

'Shite - what's going to happen now?' I thought.

My head was swirling with dilemmas. Should I take to my heels? Maybe that would only make him angrier with me. Besides, maybe he just wanted to talk. As I stepped down from the bus platform I realised I was in for another pasting all the way to my front gate. As soon as I reached the pavement he waded into me. There was no reason for him to do so. He didn't need a reason. He just kept on repeatedly kicking, punching and slapping me.

'What's this about? What's this for?' I cried in vain.

He never replied. He just kept up the mantra, 'you're going to get this you little bollix every time I fucking see you.'

I was in despair and at my wits end of what I could or should I do. Everyone, even the Garda, were afraid of these thugs. They were a law unto themselves. I had no friends as such to turn to. I didn't want my Da to be involved as this would mean he would be picked on too so all I could do was hide my ordeal from him. But my Ma was different. She was home when I fell through the door.

'Oh my God, Frank, what has happened to you? Just what is going on?' she screamed.

'Nothing, nothing,' I cried out. 'I'm okay. It's nothing. I am alright.'

Putting a wet towel to my face and holding me tightly she asked me what I had done. She didn't believe my protestations of innocence.

'You must have done something to deserve this. Tell me, son, what is it?'

'I don't know,' I wailed.

I really didn't know why I was being picked on or why I was getting these beatings with the promise of more to come. I knew in my heart that the only way to escape them was to again leave my home. But fuck it, this I was not prepared to do. Hadn't the Christian brothers tried to break me with constant beatings to no avail? This type of conduct was not going to work with me now I decided. With my Ma comforting me, I vowed to somehow deal with this mutton headed bastard regardless of the outcome.

About this time I had seen an advertisement in the local paper for helpers wanted on delivery trucks. It was a household name drinks company and so I decided to apply for the job. Riding the messenger bike was getting me down and I realised I was not cut out to be a butcher. It was time to move on.

The new job would be on St. Ignatius Road on the north side of town just off Dorset Street. The following Monday I took the day off from my messenger bike job and set out to apply for the new opportunity. Walking up from Eden Quay it was a hopeful sign that the walk from home, if I were to get the job, it would be five minutes shorter than the walk to Phibsboro.

The first thing that struck me when I got to the depot was the sheer size of the place. It was situated behind rows of terraced houses so few would have been aware of its existence. As I passed through its enormous gates I couldn't get over the enormity and complexity of it all. There were numerous trucks loading and unloading with fork lift vehicles moving rapidly all over the place. Stopping a man I asked him where was I to go to apply for the breaster's job.

Smiling he pointed to some steps leading to a first storey office.

'Up those steps, lad, and good luck to you', he added as I turned to go.

I did as he suggested and climbed the stairs to an open door and stepped inside. There in front of me was an elderly woman with neat shoulder-length grey hair sitting behind a sort of desk reception. The woman seemed nice enough and I asked her if this was where I applied for the helper's job.

'Hold on a minute son. I'll get someone to look after you' she said.

I waited around respectfully and eventually a man, who I guessed to be about forty-years of age appeared. He was dressed in a long brown overall coat or coverall, a blue shirt with navy blue trousers. He had short black hair. I noticed how shiny his shoes were.

'What can I do for you lad?'

'I am here about the helper's job on the lorries.'

He paused to look me up and down then told me that I should follow him. I did so and he went down the long corridor with me hot on his heels. We soon reached a large office and the first thing I noticed was the number of beer bottles and mineral drinks bottles carelessly scattered about the room.

He took his seat behind the desk and this too was cluttered with files and stacks of papers, many of different colours, brochures, all kinds of paraphernalia. In the middle sat a machine I was unfamiliar with. I was to learn it was a telex machine.

Again he paused and with his hand resting easily on the desk in front of him, his fingers tapping on it lightly he asked me where I lived.

In Ireland at this time getting employment had a lot to do with where you lived and Coolock was a new estate and had not as yet become lawless.

'Coolock, sir,' I replied.

'And do you have any experience of trucks or how they work?'

I thought honesty was the best policy. 'No, sir, but I pick things up very quickly.'

'And what age are you?'

'Sixteen and a half now,' I ventured, unsure of whether this might have a bearing on the job.

'And you're working at the moment. You have a job to go to, that is good,' he said when I nodded that I had work to go to in a few words that gave him enough to go on.

'When could you make a start if I offered you the job?'

'I would have to give them this weeks' notice as they need to find someone to replace me. I could start next Monday if that is okay?'

The man smiled and seemed to be pleased at my answers. Telling me that would be fine he pulled some papers towards him as he took up a pen and began to take down my particulars. When he had noted my details, address and current position that sort of thing; he placed his pen down and looked at me thoughtfully.

'Alright son. You make a start on Monday. That is next Monday you understand and I will want to see you here at 7.45 a.m. sharp. How does that sound?'

He didn't wait for me to reply:

'Call me if there is a problem with that,' he said as he handed me a piece of paper with a phone number on it.

I was elated. To me it was a step up from riding a butcher's delivery bike and more suited to my age. It would be a good opportunity for me to get into better things and at £4.2.6 the pay was much better too. There might have been opportunity for overtime but I didn't think of that for the moment. I wouldn't tell my Ma of my better circumstances so I could keep giving her the £2.10 as I had before. I reasoned it was enough to keep me but she would miss the weekend 'wrap up.'

The rest of the week flew by and there were no more unwanted meetings at the bus stop where I had been recently beaten up. I was beginning to feel much better about things and was genuinely looking forward to the new chance I had been given. The Sunday night was certainly a strain and I was restless because I was fearful that I would oversleep. If so, that would be the end of that job. As luck would have it my Da woke me and we travelled together on the docker's bus.

That Monday, it was a bright and clear morning when I alighted at Eden Quay. By then my Da had already left to pick up a connecting bus at Annesley Bridge. There, he would catch another bus that would take him on to the docks. There I was, walking along quite happy and concentrating on what might happen during the day that lay ahead of me. My mind was buzzing with the prospects of opportunity. From a big clock situated high up on a wall I saw that I was good for time. I went straight to the office where the lady I was to enquire of as to how my day would start was working.

This time quite a large man was sitting behind the counter. He too was dressed in the customary long brown coat and as I approached he was shuffling through some paperwork as he peered over his big horn-rimmed glasses at me.

'What's the story, lad?'

'I'm here to start today, sir,' I told him.

'And what's your name?'

'I'm Frank, Frank Heeney, sir.'

'Good. Yes good. You will be working here in the store for a while as that is the way we familiarise starters with how things are run here.'

He too tapped his fingers on the desk. Maybe everyone did that. A few seconds elapsed and getting to his feet he asked me to accompany him. Off we went and the route took us to a large shed where there was another lad present. He looked about the same age as me.

'Frank, this is Barry,' he said introducing us as he took a large sheet of cardboard.

Then, placing it on a machine I noticed that underneath it was what appeared to be a foot pedal. As he placed his foot on the pedal we became aware of a scraping sound as he maneuvered the box around. Then, after a moment or two the sheet of cardboard was transformed into a neat cardboard container, presumably for carrying the firm's bottled products. Then, placing it in the corner he took up another sheet of cardboard and repeated what he had just done. After making about five of these boxes, each pierced with large staples, he looked at the two of us.

'Right lads, that's how you do it. Now you just keep making them just as I did. Count them because when you reach one hundred I want you to come to my office and see me.'

With that he left the two of us to it.

'Hi Frank. Where are you from?'

'Coolock, Cromcastle. What about you?'

'Coolock, Glin.'

'By Jaysus, it is a small world now isn't it? And I was thinking it was too far away to be coming all the way here. My Da just works along the street. He gives me a lift in to work. He's got a little minivan that he does a veg round on the weekends.'

So off the pair of us went, making boxes for our living and me hoping that I wouldn't get my fucking finger stapled to one of them. Although the working day flew it did seem a bit boring to me. It was very repetitious work and once you had done one you had done the lot in a manner of speaking. Our day came to an end and my new mate Barry headed off to get a lift from his Da as I set out on the long stroll to catch my bus back home.

The next day started the same but at lunch time I decided to go to a bakery I had spotted around the corner near the canal bridge on my way into work this morning. Barry wasn't interested so I was on my own as I made my way to the cake shop. As I strolled inside there was a wonderful aroma of fresh bread and cakes. It reminded me of years earlier hanging around the bakery waiting to rob some cakes.

Inside were two girl assistants with their backs to me. I could see their figures outlined beneath their work smocks. Both had long, black hair covering their shoulders and hanging quite low on their backs. One of the two, aware of my standing there, turned to face me with a big smile on her face. It seemed to turn to apprehension. It was as though she knew me. The other girl turned around and a look of shock appeared on her face too. For the minute I was unsure what was wrong. I knew I hadn't farted and I knew also I had combed my hair this morning and there were no snots hanging from my nose.

It was then it dawned on me. Shite! They were the two daughters of the head farmer from St Joseph's Industrial School at Letterfrack. These were the girls who had cooked and ironed for the Christian Brothers, who had so often abused me when I was doing my time there, they were the Nortimer girls.

'Well, well, the dead arose and appeared to many,' I said as soon as I realised who the two girls were. 'And what the fuck are you girls doing here? When did you leave the bog?'

They just looked at me with fear in their eyes and it then began to dawn on me that I had escaped from that godforsaken place and was still officially on the run. Were they going to report me to the police? Uncomfortable with the changed circumstances I was already wishing I hadn't got the not so bright idea of buying my lunch at the bakery's shop. I am afraid I stammered as I asked them for a large slice of gur cake. This was a Dublin cake and the word Gur meant staying out overnight on the Streets.

One of them wrapped it in brown paper and asked me for payment but all the time they could not take their eyes from my face. I'm fucked now I was thinking but I took my purchase and left the shop as casually as I could.

On returning to the job my face must have been quite a shade of white.

'Have you seen a fuckin' ghost or something?' enquired Barry.

'No; No Just a blast from me past,' I replied miserably.

All went well again that day and Barry and I were becoming pals. Next day at lunch break I again went to the cake shop for lunch but the girls were gone. I never enquired why or where they had gone and I was never to see them again. It was only in later years that I was to find they were also on the run. For them it was a different kind of running. They had been part of the conspiracy of deceit and hatred showered upon us boy inmates by the religious orders. They knew what was going on. They were part of it. They now wanted to put it behind them as though they were ashamed of their past, hiding from their sins. These incidents, like shadows, would follow them wherever life was to take them. They were victims too but a different kind of victim. They were well paid and cossetted victims.

After about a week of making boxes we were both becoming tired of its tediousness but soldiered on regardless. A job after all is a job and beggars can't be choosers. On the following Monday I was given a job on one of the firm's delivery trucks as a helper. The driver was a man from Ballyfermot by the name of Des, short for Desmond presumably. A dapper sort of bloke. He had black hair combed back in a slick. I thought he likely used margarine on it as flies were attracted to his head. Otherwise he was a great geezer and fun to be with. He would start drinking the bottles of Smithwick's at lunch time and then never stopped doing so until we finished our round. This could be as late as seven o'clock or so.

I didn't know much about drinking the stuff. One day I tried a bottle and it didn't do anything for me. It just seemed to run through me. As a consequence I was bursting for a piss at the worst possible time, when he was driving. He couldn't be doing with the interruption.

'Just piss it back into the bottle,' he said.

Being modest I turned my back on him and tried but the piss was more than the bottle could hold. He was almost in tears with laughing at my discomfort and whooping, 'fuck it, fuck it,' as he drove merrily along.

Despite the experience, we got on well together. Soon afterwards Barry joined us on the round and boy was the crack mighty when the three of us were together. We younger ones soon learned that Des was on the fiddle with the empty bottles. He would miscount the empties at the public houses we delivered to. As he would get paid mostly in cash he could dock his share of his fiddle from the day's takings. Des had, it seemed, won the lottery of life.

Young Barry also got used to drinking the odd bottle and would be giddy and sometimes shouted from the lorry window at young girls walking along the streets. It was often to their surprise or in some cases their delight as Barry was a bit of a good looker himself.

All went well for a few months until one day Des had to take time off as he wasn't well. As a consequence we were given a relief driver. This driver we knew was related to one of the firm's directors. He was the type you would see behind desks in your typical office or maybe educational setting. His spectacles were as thick as milk bottle ends and he looked a right gobshite wearing a shirt and tie when driving the lorry.

We were about half way through our round at the time. Barry had sneakily downed his ritual bottles of beer. I had to admit I had also taken two so I had a glow on as well. I recall we were at a big public house in Blanchardstown.

Barry was trying to work the fiddle out on the empty bottles when we noticed gobshite keeping an eye on us. His eyes were bulging behind the thick rims of his specs.

When we were finished at the drop Barry whispered 'I've got the shillings and the job is Oxo.'

I nodded.

It was at that point we headed off in a direction I was unfamiliar with. After a while we pulled into a lay-by outside a house and gobshite leaves us in the cab and goes inside. After a little while a girl we knew who worked in the office came out to greet us and seemed to get up real close. I was later to discover that her reason for doing so was to see if she could smell alcohol on our breath. Shortly afterwards, gobshite climbed back into the cab and we set off on the return journey to the depot. Nothing untoward happened and Barry and I said our goodbyes and headed for our respective homes.

The following morning upon my arrival I was told to go up to the office. When I got there I found Barry was already there. The truth dawned on us. Gobshite had reported us for drinking and fiddling and we were both sacked on the spot.

Barry was aghast.

'What the fuck do we do now? My Da will fucking kill me.'

Rubbing my hand through my hair I pondered a response to the dilemma. I too was thinking about what my own Da was going to say because in the Heeney household no job meant no home. As we two strolled gloomily to the bus stop we decided we would remain friends and meet up the following day at the bus terminus at Greencastle Road. The idea being that the following morning we would pretend we were going to work. He would tell his Da that he was going to go on the bus with me in the future and didn't need a lift. In our minds was the thought that we could look for a job elsewhere and all would be well. Things never go as planned and this was to be the start of two years of madness.

CHAPTER 20

Next morning I told my Da I would get a later bus as I was not needed in work so early. There was no sense going to Annesley Bridge and then back to Greencastle to meet Barry. When I got to the bus stop my friend, Barry, was there waiting on me.

'What's the crack?'

I shrugged half-heartedly. 'Devil the bit. So what's the story now, will we head on into town or what?'

'Don't know,' Barry replied gloomily, 'Maybe it's better to hang out here and keep the bus fare in our pockets.'

We sauntered off like two optimistic little delinquents as happy as the day is long not knowing where or what we might do. Isn't life just great when you're sixteen and have no worries? But anxieties can easily be created as I well knew. You didn't have to have them if you knew how to make them for yourself, and make them we did.

It was about two o'clock in the afternoon when we approached an industrial estate at the back of Cadbury's Chocolate factory. Down the approaching street there were many factories and one in particular that Barry knew something of. It was a pork and bacon factory called Hearns, who were quite famous for their meat products. One of Barry's brothers already worked there and this was why he knew of it.

'Let's see if we can get a job here,' he said with a certain confidence in his voice.

There was a company shop, fronting the factory so we decided to make it our first port of call. There was a large counter that was filled with rashers, sausages, and various cuts of meat, with two girls dressed all in white standing behind it. With a big, beaming smile on his face Barry enquired about work. It didn't get us any further. We were told there were no vacancies but if we were to return before Christmas we would more likely get a start then.

'Fuck this,' said Barry. 'Let's keep trying. There is another factory in Kylemore Lane. They might take us on.'

So off we sauntered on the long walk down to Artane. By taking this route we would pass through Coolock Village where there was a small garage. Nothing ventured nothing gained. I nonchalantly strolled in and asked if there might be any jobs going. I was in luck. They wanted someone to man the petrol pumps and it was arranged for me to start the following Monday.

Naturally, I was delighted with myself and was grinning ear to ear when I came out to tell Barry. He took umbrage at my getting lucky. This left him on his own to search for work. The next thing I know, in a fit of temper, he picked up a brick and hurled it through the garage window. Having got that off his chest Barry was elated and legged it down Malahide Road.

As he did so he was howling with laughter and shouting over his shoulder, 'that's the end of your job, you gobshite.'

I was livid with anger. I couldn't believe what he had just done but that's mates for you. I took off after him and it wasn't long before I caught up with him.

'The look on your face was gas,' he chortled. 'You looked like your Ma took your dummy away. Shite, Frank. It's no problem. You will get a better job.'

Seeing the funny side of it, we carried on our way and headed on down to another industrial estate. Barry was still in very high spirits and chirpily laughed most of the route. It seemed to me that he wasn't too bothered about getting a job at all but that was all very well for him. I had no choice but to get one.

After a while we ended up outside what we could see was a jam making factory. 'I'm going in here. There might be something going here.'

'That's okay,' he smiled patiently. 'I'll wait here for you.'

Stepping inside I found an elderly lady sat behind the counter. She was busy at something and so while I waited to get her attention I had a good look around me. There were jars of all the types of jam and marmalade you could think of and more besides. All were neatly stacked along endless shelves around the walls. The woman was apparently unaware of my presence, maybe uncaring, and typing away on a big old typewriter. The clickety-clack of the keys was filling the shop.

Only after a while did she raise her head and acknowledge my presence.

'What can I do for you, young lad?'

'I was wondering if you might have any jobs missus,' I said.

'Have you filled out an application form?'

What the fuck's that I thought to myself. 'No, missus; I have not.'

'Hold on a minute,' she said. 'I will get one for you.'

Searching through some papers she found what she wanted and handed me several sheets.

'You need to fill this in. Bring it back with your references and your school report.'

I thanked her, took the sheets from her and walked towards the door. As I did so I thought to myself, 'that's the end of that job then.'

As I went back on to the street I heard a whistle and shout. 'Frank, Frank. I am over here!'

I looked from where the sound of the shout came from and spotted Barry. He was holding open the door of a green mini car.

Running over to him I said 'what's this? What are you doing?'

'Get in. Just get in' he said. 'I was able to start it, let's go for a drive.'

'Can you drive it?'

I was thrilled.

'Sure man, of course I can drive it so get in and let's fuck off.'

With that, he went screeching out of the car park and headed back towards the Malahide Road. The car's engine was screaming. It was still in first gear.

'Are you sure you can drive?' I called, as I hung on to my seat for dear life.

'Yeah, of course I can. Just hang on.'

We were still in first gear as Barry in the highest of spirits reached Glin Road. Only then did he stop the car and abandoned it just around the corner from his home.

'Me Da needs one of these,' he said as if he has just purchased the car.

It was in Barry's head that the new car would come in handy for spare parts.

'Okay, I'll be off then,' I said to him. 'I will probably see you Monday or Tuesday.'

As I said my goodbyes, I was thinking to myself, I'm not getting involved in this hare-brained idea.

I spent that weekend doing little or nothing but all the while I was thinking to myself if I went to the garage on Monday and explained would I still get the job? On balance I decided that it wasn't such a good idea.

Up bright and early on the Monday morning and with my Ma and Da blissfully unaware of my predicament, I left early enough to give the impression that for me it was work as usual. Taking the bus into town and with time hanging heavy on my hands, I wandered about Dublin's famous O'Connell Street. As I did so I noticed a sign in the window of an amusement arcade; 'Help wanted.'

Going inside, I fixed up an immediate interview with a small portly baldheaded man. As though he was well used to that sort of thing, occasionally nibbling at the end of his pen he took down my details.

'Have you any job experience?' he asked. Before I had time to answer he added 'In an amusement arcade?'

I told him I hadn't but I had been a butcher's messenger boy and I had worked on a lorry making deliveries.

Eying me up and down, something that probably told him more than could any information on an application form, he said 'The position pays £4.10s a week. Okay, follow me.'

Off we went together to where four rows of slot machines were lined up. Opening a hatch door that led in behind the machines I saw all these small buckets hanging behind each machine. He then explained to me what my job would be. When I heard money dropping into the buckets I was to take the bucket and hand it to the customer as this would be their winnings.

'Jesus,' I thought. 'This is going to be a doddle.'

I was to start the next morning.

I was so pleased with myself. I now had a job again and that night I drifted off with a smile on my face and slept like a baby. During my first day at the amusement arcade the first thought that struck me was how many customers played the slot machines from first thing in the morning to quite late in the evenings. There was a constant flow of gamblers and I was kept busy running up and down emptying the buckets behind the machines. When, on occasion a punter would make a sizeable win, I would be handed a tip for my trouble.

I was also to be introduced to the darker side of gambling. This was when a Chinese customer, a regular, asked if he could borrow some money from me. It was a totally unexpected request and I was a bit shocked by it. He was always well dressed in a suit and tie. He certainly looked respectable and he was asking me, a boy earning a pittance, if he could borrow money. I felt so sorry for him but needn't have done so. A few days later he reappeared and played the machines as if nothing had happened.

Then there was the day a lad, who was maybe a year older than me I thought, was stopped playing the machines by the Manager. The lad was, he said, too young to be playing the machines. This caused bad feelings and a squabble broke out between them. I came out from behind the machines to see if there was anything I could do to defuse the situation. I was about to meet Tosser for the first time. He was ranting and raving that he was over eighteen and the Manager would have none of it. He was telling him he had to bring in his birth certificate to prove it.

'Don't you worry,' Tosser retorted. 'I will do just that.'

A few days later Tosser reappeared with his birth certificate in his hand and mollified, the Manager allowed him to play the machines. He later told me it was his brother's birth certificate as he, Tosser, did not have one available. The newcomer was in fact a jovial type with an oval face and carrying a bit more weight than he should. He was still young, yet despite this, his brown hair was already starting to recede. As we fell to talking he told me he was unemployed and on the dole but he hoped to get a job in the whiskey distillery company where his father worked. He was living in Sherriff Street, a location which was notorious and known as '*bandit country.*'

I had an aunt and uncle who lived there and so was familiar with the area. It was made up of blocks of flats of one and two bedrooms. Despite their smallness, some families had reared up to ten children in a two bedroom flat. God only knows how they did it but coming from an area like that the opportunities available to them were slim. Many of the youngsters turned to crime as it was for them the only means of putting bread on the table. A father, if working, could never earn enough to support a large family.

As I got to know Tosser better, we became good friends and very often, rather than go straight home after work, we two would hang around town together. We would talk about our shared experiences growing up in Dublin but I never mentioned my time in Letterfrack Industrial School. I had already decided this was going to be my big secret.

The first time I met Tosser's father I remember thinking he was really just an older version of Tosser but totally bald and with a bulbous, purple coloured nose. This was no doubt due to the whiskey he consumed. I was told that at the distillery where he worked you were entitled to a daily ration. It was a good way I supposed to get you dependent and reliable from a boss's point of view.

Tosser had three older brothers and two sisters. His mother was a nondescript kind of woman who had very little to say for herself but typically would always have the kettle on.

As we got to know each other better it seemed like Tosser and the brothers were not averse to the odd petty theft or crime. One day he was describing to me how he was in Cleary's department store with the sole intention of doing a bit of shoplifting. As he was gazing at a display of cameras he was thinking to himself 'I could easily take one of these', when out of nowhere an older woman appeared beside him. As he stood there she started showing an interest in the cameras too. As she examined them he began to wonder if she was thinking the same as he was. With that thought in mind he deftly slipped one of the cameras into his jackets inside pocket and turning on his heel headed for the shop doorway. It then occurred to him that she was in his shadow and as he slipped through the doors leading to the street she grabbed his shoulder. The woman was the store detective. So much for innocent looking *'old wans'* was his way of putting it. Tosser ended up getting the Probation Act for his troubles.

I, for my part, had similar suspicions and I was always expecting my friend to suggest 'maybe we should steal something from the amusement arcade where I worked.' He never did. His dream was to carry out a major robbery and live happily ever after on the proceeds. He was mad into James Cagney gangster films.

I quite enjoyed my job at the arcade and was soon making many friends. I had noticed a girl who tried her luck frequently, a likeable sort, and we soon became friendly. The slots at the time were penny slots and the winnings would be in pennies too. On occasion customers would ask me for change. One day, as this girl asked me for change of two shillings her hand lingered on mine. It was a wonderful sensation I had to admit. From that moment on I began to take a greater interest in her.

Her name was Ann and she was from the countryside. Ann was working. She had a job at Our Lady's Hospital in Crumlin and was a few years older than me. One day, when she came into the arcade, I plucked up the courage to ask her for a date. It took every nerve on my part because of the age difference being what it was. Anyway, she accepted the suggestion and we arranged to meet on Saturday evening under the clock at Eason's.

I was out with Tosser the following evening and took the opportunity to tell him I had met this girl. Tosser wasn't going out with anyone at the time.

'See if she has any mates for me,' was his suggestion.

Saturday, the day Ann and I had decided to meet up didn't take long coming around and my feelings were those of a child at the approach of Christmas. Arriving in town early I thought it would be best to stand across the road from Eason's at Cleary's. Right then there must have been a dozen girls outside the store and the same outside Cleary's.

I thought to myself, 'Holy Jesus; what's going on here?'

I never realised how many people used this spot to meet up on Saturday evenings.

Ann arrived right on time. My new girlfriend was looking stunning in a three quarter length blue coat. As soon as we got the pleasantries out of the way it was decided we would go to the pictures as there was a Western on at the Savoy. This being my first real date I was all flummoxed about how to behave. Do we hold hands, walk side by side, what do you do on a date? Maybe Ann sensed my uncertainty. Taking my hand we went into the cinema's lobby and as we did so, I heard my name being called.

Looking around, I soon found where the voice was coming from. It was my cousin Barbara. She was an usherette at the cinema. We chatted awhile. I introduced her to Ann to which she replied she would get us two of the best seats in the house. How lucky do you get?

We followed her through the bat-wing doors and, more to the point, followed her torch's beam for the picture had started and the cinema was in darkness. I was inwardly glowing, on my first date the seats in the back row and free of charge. Things could hardly get better.

As we made our way to our seats Barbara asked over her shoulder how I was and the family, my Ma in particular. I told her all was well at home as she led us both up to the back row. I couldn't believe my good fortune. The luck continued. The film was an excellent spaghetti western with Clint Eastwood and throughout the showing we began to feel really comfortable with each other.

We were both feeling good when after the film we went to Caffola's on O'Connell Street. There we enjoyed lemonades and it was whilst there I was quite taken by the amazing blueness of Ann's eyes. They were a deep blue, quite unlike ordinary blue eyes. She told me she was a junior nurse and had a year to go before qualifying. By this time, I was feeling really relaxed as she chatted away, explaining that she lived in the hospital's living quarters for nurses.

All too soon, it was time to be going on our way. Taking her hand, we strolled to where her last bus would shortly be leaving at eleven thirty. Not surprisingly there was a lengthy queue when we reached the bus stop. There was some pushing and shoving but somehow we managed a quick cuddle and a kiss before my date hopped on her bus.

We hadn't made any future arrangements. I don't suppose it entered our minds as we were both caught up in the moment. Ann said she would see me at work during the week and with that promise in mind, I ran like the wind to Eden Quay. I too had a bus to catch. Thankfully it hadn't yet left due to something of a disturbance by several drunks. It was when I climbed aboard I saw that one of them was my father. He was giving some old feller an earful over something. Fortunately such was the heated exchanges between the two of them I was able to reach the rear of the bus unnoticed. Just how embarrassing could it get to have your drunken father on the same bus?

Throughout the journey home my Da kept getting up and pressing the bell. He thought it was hilarious but luckily for him the driver knew him well enough and let it be. Finally, after a journey that seemed to have taken far too long the bus pulled up at the unscheduled stop outside our home and my Da alighted. I stayed where I was and got off at the official bus stop.

By the time I reached home I could hear him well enough, singing one of his favourite ballads, *The Policeman's Song*. I left his performance for my mother to enjoy, hoping he wouldn't do too many encores as I slipped up the stairs to my bed. All I wanted to do was push my father out of my mind and concentrate on Ann and in my mind go over the evening we had just enjoyed together. I wanted to savour every moment as I drifted off to sleep.

CHAPTER 21

THE NEXT FEW WEEKS WENT by without too much ado. I did see Ann a few times but a date was out of the question. She was doing nights for a little while. There were some days she came to see me at the arcade. I was of course still keeping the company of my friend, Tosser. We two had, in the meantime, hooked up with another friend of Tosser's, Mick who was from Ballyfermot. The two of them had been friends for several years.

The three of us would hang around another arcade on Eden Quay. This was close to my Da's watering hole the Ace of Hearts.

One night I was to meet Mick's brother there. His nickname was Crazy Horse and being much older and tougher than we were he had a reputation as a hard man. He was outside the arcade that night when two fellers flew at him. They had earlier been slagging him off, making fun of his nose. True to say Crazy Horse's nose was the biggest I had ever seen on any human being.

In the mêlée that followed one of the attackers was stabbed by Mick's brother. To defend himself in the uneven fight he had drawn a knife. I was standing off to one side. I had no interest in getting involved but I must have been too close to what was happening. The next thing I know I was grabbed by a policeman and dragged unceremoniously towards and into the waiting police Black Maria.

I was flung to the floor and my fall from grace was followed by Mick and Tosser being thrown in with me. Needless to say the person who was at the centre of the fracas that had put us here was nowhere to be seen.

We three hapless prisoners were taken to Store Street Garda Station where we were punched, kicked and beaten by the heavy handed police. After the beating we were separated. I was gripped by my hair and dragged along to a cell whereupon I was thrown to the floor. By this time there was blood spurting from my cut and bruised mouth. I was bruised all over and shaking like a leaf at the unexpected, unfairness of what had happened.

In the cell there was a strong smell of urine. Projecting from the bare brick walls was a slab of cement or concrete that was supposed to be a bed. Taking in my surroundings I could see the walls were filled with graffiti. My head was pounding and the light set in a small cage situated on the ceiling was flickering on and off. It was surreal. There was an eeriness to what was happening, an unreality. I could hear shouting and screaming coming from outside the cell door and the sound of someone getting a good battering.

By this time the entire side of my face was becoming swollen and my fear was further agitated by the thought that the police were bound to discover that I was an escapee from Letterfrack Industrial School. They had not at that point taken down any details. That was surely to come and anyway I was sure they knew who I was.

After a while the screaming outside the row of cells ceased and things became very quiet. I had, by this time, an agonising pain in my left arm. I just sat quietly on the concrete bed unknowing what fate would befall me. A little time passed and I became aware of movement from outside the cell door and then the eye hatch being pulled across.

I heard an unseen person saying 'no, that's not him; he had nothing to do with it.'

Not long afterwards I heard the key turning in the lock. The door was flung roughly open and the cell entrance was filled by the form of a massive policeman.

'Out now,' he said to me.

Taking me by the arm the policeman led me to the front of the police station where there was another policeman in a sergeant's uniform perched on a stool behind a desk. He slid a packet of twenty cigarettes my way.

'You could be charged with resisting arrest but we have decided we won't be doing that with you. But remember, you haven't got a clean sheet. It doesn't mean you are off the hook. The charge can be filed against you in the future if we wish. Do you understand that?'

Without waiting for my reply he added 'don't let me see you here again.'

I was free to go on my way.

It was freezing outside at that time of the year and with my sore head and face, not to mention my arm, giving me considerable grief, I looked for Mick or Tosser. There was no sign of them or anyone else for that matter. I decided to light one of the cigarettes I had been given and hang around to see if they would show up.

After about fifteen minutes Mick emerged from the Garda station looking as if he had just passed the time of day with them. He looked so matter of fact casual.

As soon as he caught sight of me he said 'Jesus, Frank what have they fuckin' done to you? You're in bits and covered in blood. All I got was a few hefty kicks up my arse.'

'Where's Tosser?' I bleakly asked. 'Have they got your brother?'

'I don't know,' Mick replied. 'Don't you think we should be getting out of here?'

'No, give it a while and see if Tosser comes out. Did somebody look through the peephole of your cell?'

'Yeah, I think they were witnesses, I heard them say it wasn't me and then they let me go.'

At that moment Tosser emerged from the Garda station door. It could clearly be seen that his lip was cut, badly bruised and swollen. He also had a black eye and his shirt was ripped.

'Are you ok?' I asked.

'I'm grand but I'll be a lot fuckin' better when I get away from this place.'

With that, we three headed into Amiens Street with the intention of going into the train station toilets to clean ourselves up. Something inside me was nagging at me. Why was Mick not battered or bruised? It later transpired that his brother, Crazy Horse, was picked up in the early hours of the following morning and charged with stabbing another lad. The court appearance followed and Crazy Horse received three years in Mountjoy Prison.

I heard later that he had boasted about the stabbing, saying 'If you pull a knife use it.'

I found out that the lad he had injured had taken a knife from his pocket but had not used it. It had been an empty threat, a warning we supposed.

After cleaning ourselves up in the train station's jacks it was decided we would go our separate ways. It was time to go home. When I arrived home my head and my arm were throbbing so badly my Ma took me into the hospital on the bus. There it was found I had a fractured arm, which was fitted together again and my arm put into plaster. As a consequence I was unable to work and I lost my job at the arcade. As luck would have it I had a phone number for the nurse's station. I was able to phone Ann and keep her up to date on what was happening.

My arm was soon better as everything heals with time. Ann had been coming out to Coolock to visit me as she is the only one working at the moment. She had been studying hard for her final examinations. My Ma thought she was putting on weight and she looked at me with a mother's funny look when she said this. I had only known Ann about three months now and I didn't see the relevance of my Ma's comments.

Tosser was also out to see me the other day. He came out on the bus to talk with me. It seemed he had this master plan about doing a big safe job. He didn't have all the details yet but we were going to need a car and a driver. Tosser didn't drive and neither did Mick. I didn't think I'll be asking Barry after the way he drove the last time. It occurred to me that I would be the driver.

I had called in at the Dole office in Gardiner Street to sign on the dole to try and get some money as jobs at the moment seemed scarce. There I was told by the clerk at hatch D that I was not entitled to any money as I am under the age of eighteen. She suggested I sign on for credits as they will be of benefit to me as I became older. What a load of bollix?

In the meantime Tosser had set up the following Thursday night for the safe job he had planned. It had already been decided, we were to steal a car on the night and I was as I thought to be the driver.

Thursday afternoon came around soon enough and I caught a bus into town. Tosser's older brother had given him a load of keys to fit both Mini and Morris Minor cars. All seemed straightforward enough. Tosser got inside info on the job as one of his sisters worked there. The target was a big factory in East Wall and on the Thursday night we were led to believe the safe was to contain the entire staff salaries, a lot of money and all in cash. Tosser was certain of it and thought this is the big one.

With our heads together we were in Caffola's Restaurant having lemonade and our planning was well advanced. It had already been decided that we take a car from town, use it to do the job and then go back to Tosser's other sister's house with the safe. It was thought there isn't much room in a mini car and anyway they are lightweight. Safes tend to be unwieldy and very heavy. The car had to be a Morris Minor. That night was bitterly cold and the chill seemed to penetrate our bones as pulling our coats tight to our chests we made our way down Middle Abbey Street keeping our eyes peeled for a suitable car as we sauntered. The script was we should be able to get one while the people are at the pictures.

As the three of us made our way without hopefully drawing attention to ourselves Tosser spotted just what we are looking for. Trying to appear nonchalant I tried a key in the door. We got lucky. The car door opened and after leaning across the driver's seat I lifted the latch to allow the passenger door to open. Things were beginning to look promising. Pulling the passenger seat forward Tosser stood aside whilst Mick clambered in and then he occupied the car's front passenger seat. Fiddling with the key in the ignition the red light came on, on the dashboard. I pulled the start button and the engine started without any problems.

In truth, I was clueless how to drive the thing. Certainly my foot was on the clutch and my hands were levering the gear stick but I was fucked if I could find reverse. It was essential that I did so. When it reached the stage of futile Tosser had to jump out and push the car backward so I could get it out of the parking space. Jumping back into the car he muttered something about hoping I had by now found the right gear.

Releasing the clutch I did at least find first gear and with a jump and a shudder the car started moving forward in a manner of speaking. Thankfully there was little traffic about and this gave me the time to concentrate my attention on the maverick gear lever. I did manage to find second gear. Maybe third or fourth would come easier now that I was getting the hang of it.

My attention was so distracted by the necessity to sort the gears out; it didn't occur to me that there might be good reason for the few cars that were about flashing me with their headlights.

Somewhere from between his ears Tosser realised 'We've no fucking lights on!'

'Shite. Where's the light switch?' I was thinking to myself as I divided my attention between actually driving and finding the light switch.

Haphazardly pulling and pushing knobs and switches, pressing buttons and messing with this and that I eventually found the vehicle's light switches.

'Are you sure you can drive this fuckin' car?'

The voice was Tosser's. He was in a sweat in the seat beside me.

'Yeah, of course I can,' I told him, as we whined along the road with the car screeching in second gear. 'I am just better in a Mini Minor.'

While I was defending my hopelessness it occurred to me that I hadn't a clue how to stop the vehicle. Keeping to the middle of the road and holding my breath, though God knows what I hoped to achieve by doing that, I seemed to be doing ok so far.

'Next left,' said Tosser.

There was nothing from Mick who was deathly silent sitting in the back seat.

'Left,' said Tosser again and again more urgently.

'I am, I am,' I grunted as I was trying my best to slow down enough to take the left turn.

'Pull in,' said Tosser 'and switch the main beams off.'

Slamming my foot on the clutch and then firmly on the brake pedal I was hoping I was doing the right thing. Not from where Tosser was sitting or at least had been sitting. He was projected forward like a missile and there was a sickening thud as his head slammed against the windscreen.

'Fuck,' said Mick from the back seat, 'what ye doing? You'll kill us all.'

For my part I was thinking how the fuck am I going to get out of here with a safe in the car? Shaking like a leaf I slipped the car out of gear, thankfully without stalling it.

'Right,' said Tosser still nursing his head. 'Stay here. I will do a reccie.'

He opened the car door, climbed out and off he scarpered. As he went on his way I could see him further up the road looking furtively in all directions. A moment later he came running back to the car. Breathing heavy he told us the job is Oxo.

'What we'll do is this. There's some building work going on. We will get a plank and jam it in the boot so it is sticking out. Then we will reverse the car into the door, using the plank as a battering ram. In the door goes and in we go is that agreed?'

The factory was situated in a street with terraced houses on one side facing the factory on the other. With our plan in place all we needed now was patience as we waited for the last house lights to be extinguished and then the world was our oyster. We could make the attempt on the door. While we were sitting there I could hear the sound of heavy breathing coming from the back seat, snoring actually.

'Would you believe it,' said Tosser 'the dosser's gone to fuckin' sleep and all the idiots in the road are still wide awake?'

After a while all the lights had finally, one by one, been switched off and a decision was made to go for it. This time starting the car was a bit easier and I seem to have mastered the clutch. I never want to hear about kangaroo petrol ever again. This time we started moving slowly down the road but hopefully with less evidence of there being an amateur at the wheel.

Mick had by this time awakened and both of them got out of the car whilst I set about figuring out where the reverse gear might be. I did discover it and was guided back tentatively until I felt the nudge from the rear. The plank had made contact with the factory's office door.

'Right,' Tosser said with a sigh of relief. 'Get ready and go for it.'

With his words ringing in my ears I put the car back into reverse, pressed the accelerator until the engine was really revving and smartly released the clutch. It was not so smart actually. This is where the plan started to go wrong.

There was an unmerciful bang as the plank exploded into and through the back seats of the car. It continued its path until it slammed into the rear of my seat nearly breaking my poor back in two.

'Jaysus,' screamed Tosser, 'Christ. You're doing this all fucking wrong. Pull forward,' he bellowed.

With my back aching I placed the car into first gear and pulled forward. As soon as I had made some space Tosser adjusted the battering ram plank so its end was wedged up against a cross member in the car's boot. That would stop it going in the wrong direction.

Once again I got it into reverse and once again it went flying backwards. This was followed by yet another unearthly bang but this time it was the factory door, not the car seats that were splinted into two sections.

This was when the lights started flickering on in the homes across the roads. What a commotion we had caused.

'Quick,' I called 'Get in, get the safe in.'

'And let's hope none of those fuckers in the houses have got a telephone,' added Mick.

'Don't worry, no one will come out,' I called reassuringly as the three of us ran up the inside office stairs. Tosser had told us it is the first room on the right. As we darted inside we saw the safe illuminated by the street lights clearly enough. It was in the corner and at a guess I would say about three feet high.

'Let's grab it then' said a breathless Tosser.

'Jesus,' said Mike; 'we can't lift it. It's too heavy.'

'Roll it then,' I suggested. 'Keep tipping it over towards the stairs.'

'But we can't get it down the stairs,' said a clearly exasperated Tosser.

'Just fucking roll it will you,' I called, increasingly concerned at the noise we have made and the reaction we must be causing.

So we just pushed and rolled, heaved it until we had levered the damned thing to the top of the wooden stairs. From there we just heaved and watched it as it tumbled all the way down the staircase smashing the stairs as it went on its merry way. We then scampered down what was left of the splintered wreckage and by levering, lifting and maneuvering we used the plank in a vain attempted to get the rogue safe into the boot of the car.

'Jaysus,' said Tosser, 'It won't fit in the boot. It's too big. It's half in and half out.'

As we contemplated the latest miscalculation more and more lights were coming on in the terraced homes facing us.

'We've gotta get out of here,' I said. 'Someone's going to come out of the houses.'

'You get in and drive,' said Tosser, 'Mike and I will hold it in the boot. You drive slow we'll run behind it.'

I put the car into first gear and off we went with my two mates running behind holding the heavy safe which was sticking out of the car's boot. The two lads were trying to keep it from falling out on to the road. I was surprised the car's front wheels were still on the road because of the ridiculous weight in the rear. Thankfully we only had a five minute drive to Tosser's sister's house and the forlorn hope that the police didn't arrive on the scene of what has turned into a farce.

Pulling up outside his sister's home, Tosser banged on the door. It was soon answered by his sister.

'Jesus, what are you doing for God's sake?' she asked, standing there in a short nightdress.

'We've got the safe. Now we have to get it in,' gasped her brother.

With that, he went into the house and emerged moments later with a trolley. From there we all helped to manoeuvre the safe onto the trolley, somehow got it inside the house and then as quickly through the back door and into the rear garden. It was my job to get shut of the car and we arranged to rendezvous at Tosser's house where we would all sleep on the floor for what was left of the night.

It was the rattling of cups that awoke me.

'I've told you before about bringing your mates back here.'

That was Tosser's mother calling through from the kitchen.

'I hope you weren't up to no good last night.'

I hear Tosser's voice, 'that is a lovely cup of tea, Ma.'

After the tea I headed off home.

Two days were to pass before I met up with Tosser again. This, as arranged, was at his sister's house. There I found Mike in the kitchen enjoying his cup of tea. Sounds from the garden could be heard; a muffled sound.

'What's happening?' I asked Mike.

'It's Tosser he's out in the garden and has nearly got the back off the safe.'

Going out through the back door and into the garden I found that Tosser, by now, has a heavy bar wedged into the back of the safe. He was levering and pulling at it frantically. Beads of sweat were standing out on his brow. I was puzzled. I could smell something strange coming from the rear of the safe. Tosser looked at me with a lopsided grin.

'This is it' he said, 'pay dirt.'

With that he wrenched off the back cover of the safe and we pair kneeled to peer inside. As soon as we did so Tosser let out a roar,

'For fuck's sake.'

Putting his hand inside, he pulled out a tin of plasters and the remains of a smashed bottle of iodine. The safe's total contents. Such was the ignominious beginning of our safe cracking careers. It must be said it was also the end of that particular vocation. If I wasn't there when he got it open I would never have believed it. Mike spluttered and very nearly choked on his tea when we gave him the news.

Tosser's sister had been off work that week. When she returned to her job she was to hear sweet words about the idiots who wrecked the place robbing the safe when the wages were all on the desk three feet from the safe. The idiots must have walked past the neatly placed stacks. To rub salt into our wounds, we also learned that the keys to the safe were hanging on the hook just above it. There had never been a need to remove the safe at all.

CHAPTER 22

I WAS WALKING DOWN DUBLIN's Parnell Street and my bum was freezing with the cold. I was wearing a short jacket that for very good reason is known as a bum freezer. I hadn't seen any of the lads since the safe cracking fiasco and I was now on my way to meet Ann outside Cleary's Department Store where we had arranged to meet up. When I arrived she was waiting for me.

'How are you?'

'I am grand,' she smiled. 'I have got tomorrow off by the way.'

With that, I took her by the hand and we thought best to head for Wexford Street. There we found a cosy public house with a popular ballad group doing the entertaining.

'You look freezing,' she said as we are walking along. 'Don't you have an overcoat?'

Only then did it dawn on me that I had never in my life owned an overcoat. It wasn't a good start to our date for, when we arrived at our chosen pub; I was turned away on the grounds that I was too young to be admitted.

'I suppose we just better go to the pictures,' I suggested and we made our near dejected way in the direction of the Adelphi Cinema only to be turned away from there too. The movies that day were all X rated. You needed to be eighteen-years old to be admitted.

There was little else to do but to hop a bus out to Crumlin to where Ann worked. Once there and close to the hospital's entrance I suppose we held each other tight to keep the cold at bay and other reasons. For a start there was the passion even in the bitter cold. There was another reason. She was warm, very warm to me and I imagined I was to Ann too.

Following a brief but heavy kissing spell she asked me 'Do you like red, the colour red?'

I had little need to decide whether I did or not. Before she had finished her question she opened the front of her coat to show me her red dress. My eyeballs went like organ stops.

'Er, yes. I definitely like red.'

'I thought you would. It's nice isn't it? I don't know how we are going to work this but I would love you to come up to my room and spend the night. There is no way you can come in through the hospital main doors but maybe, just maybe you could climb up from outside,' she suggested whimsically.

I was always open to such suggestions and together we made our way around the side of the hospital. At a certain point Ann pointed up to a row of darkened windows.

'I will go on in and switch on the light. Then you will be able to see from here where my room is.'

Giving me a big hug and kiss off she went. I waited nervously and then after what must have been five minutes I saw a light come on in one of the rooms and then shortly afterwards Ann waving in my direction from the window. Not knowing if she could see me I waved back but first there was the wall to be gotten over. From where I was standing I could see a drainpipe running up the building that passed by her room. Up I climbed though my hands were freezing cold. There wasn't a thought in my head as to the danger I was putting myself in. Only the pleasurable anticipation of what reward was awaiting me. Luckily it was not a high climb only to the first floor.

Grunting with exertion I finally pulled myself in through the window. Ann's was a small room with the walls painted a more or less tasteful pink and there was a small iron framed single bed. In the room was a single wardrobe and dressing table with a dansette record player placed on top.

Ann, in her red dress, was visibly impressed. She was looking at me in mild bewilderment that I had gone to such risk to get here.

'Shhhh. Don't talk, not a word,' she whispered. 'If anyone hears a man's voice I will be sacked and thrown out of the hospital.'

In whispers, she explained to me that she was a student nurse and the accommodation came with the job. I was later to find out that this was just a story to cover the real reason she was there. My head was elsewhere as this was the first time I had been alone with her in her room.

Ann was very experienced in her lovemaking and although I was more or less an amateur she knew how to get the best out of me. We spent days together in her small room making love in every way. She called it killing her and she was constantly wanting to be killed!!

When I needed to go to the bathroom Ann would keep watch in the corridor as I crept out, sneaking along like a shadow and hoping that we would not be caught.

But sadly I had to leave as Ann had to get back to work.

Boy was that a few days to remember!

I had agreed to meet Tosser and Mike in town on Saturday night to go for a drink in one of the cafes that were dotted around Grafton Street. We were all at loose ends as to where our next 'JOB' was to be. Tosser was more interested in maybe doing over a shop. But Mike knew of a pub off Moore Street that he said was a doddle.

Over a few soft drinks we decided that we would maybe try the pub as it seemed the better option with a lot of cigarettes and drink to be had there. We scouted around the area after dark to see what the possibilities were. The pub seemed to be packed and it looked like the best proposition, so we decided to do it on the next Saturday night.

I did see Ann on a couple of evenings over the next week but was not invited back to the hospital room as she had too much work on and had to be up early every morning. Things at home were still not the best and I was considering maybe getting a flat in town with Tosser and Mike.

I was in the front room on the next Saturday morning with my Da who was looking out the front window when he piped up.

'There's yer man Barry, your friend, he has just pulled up outside on a motorbike. If only you could be like him. He must have a good job to be able to afford a motorbike at his age.'

'Yea' I answered in my head, 'it's a fucking robbed bike you idiot.'

But out loud I replied 'I am doing my best Da and looking all the time for work.'

With that Barry knocked on the door.

As I opened it he asked 'What's the script I haven't heard from you in ages?'

'Oh, this and that' I replied.

'Shush keep your voice down. Me auld fella is in the living room' I said as I directed him out to the front garden where we can talk.

'I have been going out with this girl' I explained to him so I have been off the scene for a while,' not telling him about Tosser and Mike.'

'What have you been up to?' I asked.

'Not a lot,' he replied and looking in the direction of the bike he said 'got that one about two weeks ago from the north. It's a dandy bike and no traces back from it I'm told once they come from up there.'

'Geez, is that right? Can they not trace it then?'

'No' he replied 'I've got a duplicate log book and it's kosher.'

'Good on, yea then' I replied.

'Listen,' Barry said 'you can get cars up there also but we would need log books first.'

I was not too keen on this idea I thought but kept my thoughts to myself as Barry was quite pushy and got annoyed at the least thing.

'Yea great,' I replied.

'Okay then. I'll let you know when we are heading up north again and you can come with us.'

Fuck that, I thought, but kept it to myself.

'Yea okay then let me know. See ya,' I answered.

Barry hopped up on his motorbike and headed up the road. When I next saw him he was driving a Triumph Vitesse car that he had ringed with false number plates, but that's another story.

CHAPTER 23

I MET ANN OUTSIDE EASON'S. It was a cold night and everyone was hustling and bustling about as if they all had a special place to go. I wrapped my arms around Ann and could feel the warmth of her beautiful body. We kissed slowly and I lost myself in her.

'What are we doing?' I asked.

'Can we go up to the Richmond Hospital? I need to see a friend there' she asked.

'Anything you like my loveliness.'

With that we held hands. She had on black gloves and they kept my bare hand warm. We sauntered up O'Connell Street, past the Rotunda Hospital and around Parnell Square. We went right by the door of St Joseph's Orphanage where I was incarcerated when I was younger.

Are all these perverted hell holes named after Saints I thought to myself, never letting Ann know my thoughts. Too ashamed to tell this nice girl of my past. [We will get back to the Nice Bit later!!]

When we got to the Richmond Hospital, which is a red bricked building, Ann asked 'Do you mind hanging around here Frank? I won't be too long.'

'No problem,' I replied.

With that she set off up the driveway.

After a while I got cold and bored and decided to take a recce around the grounds. I sauntered by the main entrance and went around the back where I saw some lights on. I started to peep into some of the windows to see if I could locate Ann but the rooms all seemed to be empty. I came across one that had a window partly open and looking inside I saw a transistor radio on a table inside. Looking around I could see the coast was clear so I hopped up onto the windowsill. Leaning my upper body into the small top window I tried to loosen the catch on the bigger window, but to no avail as it seemed to be stuck solid. I reached in and got my hand on to the top of a wardrobe. I did this and was able to pull myself through the window. I grabbed the radio and scampered back out the window. Slowly lowering myself down to the ground I placed the radio in the grass and went back and closed the window to the way it was.

Unknown to me, I had left a fingerprint on the top of the wardrobe and that was to be my downfall. I hurried back to the main gate. There was no sign of Ann there, so standing in the shadows I waited for her. It was not too long before she arrived back.

'Sorry I was so long but Mary never shuts up, she just goes on and on, she is like a talking machine.'

'Talking machine? I know what that's like to listen to.'

Just a load of crap to me.

She then spotted the radio.

'What's that?' she said, pointing at it.

'Oh, one of my mates was passing and he gave it to me'

'Some mate?' And she looked at me with a knowing smile.

We set off hand in hand with me holding the radio on my right hand side by its handle as it's regarded by Dubliners that the lady walks on the inside and holds your left hand. It's something to do with olden times when men needed to have their right hand free to get to their sword.

All of a sudden I heard the screeching of brakes and lo and behold a Garda car came to a halt just beside us. Well to say I nearly shit myself would be an understatement. My fucking heart stopped. With that, four of the biggest Gardaí I had ever seen leaped out of the car. We were standing dumb struck, waiting for them to pounce on us, and with nowhere to run or nowhere to throw the transistor. We were just riveted to the spot when they flew past and into a Public House.

'Jaysus' I said when I could speak, 'I thought they were for us.'

With that we both quickened our pace to Ann's bus stop. Up the drain pipe again, for another night of passion. I don't think many sixteen year olds were having this life.

So in the early hours, leaving the radio behind me I slipped out the window and headed home.

I headed in to town on the bus that afternoon, making sure my Da was not on it as I didn't want him asking questions of where I'm going to. It was quite cold when I met up with Tosser and Mike. Tosser was wearing a fawn coloured; camel haired overcoat and what looked like a tea cosy on his head. He looked like a real dope. Mike had a long, grey overcoat and scarf and looked the real gent. And me, well I had got the pissing bum freezer on and my bum was frozen.

'Right lads' I asked 'what shall we do?'

'Let's just have a scout around' said Tosser. And we headed off in the direction of Moore Street. It was a very cold evening and we could see the mist coming from people's mouths as we passed them in the street.

There was a big queue outside the Adelphi cinema as we passed by. All the young boys and girls were huddled together trying to keep warm.

'Jesus wouldn't that be just grand,' said Mike, 'if I only had a girlfriend and could go to the pictures with her?'

'Yeah' said Tosser 'you'd be up in the back row with your hand down her knickers.'

'Divil the bit' said Mike.

We slid along Henry Street, looking cool and nonchalant like three buddies out for an evening stroll, but we had deadlier things on our minds.

'Over there' gestured Mike, 'would you just look at that?'

We looked and could see the second floor window of the pub we were going to hit tonight.

'Jaysus 'said Tosser 'if they leave that open we're home and dry.'

'Let's keep moving' I said. 'Don't draw suspicion to ourselves.'

We headed back up to Caffola's so we could get in from the cold and while away the time. The cafe was packed and filled with smoke and we could hear the buzz of the chatter and the clatter of plates and cups. We slid into a booth at the back. It was not long before closing time came around and we were turfed out onto the cold streets. Even though it was after half eleven and the last buses were gone on their final journey, there were still lots of people milling around. We decided to just wander around to let the city quieten down.

It was near three in the morning and there was just the odd taxi moving around as we approached the pub.

'Be Jaysus,' cried Tosser 'the window is still open. Our luck is in. Right lads, let's go for it.'

Here we were, the no brain gang, robbing a pub in the middle of the night, with no transport and no way of taking away the illicit goods. Tosser gave Mike a bunch up. He gripped hold of the window sill and pulled himself up and then in through the window. After what felt like an eternity, he stuck his head out the window.

'It's safe, come on in.'

I said to Tosser 'you go on up and you can open the front door for me and I'll come in that way.'

'No, no' said Tosser, 'the door might be bugged. It's better if we all come up through the window.'

So up we climbed up and in through the window. We were in what I could only describe as a storeroom. It was pitch black.

'Let's head downstairs' said Mike 'the coast is clear.'

We sneaked downstairs in a line holding our breath but all we could hear was the humming of fridges.

'See if there's any money' said Tosser as he went in behind the bar counter. Mike had found some bags and I and he were scooping all the fags off the shelves into them. In the meantime, Tosser was opening the till.

'There's only fuckin coppers in here' he said.

'Coppers are money 'I said 'put them in your pocket.'

By now, we had all the cigarettes packed away. I was not too keen on taking drink as it was heavy but Mike knew of a man that will buy drink. He suggested we take as much drink as we can carry with the fags.

As they were filling more bags with all the drink they could carry, I decided to look out the window, although it was still pitch black. My eyes had not fully adjusted, so I was making slow progress and something soft and furry brushed against the back of my right hand. I nearly shit myself and let out a scream, and with that there was this growl. Grrrrr…….

Tosser came running from behind the counter and lit a match. I was standing there in shock and could feel the hairs standing up on the back of my neck. I could see, in the light of the match, this big black German Sheppard, with his tongue hanging out between his big sharp teeth and his tail wagging.

'Here boy, here boy, that's a good boy now' said Tosser as he approached the dog and started rubbing its head.

'Look Frank, it's as good as gold, He won't bite ye.'

I carried on over towards the window while Tosser was talking gibberish to the dog. I pulled back the curtains slightly so I could look out. To my amazement I could see across the road, what looked like about ten people grouped up against the shops and looking over this way?

'Quick lads' I said 'come look at this.'

With that, Tosser and Mike came over. The three of us were peering out the window, while the crowd starts pointing in our direction and waving.

'Fuck' said Tosser. 'I think the cops must be outside.'

'They can't be' I said. 'We didn't make any noise. How would they know we're here?'

Then, a big mutton head appeared in the window. We dropped the curtain and in unison, we jumped back in shock.

Tosser fell to his knees and putting his head in his hands he said 'I'm fucked' I'm going down for this. I have other charges outstanding.'

'Well I'm not going down for anything' said Mick as he stuffed packets of cigarettes in his pockets.

I was thinking this is like déjà vu. It was just like the Town and Muck all over again where I was caught and sent to Letterfrack. I went back to the window and pulled the curtain back slowly and peered out. There seemed to be a larger crowd forming across the road and some of them seemed to be raising two fingers in the air.

I dropped the curtain back and said to the lads 'I think there is only two coppers outside, so we have a chance. We'll open the main door, two run left and one run right and we might get away if we're fast enough.'

Unlocking the door, I pulled it open and Mick ran straight through it and turned right and Tosser turned left. I decided to go right and all the while you could hear cheers and whoops from the crowd. I ran straight into the arms of a big copper who pulled me to the ground and sat on me. In the mêlée that followed, the crowd decided to come to our aid, but to no avail as two black Marias screeched to a halt at the kerb. Coppers started alighting from the back doors. We three were hauled into the back of one and taken slipping and sliding and holding on for dear life in the back of the van as it sped through the streets to Store Street Garda station.

The three of us were dragged from the back of the van into the station, where we were brought before the Sergeant who was sitting behind the desk. He looked up at the three disheveled youngsters and asked individually

'What's your name, date of birth and address?'

We proceeded to give these. Then we were taken separately and pushed ungracefully into separate cells. As the cell door slammed behind me, the pain and anguish filled up inside me. God, what have I gone and done now? Am I just stupid or dumb, or maybe I'm both? With my hands in my pockets and head bowed in dejection, I paced up and down the cold cell. All seemed eerily silent, so unlike the last time I was here. I tried to turn my thoughts to better things but darkness surrounded me. I felt like I had just come in from a fog of unreality. Is this another misty morning? I searched through my pockets and I find one fag and one match. I bent down in a corner of the cold cell; putting the fag into my mouth I scraped the match on the cold floor. As the flame sprang to life I lit the fag, quickly inhaling. I felt light headed with the infusion of nicotine reaching my bloodstream. I slowly began to relax and tried to ponder my future but nothing came to mind. The only future I could see was a prison cell.

My fag was now finished and I sat on the cold stone bed. Although I was tired I could not doze off due to the intensity of the cold. I huddled down into a foetal position to try keep warm. After what felt like an eternity I heard a key scraping in the lock. With that, the cell door opened and standing there was a slightly built copper. His size looked unusual to me and his accent was from Dublin.

'Out here, Heeney,' he said, gripping my arm above the elbow he led me along to a room.

I had been in this room before. It was the one where the table and chairs were bolted to the floor. There was an official notepad and pen on the table.

'Sit down there' he gestured at one of the chairs.

'Would you like some tea?' he asked.

'Yes' I replied 'Three sugars.'

He left the room and I could hear the key turning in the door to lock it. As I sat alone, I wondered where Tosser and Mike were. It was all of about ten minutes when I heard the key in the door and in came the copper with a steaming tin mug of tea; placing it in front of me He said 'Get that into you boy. It will liven you up.'

He took a seat and taking a pen in his hand he said 'Ok let's have it, name address and date of birth. I am now going to write a statement of what occurred this evening between the hours of ten p.m. and two a.m. at the premises of Ten to Eleven, Moore Street in the city of Dublin. But before I start, I wish to inform you, that you were caught red handed inside the said premises, and you will be charged with burglary. Now what do you have to say?'

Thinking as fast as I could, I replied, 'It must have been about midnight, when I was walking alone down Moore Street when I spotted the pub door open and I decided to go in and take a piss, although the pub was in darkness. I found my way to the toilet and after emptying my bladder, I was about to leave, when I spotted a big German Sheppard dog. Me being terrified of dogs, I ran back into the toilet and shut the door. I must have been about an hour there cowering behind the door when a heard a big commotion. Opening the door a crack, I peered out. I could see that the outside doors were wide open and there was no sign of the dog, so I decided to make a run for it and ran straight into one of your rozzer mate's arms. That's all I have to say on the matter.'

He looked at me with piercing eyes and said 'Do I look like I came up the Liffey on a fucking banana boat? Going for a piss! My fucking arse. I'll give you piss in a minute, now tell me the truth of what really happened cause you know your mates will and you will be worse off.'

'That's my statement' I replied 'and that's all I'm prepared to say.'

With that he jumped from his chair and came around and boxed me straight into the side of my head.

I fell to the floor and he started to kick me into the stomach and chest screaming 'You will sign the statement or you will be battered until you do. You fucking little bastard, your mother is a whore and god knows who your fucking father was.'

'Fuck off you bastard I'll not sign anything for you,' I replied.

He then pulled me to my feet and with spittle flying from his mouth he said 'Boyo you know the score. You will sign one way or the other.'

He then boxed me to the head again. I felt very dizzy after this and threw up what little I had in my stomach.

'You dirty little fucker you will clean up that mess,' he screamed.

He then backhanded me across the face and left the room. I was in a terrible state crying and trying to breathe with snot and spittle dribbling from my mouth and nose.

What was I going to do? He was going to keep laying into me until I signed his statement; I did not have much of an option but to sign it. But then I decided that I would just scribble my signature and I could explain to the Judge in court I did not sign it. With this plan in mind I waited for the Garda to come back into the room.

He had a phone book under his arm. I had heard stories about the phone book; they would hit you over the head and shoulders with it as it left no bruises. He threw the phone book on the table, and with a mad look in his eye he left the room again.

I was in no doubt that when he returned I was going to get a battering with the book. My heart was racing and banging like a drum. I just wanted my Mammy. I just wanted to go home. The tears fell from my eyes like rain and my shoulders were shaking like leaves on a stormy winter's day.

After a while he returned with a mop and steel bucket.

Throwing them at me, he bellowed 'Mop up your fucking mess and stop snivelling, you little bollix.'

As I mopped up he started to write on the pad he had in front of him.

After some time he said 'I have your statement ready now for you to sign. I will not read it to you as I want to bring you out in the car for a run.'

'Why?' I asked.

'We have some burglaries we need to have cleared up and I know that you have done them so I will take you out in the car so as we can have them identified and cleared up. Okay? If you refuse to do as told, I will have no option, but to use the phone book. Do you know what that means?'

I was not very happy with this but didn't seem to have much choice.

He then took a handkerchief from his pocket and gave it to me saying, 'Clean up your snotty face.'

Taking me by the arm, he took me from the room and along the corridor to the main entrance room where we met up with another detective. This one was burlier with black hair combed back. He was dressed for outdoors with a big, black overcoat.

He spoke with a country accent when he said 'So, this is the little fucker that is robbing everyone's gas meters in the area. No loyalty among thieves then, when you rob your own type' he roared.

With one Garda on either side of me, they marched me out to the yard where their unmarked blue squad car was parked. The smaller one of the two took the driving seat and I was shoved into the rear seat by the larger one, who pushed me into the corner of the rear seat up against the far door.

'Don't even think about it' he said as I looked out of the window. 'The doors are locked.'

With that we drove out of the Garda station.

The small one, the driver, explained 'We will pass properties and point out to you the ones that have been robbed. I need you to admit to robbing them so as we can eliminate them from our lists. The judge will go easy with you for being so cooperative.'

It was recognised by all and sundry in the Garda force that the thief would agree to doing 'jobs' they had not committed due to the fact that they had maybe gotten away with other thefts in the past.

'I am not admitting to anything' I replied to him.

Whack into the side of my head with a fist from the big one in the back of the car with me.

'You will do as you are asked' he bellowed.

Whack again this time into my upper arm.

I started to cry and was getting very upset and was very fearful of what they were going to do to me.

We stopped outside a block of flats and the driver said to me 'In here we have four flats that been done over by you, you little shite ok?'

'No. No. I have not done any of this' I shouted.

Whack into the side of my head by the big one in the back.

By now my head was ringing like a bell and the pain in my upper arm was excruciating.

'You will do as you are told, boyo, or you will end up in the hospital' the big one grunted.

I was in a state and could only think of getting out of this mess as soon as possible, so I said I would agree to what they wanted. I would have agreed to anything at this stage.

'Ok then' said the driver. 'We have the ones here that you robbed and we are now going to make two more stops and we will point out to you the other flats you have robbed.'

After about another thirty minutes or so and the driver pointing out various flats we went back to Store Street Garda Station.

I was led into a cell and the door was locked behind me. With my head in my hands and trembling from both cold and fear I awaited my fate. I could hear footsteps approaching my cell and then the clatter of keys in the lock. The door swung open to reveal the smaller detective standing there with a tin tray in his hand.

'Here is some nosh for you. Get it into you as you will be here overnight for court tomorrow morning.'

With that he placed the tray on the floor and left, banging the door behind him. With a sigh I picked up the tray to inspect its contents. It had a tin mug of tea and fish and chips on a tin plate. There was no knife or fork but I was starving and laid into the food with my bare hands all the while thinking have the bastards spit into it. After finishing the food I felt sick to the stomach. I was not sure if it was from rushing the food or from all the bangs on the head.

After some time I again heard the key rattling in the door lock, the door flung open and a uniformed Garda stood there. He had a blanket in his hand that he flung at me.

'You will need this for your sleep over' he barked.

I could hear his laughter as he banged the door behind him. There was a horrible smell from the threadbare blanket but I had to put it around me to try and stave off the cold. Needless to say, I had a sleepless night, with wild thoughts running through my head.

I had not heard a word about Tosser or Mike and was hoping that they were not been treated as badly as I was. It was not unheard of for someone to die in Garda custody and no one was ever held responsible for it.

I somehow must have nodded off and was awakened by the sound of the key in the lock and a big burly Garda standing there with a mug of tea in his hand.

'Have this and then you can come out and empty your pisspot' he said as he handed me the tin mug of tea.

'Shit' I cried as it nearly burned the fucking hand off me. It was a cup of hot scald pretending to be tea.

Laughing he slammed the door. Were they all a bunch of comedians here, or were they just sadists?

A short while later I was taken out to the interview room again by the small detective. The big one was already seated when we got there.

'Ok, so this is how it works' said the small one.

'We have prepared your statement for you and you need to sign it here just at the end of the writing' as he pointed to a part of the page with his index finger.

I scribbled where he had pointed to, but it no way resembled my signature.
'Good. Good' he said.

'Now if you would just put your initials here and here' he gestured with his finger.

I gave a bit of a squiggle that did not resemble my initials in any way.

'Ok, that's us done here' the big Garda said.

With that they both, again with one on either side of me, took me out to the car park. One in the back and one in the front as before. We headed off to the court house. I was taken into a holding cell where Tosser and Mike were.

'What's going on?' I asked on seeing them.

'Don't know' they both replied. 'The fuckers have had us locked up all night and are talking about a week's remand.'

'A what' I asked.

'A fucking weeks remand' Tosser replied.

With that our names were called out and we were taken up a dimly lit stairway into the courtroom.

'Go over there' we were told by the Guards as they pointed to a dock in front of the Judges' bench.

There was a spattering of people in the courtroom, and some Gardaí leaning against a wall with papers in their hands.

'All rise' someone said and with that we all stood up for the Judge's arrival in the court room.

He was a medium sized man with grey hair combed back, wearing a black outfit like a cloak. He had on glasses that he would peer over when addressing the Garda. A man seated in front of the Judge handed him some papers and the small detective was called to give evidence.

He stated that two of the defendants were pleading not guilty but Heeney had pled guilty to the public house burglary and had asked for twelve more cases of house burglary to be taken into consideration. One of these included the theft of the transistor radio from the nurses' accommodation.

'Tosser and Mike stand up,' said the Judge.

Looking at me in aghast both Tosser and Mike stood up to face the Judge.

'You have both pleaded not guilty to the case of burglary of a public house on the night of such and such in the time aforementioned. I will ask you again how you plead to these charges.'

Both of them replied in unison.

'Not guilty, your Honour.'

'In that case, I remand both of you for one week to St. Patrick's Institution without bail.'

And looking at the Garda he enquired 'Will this be sufficient time for you Guard?'

'Yes your Honour that's fine,' replied the Garda.

'In the matter of Heeney, I will not remand him for one week to St. Patrick's Institution without bail as he has pled guilty.'

I tried to speak to the Judge.

'Your Honour I am not guilty. They have made up my statement and I have not signed it.'

'Quiet, quiet in the courtroom,' the clerk said.

'Take them down' said the Judge, gesturing to Jimmy and Tom.

With that they were bundled down the stairs from the courtroom.

'I will deal with Heeney now' said the Judge. 'Does he have any form Guard?'

With that the guard approached the bench and taking out his notebook he replied 'He has done some time in Letterfrack Industrial School from 1/07/1964 to 13/10/1967 and did abscond from there before his sentence was finished. He also served one month in Marlborough House from 18/03/1964 for larceny.'

'He is over sixteen now and that is irrelevant. Has he had any other charges brought up or does he have any outstanding?' said the Judge.

'No, your Honour. Nothing outstanding to my knowledge.'

'Ok Heeney move forward. Do you understand what you are here for today? It is a very serious matter indeed.'

'I was forced to sign a confession your honour. I did not do all the burglaries and I never stole the Transistor Radio.'

'Mmm, Mmm Guard is this correct?'

'His fingerprint was found on top of the wardrobe in the nurse's quarters. This proved his guilt in the case of the theft of the transistor radio, your Honour. What else he says is only a tissue of lies, your Honour. He is as guilty as sin in all the other cases.'

'I see. Well then, due to the seriousness of the charges I can only impose a custodial sentence. Twelve months detention in St. Patrick's Institution. Take him down.'

It was the 18th June 1968. I was sixteen and a half years old and I was being sent to prison.

When I reached the cell I asked 'What's going on?'

'We have been remanded to St. Pats for a week' Tosser said. 'And no fucking bail. Why did you plead guilty? You are now fucked. You'll get twelve months.'

'I have just got twelve months' I said. 'Because they battered me and I was hoping to tell the Judge that but he would not listen.'

'Listen. A fucking judge listens to an urchin like you. Are you mad? They only take the coppers word for everything.'

'What are we going to do? What will become of us now?' asked Mike.

'We will be ok. It's only a week's remand and then we will get bail. If it's going to drag out any longer they will give bail if you plead not guilty, not like this gobshite Heeney pleading guilty. He won't get out now for twelve months' piped up Tosser.

They brought us some food not long after and we wolfed it down. My head was all over the place and I could see no way out of this mess. I had been done for twelve burglaries plus the pub. A lenient sentence some might think. But I had not committed the burglaries, and the Garda had got them solved. Hey presto into thin air, the corrupt bastard.

Rattle of keys coming down the corridor and the door opened.

'Right me boyos. The van is here to take you to St. Pats. Look lively now' shouted out the jailer.

'Not you Heeney the detectives will be here for you shortly.'

CHAPTER 24

It felt that everything was falling down around me. Holding my head in my hands, I asked myself over and over again, 'what can I do, what can I do?'

I was beginning to lose touch with reality but was brought back to my senses by the metallic sounds of a key being turned in the door.

'Okay, boyo,' grunted the guard as he gestured towards the now open door. 'It is time for you to go now. They are waiting for you up at Saint Pat's.'

As he motioned with his upturned thumb he laughed softly to himself. Behind him stood two plain-clothed Gardaí. Each taking one of my arms I was led out to the waiting car. Pushing me roughly into the back-seat, I sat between the two Gardaí officers awaiting my fate. The smell of their gabardine coats was overpowering. The driver was in uniform and like his companions was well built. Sandwiched between the two uniformed men I was aware of the car moving off, approaching the gates and these being swung open by more uniformed guards. All this for one little laddie.

As the car wended its way through Dublin's heavy traffic each of the Gardaí kept a firm grip of my arm. A bit pointless as there was no chance of my making my escape. Familiar sights came into view. I passed the butcher's shop where I had worked. I felt emotional as I saw my bicycle propped up against the shop window. That past life seemed now to be a distant dream. Five minutes later we reached the imposing edifice of St. Patrick's Prison. Within moments of the driver sounding his horn, the house-sized heavy grey doors began to open.

'Come on, lad. We're there.'

With those few spoken words, I was pulled from the car into what appeared to be an inner prison yard. There were the prison gates behind me, now closed. Closed also, the barred gates in front of me. I was in a holding area which was somehow daunting in its medieval aspects. This was where a prison screw took over from the two detectives. Taking me by the arm I was led inside through the barred gates. The screw holding my arm was tall and thin and his mousy hair was like the thatch on a cottage roof.

'I will sign for him and take it from here,' he said as he wrote his name on the desk-pad in front of him.

Taking me to a room he told me to wait here and leaving me, he turned the key in the door behind him. There was a moment for reflection as I sat on a seat and looked around the room's bare walls. It was a big grey-painted room and again I felt dreadfully small and vulnerable. There were barred windows though they were so grimy with the passage of time it was impossible to see through them. Soon afterwards, I heard the key turning in the lock.

'Okay, boyo. You're going to the big house.'

I had little choice but to accompany him as we passed through a large gate. The guard rattled his keys as though to assert his authority as we passed prisoners tending to the garden's flower beds. They looked up at me but they kept their thoughts to themselves as I passed. Reaching an open heavy door we two went in to where I am scowled at by a heavily built guard.

'This is your man, Heeney. He is the only one today. Twelve months for burglary.'

'Good, I will take him. What's your religion, boy?'

'Roman Catholic.'

'Right, now you go on over there and take off all of your clothes. That means everything. You understand?'

Nodding, I did as he instructed and went into one of the five closets. I left the entrance open as it didn't seem to matter much. The bat-wing doors offered little opportunity for modesty. Undressing, I did try to keep my private parts covered whilst trying my best to look unconcerned and like I did this every day.

Handing me a clutch of clothing I saw I now have underpants and trousers, a shirt, jacket, shoes and socks. There was a pillow case, two sheets and a towel. This then was to be my wear from here on. Any departure from the grim uniformity was taken as rebelliousness when one was put on a charge. The guard made this clear to me and added that repeated offences led to loss of remission.

'You are now in the care of the State. Our task is to make absolutely certain that when eventually you leave Saint Patrick's prison you will not re-offend. Do you understand, Heeney?'

I nodded. What else could I do?

'We take great pride in how we break little bastards like you. Now, keep your nose clean and you will come to no harm. Step out of line and you will not know what hit you. Sign here for your belongings. You will be reunited with them when you leave. This will be in nine months' time if you are a model prisoner. If not, you will be here for 12 months and this could be longer.

'One more thing,' he added. 'You are no longer Heeney. You are 0095. Now, follow me to your cell, 0095.'

Following the guard we passed along several grey-painted passageways. Up a steel stairway, through several heavy doors, all the while his keys jangling as we went on our way. We then entered what is known as a prison wing, 'B Wing' as I was too soon learn. I was surprised at how narrow the wing was and judged it to be no more than 20 feet in breadth. Like the inside of a church the ceiling or roof was very high and the only light entered through skylights. There were rows of closed, dark green cell doors on either side of the granite floored wing. Each had a small square, presumably an observation window, and a small aperture in which a card was placed. These cards contained the information relevant to the prisoner held inside. Name, number, date of birth, religion, and crime one has been charged with. There are no secrets here. Taking in the wing, I saw two flights of steel stairs leading upwards to the further three wings. Along each guard rail were safety nets to dissuade anyone who might be inclined to end it all by throwing themselves over the rail.

Staying on this floor, I was taken to a cell and I found myself in what was to be my home from here on. In the cell there was a small steel bed placed against the wall, a chair, a small table, and beneath it a chamber pot. There were no other furnishings, the walls were grey painted and inset was a small barred window. It appeared that this could be slightly opened. A pipe ran across the floor and under the window. This I learned had, in the winter months, hot water coursing through it to keep the temperatures up a little.

'You will get a meal later, brought to you. Tomorrow you see the governor.'

With that the door slammed shut, the key turned and I was left to mull my fate.

The Governor at the time was a Mr. K, a namesake of Justice E. K. who presided over the Children's Court. Each week she sent, to their uncertain fates, many children brought before her, many of whom were charged on the most minor of pretexts. These small prisoners, victims of fate and circumstances not of their own making, were, after sentencing, sent like cattle to diverse children's penitentiaries euphemistically known as Industrial Schools. It crossed my mind that these two K named persons might be related. It was the way things were run in Ireland. You got a job in a safe career, not because of your ability or experience but simply because you were related or a friend of a person of influence in the same calling.

I had two blankets laid out on a crumpled mattress. Deciding to make the bed, such as it was, I first sniffed the pillow. In a word, it stank as did the mattress. I doubted if either ever saw a cleaning. Folding the blankets on the bed to better cushion myself, I lay there trying to gather my thoughts, to make some sense out of my situation. I was still there when later, a key turned in the door and a screw holding a steel tray entered.

Two words only were uttered. 'Your supper.'

Under the circumstances those words were surplus to requirements. That much was painfully evident. The door slammed shut, the key was turned. It had been the briefest of interruptions to the stultifying solitariness of the bare cell. What was in the bowl, in ordinary circumstances, looked like slop dressed up as stew? There was besides a metal cup which held tea so hot it was best sipped carefully. Hungrily, I wolfed the meal down and then, picking up one of the four cigarettes taken from my belongings. I lit the match and drew heavily on the nicotine. I was now beginning to feel better. By listening carefully I could make out the noises made by fellow inmates, the coming and going of mundane prison life. I could even hear the soft tones of a melody and I felt a little less lonely as a consequence. I was isolated but no longer felt as though I were on my own. My earlier fears had somewhat abated and I relaxed a little. The fear of the unknown is always far greater than the fear of the known.

It was still a restless night and not long after I fell into a sleep I heard the rattle of keys outside my cell. A guard, accompanied by a prisoner known as a trustee, came inside my cell. A tray was placed upon the small table.

'Your breakfast.'

By now, I was beginning to wonder if there were more than two words to any conversation in this grim prison. The porridge was - porridge but went down with relish. Afterwards, I savoured the second of my cigarettes whilst I again sipped tea. Outside there was much coming and going on the landing but I was left to ponder my own fate, clueless as to what the system had in mind for me. My mind was increasingly concentrated on the chamber pot, which, after the last pee was now filled to the brim. If I had the other call of nature I was well and truly in a mess. Making my bed, I then ran my fingers through my hair, the most rudimentary of combs. There was now little for me to do but to await my fate. When it did arrive it was in the shape of a guard built like a brick shithouse.

'Get your piss pot, son. Take it to the end and empty it.'

Struggling to balance the bowl as I walked, for I had no wish for its contents to slop over the brim, I followed the guard along the landing until we entered a recess. This small side room held two sinks and a couple of bat-winged door closets.

'Dump your piss in one of them toilets and then wash your face and hands.'

Other than cold running water there was no means of cleaning the bowl. Then, placing it on the bare paved floor I ran a little water through my hands and over my face to freshen up. There were no towels to dry myself. I didn't ask. All I could do was follow the guard back to my cell. Before turning the key he told me that I would be going to see the governor in a short time. As good as his word he did soon reappear, this time accompanied by a skinnier fellow. As I fell in behind them we three went along the block, through gates and along to a better furnished corridor. Upon slightly knocking on the varnished paneled door I heard a voice.

'Come in.'

Moments later I found myself standing before the polished desk of the prison governor. Wearing a suit and tie, he rifled through the paperwork before him before raising his eyes to meet mine.

'So, you're Heeney and you are with us for nine months.'

I nodded.

'We are here to rehabilitate you, to get you back on the straight and narrow. For us to do this we need you to be on your very best behaviour. Had you been better behaved in the past you would not be here but at your home, not mine? You must follow all instructions and not interfere with other prisoners. Do you understand me?'

I told him I did at which point, talking almost to himself; he said he would place me in the wood yard for a few days.

'Take him to his cell and make sure he has everything that he needs.'

'Of course, governor,' the larger of the two guards nodded.

After my being returned to my cell one guard told me that my gear would be with me shortly. I was once again on my own. It occurred to me that at no time had enquiry been made as to my ability. They had no idea if I could read or write, if I had the ability to do basic arithmetic, how best I might be rehabilitated. No, I was just a slave in the Irish Gulag, its prisoner system, a workhorse. I couldn't figure out how this was going to rehabilitate me.

Later, I was taken to yet another room, a storeroom in which appeared to be kept cell bedding. As soon as I appeared, a young prisoner reached the small counter and looked enquiringly at the guard who had brought me to this place.

'Give the lad the full kit including a change of clothes.'

With that the lad behind the counter pulled down a pillow case and started to pile everything into it. When it was filled he handed it to me. Not a word passed between us. On later examining the contents of the pillowcase I saw that I had the usual change of clothing but this time a towel and a toothbrush too.

'Such sweet charity,' I smiled to myself.

The next undertaking was to have my hair cut. Here, in what passed as the prison barbers, a youth was working. He told me that the cut for me would be a short back and sides. This amounted to my head being closely cropped and my locks, which I had taken great pride in, were soon scattered across the barber shop floor. From there on I settled into the prison routine until I was to blend in with the other inmates.

Days were pretty much routine and I worked at the steady monotonous pace of the prison's clock - the awakening in the morning, chamber pot emptied, washed, breakfast, which was queued for, each prisoner standing in line. There was no canteen so meals were eaten in one's cell. This went some way to explaining the extraordinary mixture of odours that permeated the prisoner. I did learn to use a sheet of newspaper to cover the contents of the chamber pot. In between times, each prisoner was assigned to his work routine. This might be kitchen or laundry routines, cleaning the prison wing's floors, working in the wood yard, or attending lessons.

Recreation, or at least a stroll around the prison yard, depended much upon the weather. There were no drying facilities so if it was raining, which in Dublin it often is, there would be no exercise that day. For many of us, prison meant exactly that, we were confined to our cells for twenty-three or, if the weather was bad, twenty four hours each day. The one break from such monotony was an hour allowed in the prisoner's recreation room. One could watch the television for one hour on a Saturday only. There was little of interest to us and the only programme looked forward to was Top of the Pops. Somehow, the show's start always coincided with the screws turning up to return us to our cells. This resulted in a chorus of protests but these were futile.

Some of the lads could look forward to visits from family to break the monotony. Although I was entitled to weekly visits in St. Pats, for one reason or the other my Ma and Da never came to visit, but they did leave me money from time to time so as I could buy cigarettes and toothpaste etc. Ann had come to try and visit on a number of occasions to no avail as she was not in receipt of a visiting order. They were sent to my Ma and Da and went unused.

The prison church on Sunday was packed in contrast to the half-empty churches in the outside community. This did not suggest that prisoners were more religious or penitent than the freer city residents. It did mean prisoners were much more bored and desperate for a break in the monotonous routine of prison life. I found a small prison library in which I could browse the books. This activity was much looked forward to and I derived much more from reading than I did from anything else.

CHAPTER 25

SITUATED IN THE NORTH-EAST CORNER of the prison, the tin roof wood shed and yard was where the firewood was made. This was boring and repetitive work. It was also sore on one's hands. No protective gloves or anything else were provided. This activity did help to build my cache of cigarettes. You see, we were only allowed four cigarettes a day. I soon acquired the skill to split a match in two. By doing so I could enjoy eight rather than four smokes each day. I even saved the contents of the butts and by doing so I gained an extra cigarette. This was the only good thing about San Izal toilet paper. The paper's shininess made it easier to use as a makeshift cigarette paper. As I fell into the routine of prison life I kept my head down and I kept myself to myself. It was what gave me security but I joined in the occasional card game.

Once a week we would shower and we prisoners did so in small groups, usually six convicts. Some were modest and when showering kept their underpants on, others were happy to be seen as nature intended.

It was on my fifth or sixth week there when, accompanied by a solidly built guard, I found myself in the shower room on my own. Unusual, this had never happened before and I was a little taken aback. On this occasion instinct suggested I keep my underpants on. I guessed he might be pervy and wanted a peek. Besides, being on my own I felt strangely vulnerable. Busily washing my body with the bar of carbolic soap I became aware of a presence behind me. Turning, I was horrified to see the guard, the front of his uniformed trousers open, with a full erection in his hand. He was making a beeline for me. His intentions were clear. He wanted sex with me.

'Shit!' I thought to myself. 'What the fuck is happening?'

'Use the soap to grease up your arse, lad. This will only take a moment. You'll get used to it. Don't make a fuss.'

Terrified, I spun to face him and with my head down like a charging bull I ran at full speed towards him and bowled him over.

As I did so I began to scream: 'Help me! Help me!'

As the guard picked himself up off the floor two guards with batons in their hands came running into the shower room.

'Get him, get the bugger,' the guard screamed. 'The little bastard has just assaulted me.'

'No, I didn't,' I cried out. 'He tried to rape me. Honest.'

I was wasting my breath. One officer grabbed me around the neck, the other by my ankles. From there I was dragged from the shower room with the would-be rapist aiming blows at my chest. Now screaming with pain and fear, I was dragged protesting down to what I was later to learn was the chokey. There, two other guards were waiting making five of them in all. One of these officers was holding a dark grey garment of some kind.

'Hold him down,' he barked.

I was no match for the guards as they wrestled me to the stone floor in the near bare cell. Then, tied up in a garment I had heard about but never before experienced, I was being trussed like an animal in a straitjacket. First my arms were outstretched to allow the harness to be better slipped down my body. My arms were then roughly placed on my back and the harness pulled tight with straps. Unable to move at all, such was the restraint of this diabolical harness, I heard one of them speaking to his colleagues.

'Okay, leave the little bastard to his own devices. Three days and he will think twice before he raises a hand to a prison officer again.'

'You dirty little fucker,' one of the officers snarled.

Another of the squad contemptuously kicked me in my midriff which hurt and winded me. Then I heard the cell door slam shut behind their departing figures. The turning of the key could have only been symbolic. Such was the tightness of the harness and the claustrophobic sensation I could not move a muscle let alone remove myself from the chokey.

I was later to learn that you could only be put into the 'Base', known as the chokey on the instruction of the Governor. This requirement was never adopted by the prison's guards. These men were unaccountable and they acted accordingly.

Whimpering like a wounded animal, my mind reeling, I uselessly rolled about on the concrete slabbed floor and strangely enough was now aware of my wet underpants. The room was almost completely dark but my eyes had adjusted. There was a blanket on the floor where it had been tossed but no bed. Wriggling like a snake I made my way to the blanket. However, with my hands and arms securely lashed behind me there was no possibility of my wrapping the bedding around me. Instead, I derived a little comfort from sitting on it and using it as a protection from the cold bare floor. Looking around me I took in my situation.

I was in a small cell with no window with bare walls and an uncovered concrete floor. There was no natural or artificial light. I could only imagine that the little light that did seep in came from under and around the door. As an added twist in the screw, I was to discover that there was a ceiling light. This was switched on at night when one might wish the darkness to sleep better.

Shivering with the cold I wanted to do a piss but could see no chamber pot. Even if there was such a thing how could l use it when trussed in a straitjacket? Somehow, being young and lithe, I was able to get on to my feet and I made my way over to the corner. There, I just stood, had a pee and felt the warm fluid running down my thighs. I was more and more focused on what happens when I need a shite?

Time passed slowly or quickly. You never know in such circumstances. Later I heard footsteps approaching and a key turning in the lock. Squinting my eyes I could make out a screw who I had never set eyes on before. Guided by the little light available he placed a tin mug and a little bread on the floor beside me.

'You have three days on bread and water you little fucker. Maybe it will help to remind you to keep your hands to yourself.'

With that remark he left the cell and I heard the key turning in the heavy door.

He did so without explaining how I might eat or drink whilst trussed up in a straitjacket unable to do more than wriggle my fingers and my arms strapped securely behind me.

Time passed but without me having the foggiest idea of the time. I was held in a vice, unable to move, unable to do any of the body movements that we take for granted. I was virtually paralysed from the neck down. This was not because of a stroke, a paralysis such as you suffer from in a road accident. This was diabolical evilness that grown men could do such a thing to a child. It was proof that no one has to be occupied by an enemy nation to suffer to the extreme. One's own nationals have the capacity to do an occupier's work for him. All I had to give me comfort was my own thoughts, my recollections. I was mothering myself. I had determined that no matter what the guards did to me I would survive and, hopefully, I would do so to tell the tale. My only sanctuary was in life itself. My tormentors had no sanctuary.

Sometime later, I have no idea how long later, I heard footsteps approaching, a key was turned and the same screw slammed open the door.

'Get yourself a good night's sleep,' he chortled as he contemptuously dragged a mattress in and left it on the cell's bare floor.

The door then slammed shut behind him. Out of sight, out of mind. I shivered from the cold. I tried in vain to move my body. My limbs were aching from being seized so tightly. I wondered if it was possible to lose one's mind. I started then to shiver uncontrollably. It might have been the cold or a reaction to the trauma of being trussed like a pig.

Now, I thought to myself. Cruel it is the way man treats animals but they are not tortured for pleasure as I was. And I, just a boy who could have been the son or nephew of any of these men. What possesses Man to treat his fellows in such a way? They decry drugs yet these guards could never excuse their behaviour towards me, and presumably others, by claiming drunkenness or the effects of drugs. They were of clear and calculating mind.

I then became hot. It was a burning heat and then oblivion when I fell asleep or perhaps unconscious. Did it matter? The only reason I knew that it was night was because the mattress had been dragged in to my cell. The only way I knew it to be morning was that it was taken from the cell. The guard at the same time would take away the water, which had not been drunk, the bread which had not been eaten. These would be replaced as if to taunt me.

So the torture went on for three days and three nights, which for me might as easily been three years. During those endless, often sleepless foot-dragging hours, I had only my thoughts to keep me company. There were no sounds of normal human behavior.

I had heard of a book written by the American author, Jack London. He too, in I think Alcatraz or Sing-Sing Prisons, had been strapped in a strait-jacket. In writing of his experience he told of his success in creating out of body experiences. Such things were beyond my childhood comprehension. I was fully in touch with every protest made by my body. My own self seemed to be punishing me by hurting me. The only relief was when I felt parts of my body become numb. It seemed to me that my body was frozen like a carcass in a butcher's freezer.

It occurred to me that had I been trapped in a similarly restrictive way, in a mine for example, the world and its expertise would have rushed to my aid. The world would have held its breath until I was rescued. Yet Man did this to a mere child and derived satisfaction from doing so. One doesn't have to believe in the supernatural for the mysteries of life exist in our everyday world.

Bizarrely, there was only one thing from which I could derive some comfort. Over the three days I was never to release my bowels. And, after the first 24-hour section I stopped peeing. I was empty. How strange that, under such extremities, one can still be responsive to human dignities.

There was however a body odour, which I could do little about. There was also, I guessed, a rash developing on my inner thighs. The only thing the guards could not stop was the clock. On the third day the mattress was removed and so was the harness. Without assistance, I was accompanied to the shower room where my ordeal had begun. I recalled the words of the guard on the day I had been signed for:

'We take great pride in how we break little bastards like you.'

So, this was a source of their pride thought I, as I stiffly used my hands to vainly wash three days odour, stiffness and paralysing effrontery from my tortured body. When dried and dressed I was returned to my cell.

Dropping to my knees I scrabbled for my cache of fags. Then, trying to come to terms and to make some sense of the unreality of it all, I smoked my brains out over the next thirty minutes. I soon was to gather that I was now confined to my cell. Food was brought, I wolfed it down and unashamedly I licked the plate.

I was never taken before the governor, never given opportunity to state my own defense. I should have realised that here in this awful prison there was a uniformed self-protective circle. This was the way it had been at the Letterfrack Industrial School for children. It was an institutional thing. Why would it be any different in Saint Patrick's Prison? They were all of the same mind-set, which is quite alien to those whose lives are relatively normal. Here too, in this place of incarceration was where sexual abuse was not only rife but seen as a perk of the job. It was a bonus for those that way inclined. This too was institutionalised, accepted and protected. Sexual abuse of prisoners was however never spoken about even by those who abused their positions and youthful charges. We were tit-bits to be sampled if a guard's whim suggested he do so. I was naïve. I thought had the public outside the prison walls been aware of such endemic abuse of young prisoners they would stop it. Would they?

In the weeks that followed things in the prison seemed to quieten down and I was never again approached by the fat guard who had tried to rape me. If anything, he was steering clear of me. Time was moving on, I was keeping myself to myself and, wishing my miserable life away. I waited for the golden day when I would walk through the gates a free man.

There had been talk of a new detention centre in Shankhill that was about to be opened. This was to be for boys like me whose behaviour had been good. Word was that it was without walls or barred windows. An 'open prison' based on trust. It was paradise compared to Saint Patrick's Prison in Dublin. Inspired by the hope that I might be fortunate enough to be chosen to be transferred there, for the governor would have been unaware of my experience in the chokey, I became very much a goody-goody two-shoes. I was not alone. The behaviour of everyone in the prison improved. The only thing that caused me disquiet was my addiction to smoking cigarettes. I became fixated by the lure of the next cigarette, and then the next and so on. The food in this child prison was unpalatable. None ate it except to keep body and soul together. So there was very little meat on me. I was by now skeletal.

The days passed and I was putting much of my time to good use by reading every book I could lay my hands on. Studious, I was also writing a great deal, laboriously penning words copied from books, memorising their spellings, noting the grammar. I was also learning arithmetic, adding and subtracting, multiplying too in both my head and on paper. Aware that the priority on release would be finding work I knew that the better read I was then the better my chances of becoming employed. All I could otherwise do was count the days and hope that one day before my release I would be told that I was to be sent to the nearly completed open prison. This was one of the carrots on my stick.

It was now October. The nights were drawing in, the weather was much colder and I had spent five months in Dublin's notorious Saint Patrick's Prison. The rumour mill was telling that there was to be a meeting attended by the prison's officials. Governor K and Chief Prison Officer J. K would be joined by the prison's Chaplain and the welfare officer. Between them they would decide on who were to be fortunate enough to be transferred to the newly renovated Shanganagh Castle Prison. The only thing that was news to me was that Saint Patrick's had a Welfare Officer. I had never met him and no one else had ever mentioned him. Had I had the opportunity to meet him it might have given me the opportunity to tell him of my bathroom and chokey experience. He might even have helped guide me through my studies. Was he there just to make the numbers up, to look good on the roll-call of do-gooders?

The day I had been praying for arrived. Called to the governor's office, I was told that I was to be transferred to Shanganagh Castle to complete my sentence. This would take place over the weekend of November 5th 1968.

When told it seemed to me that I was enjoying all my Christmases in one. How I skipped back to my cell, my heart filled with joy. I can think only of complete release that would have equaled my joy and brought about such high spirits. From day one I started counting the hours until I would hear for the last time the keys turning in the door of my Saint Patrick's Prison cell.

Lying on my dirty mattress that evening, enjoying my reveries, I could hear from somewhere distant a song being played. It was the Equals singing, *Baby Come Back*. Each prison wing had a speaker placed on a chain dangling from the roof eaves. From time to time you could make out the strains of melodies carrying over the general noise generated by boisterous prisoners scattered along each of the prison's wings. That song stuck in my memory and I afterwards bought the track whereupon I played it over and over again. That week I even went to Mass to better focus my thoughts and to break up the slow passage of time.

After my years in Letterfrack Industrial 'School', and experiencing and witnessing the calculated and again institutionalised abuse of youngsters by both the Christian Brothers and State functionaries, I had given up on God. There was to me no evidence of His presence on earth. It had not passed my notice that in Ireland, Halloween is a public holiday. Perhaps the liberation from British rule had opened the doors to those far more iniquitous. They had, it seemed, opened the door to the worship of dark forces. They were to henceforth run the Irish State according to their new beliefs. Whatever name was given to government institutions, they were to me simply departments of Hell's Kitchen disciples.

As our last night at Saint Patrick's Prison approached there was a lot of good humour mixed with sourness between those who were to be transferred and those not so fortunate. There was much rivalry with those fortunate enough to await shipping out being cat-called 'squealers' and 'screws pets.' I cared not. All that mattered to me was that I was one of the lucky ones. I was going tomorrow.

The next morning I was all ready with my stuff in my bag standing at the cell doorway when the key in the lock turned.

'Okay, smart arse. You are off on your holidays,' the screw sneered.

By this time there was a general din of banging plates on doors throughout the wings of Saint Patrick's Prison and then as we were brought to reception and departure desks.

'Line up you lot. You are not out of here yet.'

The order was given by the fat screw who had tried it on with me. Perhaps uncomfortable, he avoided eye contact with me. It was as if I was not there.

The thought of what he had intended to do to me that day stayed with me throughout the rest of my life. His intention filled me with revulsion. Did these sadistic perverts realise the effect of their actions on children, or was it that they simply did not care? Maybe the terror and humiliation was part of the thrill that drove them to be what they are. Their power over those they were charged to protect.

Recovering the clothes I had been wearing when I arrived at Saint Patrick's, I started to dress myself. They were little more than rags but how good I felt wearing them. Putting on my own clothes made me feel better, even if they were rags. It is impossible to describe one's feelings if poverty stricken. Even rags that belong to you hold a significant part of your self-esteem together. And so, with such elation and thoughts in my mind, I and seven other inmates trooped across to the blue Bedford van awaiting us. Scrambling on board, we elbowed each other out of the way to get what we thought was the best position. The trip across Dublin, that would take us to and through its better heeled communities, would take up to an hour. Never have I looked forward to a single hour so much in my life. I had so far spent five months at Saint Patrick's Prison. To me time was meaningless. I felt as though I had spent my entire life in that awful place of iniquity.

Our van passed through the Ringsend borough. Excitedly, I kept my eyes open to see if I could catch a glimpse of my grandmother's home, and my uncle's too. Such was my attention that our taking a driveway up through a castle's entrance came as something of a surprise. Yes, it really was a castle. After alighting, our small group was led to a reception area. Here, we discovered, there were no uniforms. Those in charge wore civilian clothes. After registration we were shown to our dormitory. Here, the beds on either side were set out in rows. We were then given a tour of the castle to familiarise ourselves with our new home.

Here there were classrooms, a recreation room with seats, tables, a darts board, a few books scattered around, even a television. Here was heaven compared to Saint Patrick's Prison. There were even gardens in which we could spend our time in. There was also a kitchen and we were welcome to make use of it. Who said crime doesn't pay? Here beckoned a life superior to the lives led by many who had never strayed from the straight and narrow. I was even able to telephone Ann at the hospital where she worked to tell her my good news. Laughing at my excitement she told me that she had a day off on the coming Sunday and she would visit me.

'It is a long way for you to come,' I queried. 'It is difficult to get to?'

'Don't worry about that, Frank. I will get there. Do not worry. I am a country girl, you know that. I am used to such things.'

During the familiarity tour we boys were told that we were allowed out of the castle's grounds. But, we could only visit the shop to purchase confectionery or cigarettes. We were duty and honour bound to be on our best behaviour. There were no walls, no bars, and no threats. Only the warning that if we were to misbehave, then, it was back to Saint Patrick's for us. There was no reason then for bars, gates or walls. This fear was enough to keep us well behaved.

Each of us was given duties to carry out. I was to assist in the kitchens, though for some reason this was never mentioned in my Freedom of Information entry. This had me as assisting in the gardens, which I never did. Such records are far from accurate.

I liked the place of course and my attitude towards other inmates changed. Whereas at Saint Patrick's I had drawn into myself, here I mixed well. It was also opportunity for me to continue my studies. The facilities for doing so were far better. Unfortunately, the opportunity was denied to me. They thought my education was perfectly adequate; that the place was better given to someone who lacked my abilities. There was also an aspect of favouritism too so this might have just been an excuse to fob me off. I thought it best not to mention my suspicions. That was another lesson I had learned.

CHAPTER 26

THE WEEK PASSED MUCH MORE quickly than the weeks spent in Saint Patrick's, much more pleasantly too. I was now eagerly counting the days off the calendar until Sunday when I could expect a visit from Ann. I couldn't figure why a lovely girl like her would want anything to do with a jailbird like me. I was just appreciative that she did so. That day when I awaited her arrival I was glued to the windows. Eventually, I could see her in the distance as she made her way up the long driveway to the castle itself. I wondered if she would be as impressed as we had been. I quickly left my spot at the window and made my way towards her approaching figure.

Sweet romance, our meeting was like something out of an Emily Bronte story. Breathing with anticipation, as we drew closer, we two broke into a trot and we fell into each other's arms. How long we kissed, hugged and whispered sweet endearments to each other I cannot tell. How much better it was to hold her in my arms, to breathe in her fragrance, to feel her warmth. This was a million miles removed from the grim austerity of the previous prison. When she eventually managed to get a visitor pass we had sat opposite each other at a table. We were forbidden to touch each other, not even a stroke of the hand.

I think we both brushed a tear or two from our eyes that day. Holding hands we walked around the castle grounds. My questions were coming as quickly as a nest-building woodpecker tapped at a tree with its beak. I couldn't remember when I had last been so happy.

Many boys, when sent to prisons, were soon afterwards to receive Dear John letters from their girlfriends. Some took the news very badly, more than they had the sentence itself. There had been cases of suicides and attempted suicides due to such letters being sent. Quiet boys became rebellious, constantly looking for a means of getting their frustration out of the way by fighting other inmates. It seemed to me that Ann was well and truly on my side. I resolved that as soon as I was released then I would do the manly thing. I would find work and take care of her. Little did I know?

That blissful hour or so we couldn't keep our hands off each other. Caught up in a ring of fire we bragged about how we would constantly make love when we were able to. As with all good things the time came when her bus was due. Again, exchanging endearments, I watched Ann climb on to the bus and I waved until the bus was out of sight. I savoured her promise that she would return the following week. Comforting myself that the week would quickly pass I returned to the castle.

On the Monday, my job in the kitchen taught me what Welsh rarebit was. The kitchen was a good working environment and there were four or five of us working in there. The tutor screw there was friendly enough. Mind you, after the experience at the other prison I was constantly on my guard. I no longer trusted anyone. In my view, even the well intentioned might have had ulterior motives. They were staff members here rather than guards. A streetwise boy instinctively knows if an interest in him has sinister undertones. Some of the staff, I guessed, were inclined towards same gender sex. One boy who was a little on the plump side, was the son of a well-known South Dublin builder. It was a matter of some debate as to why he was in prison. Most of, but not all, us had come from grinding poverty and places of considerable social deprivation. There was no way that this boy could be included in those considered poor and unfortunate.

There were whispers. One commonly heard was, 'He is one of them and his Dad has sent him here to teach him a lesson.'

The term 'one of them' meant there was likelihood that the boy was more feminine than he was masculine. He did have an effeminate look about him and he was given to mannerisms that are not particularly male. Furthermore, the youngster mixed within a circle that regarded themselves as a little above the rest of us. Was it because they had something in common, something to protect and needed ring-fencing? As far as I was concerned, what the others did was their business and I kept myself to myself. There were times when I felt it best to distance myself from what I thought might be a bad situation. All I wanted to do was finish my sentence with a clean bill of health. Everyone did the same and the ongoing conversational topic was the record hits of the day.

The following Sunday and I was again sat at the window expectantly awaiting the arrival of Ann. I wasn't alone. Others among us were expecting their visitors too. There was great excitement. Some were pacing anxiously around the gardens waiting for the bus. The cold November snap did little to cool our ardour.

Before too long my much looked forward to visitor arrived and again we fell into each other's arms. This simple show of affection was to me the most beautiful thing that could happen to a man and a woman. From that moment on we talked incessantly about ourselves, our feelings and our plans when we would be united together.

'You seem to have lost some weight, Ann. Are you alright, is everything okay with you?'

I had noticed her thinness during my girlfriend's earlier visit. I had then chosen not to mention it in case it came across as a criticism.

In answer to my question she shrugged. 'Ah, do not bother about such things. It is a woman thing you know.'

I dropped the subject and strolling purposefully we sneaked behind a tree to continue our amorous interest in each other. We two kissed and fondled but the situation not to mention the cold meant that we were unlikely to get to heavy petting. As for anything else we had in mind there was no way one could lie stretched out on ground that already was near frozen. Not to endure my disappointment, Ann gently took my hand and placed it under her skirt.

'Oh, Frank. Kill me now.'

This was a term she commonly used to suggest making love.

Shite, I thought to myself. How on earth was I going to achieve that? We were out in the open parkland. The tree certainly provided enough cover for that sort of adventure. Tugging at my trouser zip and deftly taking my fully erect manhood in her hand, Ann whispered words of love in my ear. With an almost practised ease, she pulled the gusset of her panties to one side and lifting her thigh she skillfully guided me into her. I was in raptures. How many inmates get the opportunity to grab a ride in the open on a freezing cold November day? In terms of lovemaking it was a memorable one-off, the recollections of which were to stay with me, to be savoured again and again, for the rest of my life. There was such longing as I again waved her off and, as on the previous Sunday, I waved until her bus disappeared over the rural landscapes.

I still held the £2 she had pressed into my hand.

'Here, and don't you be smoking too many cigarettes,' she whispered.

There could be no visit on the following Sunday. Ann was obliged to work. Still, two weeks waiting I could live with. I had little choice. In the meantime I got on with the routine. The days and the weeks slipped by and Saturday, November 23, 1968 was quickly approaching. This was a day upon which events occurred that would scar me for the rest of my life.

It was about 11 a.m. that morning and I decided to retrieve my coat from the dormitory. I had it in mind to pop out to the shop. The place was quiet. There was nothing unusual in that but as I approached the dormitory I was aware of a gasping, a moaning and muted protests coming from a far corner of the dormitory. Slowing my pace and treading more cautiously I decided to investigate the strange disturbance. As I drew closer the sighing and the grunts became clearer.

'Shite, there is something going on in here,' I whispered to myself as I cautiously edged forward.

I was totally unprepared for the sight that met my eyes. On a dormitory bed was the builder's son, on his hands and knees and his pants pulled down around his ankles. Astride him, with his shirt pulled up and trousers down his bare thighs, the prison officer was grunting and sighing with pleasure as he pleasured himself on the mildly protesting builder's son.

From me, there was an impulsive snort, a mixture of shock and amusement, which caused a pause in the sexual activity taking place. Now aware of my watching them, the officer stopped what he was doing. Horror filled his face as he turned and looked directly into my eyes. Furious at being caught in such an embarrassing and possibly illegal activity he had the look of a maniacal vampire. I have never been subjected to such venomous hatred. Startled, my head spinning, turning on my heel, I grabbed my coat and I fled the scene. Rushing out of the building and down the castle's long driveway I reached the gate as a bus was approaching. Terrified, not so much by what I had seen but by the possible consequences of my being a witness to it, without thinking, I leaped on to the bus.

'Oh God, what will I do now,' I kept asking myself. 'The officer will fit me up or worse. They can do what they like and I knew it.'

'Tickets please.'

I snapped into reality.

'Can I give you my name and address as I have no money?'

'You are from the castle?'

I nodded and the conductor smiled reassuringly, 'it's okay. Don't worry about it.'

Throughout the bus trip I sat petrified waiting to hear the sirens of a following Garda car. Again, I was running away from a situation that was not of my making and which I had no control over. Alighting from the bus at the terminus, I headed straight for Sheriff Street flats where I expected Tosser to be. Knocking on the door brought his mother to answer it.

'He is no longer living here,' she said in answer to my query. 'He is living in Capel Street. He has a flat there.'

'Do you know where in Capel Street?' I asked.

'Yes, it is under the Varna Brush Company, in the basement at the Bolton Street end.'

Thanking her I quickly made my way to see if I could find Tosser. I still had ten shillings left over from the £2 that Ann had given me during her last visit.

CHAPTER 27

23/11/1968

AFTER LEAVING TOSSER'S HOUSE IN Sheriff Street I headed up Talbot Street passing the Electric Cinema on my right under the railway bridge. I was thinking of when I used to go there on a Saturday morning in the past to watch the cowboy films and the fun I had there. It was an overcast afternoon and the rain was doing its best to come down and it seemed to be getting a lot colder as I approached Capel Street.

I stood at the corner of Capel and Parnell Street gazing across at the row of shops and houses on the far side. I was looking for some indication of where the flat might be. There was a pawn office immediately in front and as I looked further to the right I could see a sign over a basement advertising Varna Brushes. That's it, I thought and stepping from the pavement I headed across the road. On arrival outside the main entrance I could see a gate that led to steps that would take me down to the basement door. On knocking at the door I could hear some shuffling as noise was coming from inside but no one answered the door.

They are afraid of what was outside I was thinking so I yelled out 'its ok lads it's not the Guards.'

With a clatter of bolts and a shuffling of locks the large door opened to show Mike standing there.

With a look of surprise on his face he exclaimed 'What the fuck? How did you get here?'

'It's only Heeney' he shouted over his shoulder to someone unseen.

'How are ye Mike?' I asked. 'I have only gone and escaped from the big house.'

'Come in, come in ye terror and tell us all about it.'

On entering the flat I could get a deep smell of mould and dampness, and the lighting was a bit dull to say the least. Mike was sitting at the kitchen table with a bottle of whiskey and a glass in front of him.

'A bit early for that' I said.

'Just thinking about it for now' Mike replied.

'How are you? Sit here and tell me all about how you're here' He said pointing to a rather decrepit looking armchair in the corner.

'Well it's a long story but I'm here now and that all that matters. Maybe I can stay with you lads for a while or until I get on my feet.'

'You can stay as long as you like,' they both piped up.

'Do you want a cup of tea? You look famished' Mike said.

Not wanting to show disrespect I said 'yes', but I did not like the look of the pile of cups and dishes in the sink and the damp smell was getting to me.

I explained to the both of them about my escape from Shanaghan House and going to Sheriff Street and Tosser's Ma telling me where they were.

'You will have to be careful and not get caught as they will put another six months on your sentence' said Mike.

Looking around the room we were in, it was quite dingy and dark. It was kitchen and living room in one with a small table and four chairs. There was also a three seater couch to go with the armchair I was sitting on and it looked just as rancid. It turned into a bed I later found out as I had to sleep on it. I was thinking of getting a clothes peg for my nose to alleviate the smell, but beggars can't be choosers, they say.

We three went out for a walk later in the evening so as the lads could familiarise me with the area and its goings on. They had not been long in the flat and were on the lookout for something better but money was tight and work was not easy to come by. The idea was to maybe do a few break-ins to keep the money flowing, but up to now they had not come across any opportunities in this sphere.

It was quite late and very cold when we got back to the flat. No opportunities had presented to us and the streets were deserted. There was no heating in the flat so I went to bed in the clothes I was standing in. Mike had given me some blankets to throw over me to try to keep me warm. The two boys had a bedroom each and the finery of a double bed.

I slept a sleep of the dead and only awoke on Sunday morning to the sound of Tosser farting in the living room. It was a big bloomer.

'What's up, my man?' he said to me as his nose scanned the air around him.

'Oh lovely. Eggs. The best smell to wake one up!' He bellowed.

'Jaysus, rotten eggs you mean' I said.

Pulling myself up from the couch bed I was lost in thought about clothes and where I would get some to wear as all I had at the moment were the rags on my back and they were already starting to smell.

'There are a lot of spare clothes in my room if you want any. They are in the blue bags. Just root around them and take what fits. You can put dirty clothes in the black bags as my sister will wash them in the washeteria as she works there. She then puts the clean ones in blue bags. So it black for dirty ones blue for clean ones. Got it?' said Tosser.

'That's fantastic. I was just pondering what I would do for clothes. Good on ye'.

With that, Mike came out of his bedroom, hair all tousled and looking as if he had a lot to drink the previous night.

'What's the smell? Oh man! It's like someone crawled up your hole and died.'

'You will get used to his smells, Frank. He has the worst smelling hole ever' he said grinning.

I could hear church bells ringing somewhere in the distance, and peering out of the window the day looked just like any other November day. It was just beginning to reach my brain what I had done in escaping. I was on the run again, but for how long could I stay out of prison was anybody's guess.

I knew the inevitable was that I would be caught and sent back. But, how was I going to explain why I ran? It just looked like an impossible situation for me as no one would believe me as to what I had witnessed. It was the same in Letterfrack. No one would listen to or believe the boys. This was just another brick in my wall of the system and the life I had been born into.

Over the next week not a lot happened. We just dossed around the flat as the rain was pouring down every day. We caught up on things and talked of things we would change in our lives if we could. If we could get a steady job or if we could pull off a big robbery, just boys things. I was sixteen years old and the two boys were of a similar age maybe one year older. All our lives ahead of us, but no way of living it without work.

I decided that I would head over to my Nan's to see Vincent and catch up with him. Vincent was really my half-brother but all my life I had been led to believe he was my uncle. I was too afraid to go home to my house in case the Gardaí had it staked out and I might get caught. I thought to myself I had been watching too many films.

Tosser gave me the loan of a couple of quid and I caught the bus over to Ringsend. I got off the bus at the chapel and walked to Ringsend Park.

Knocking on the door Vincent opened it.

'What's the story? What are you doing here?' he asked.

'Nothing. I just dropped over to see you and have a chat.'

'Come in then. You look freezing'.

He had been playing his guitar and it was out on the chair. Picking it up he started strumming it.

'What's this?' strumming away.

It was *Paperback Writer* by the Beatles. I recognised the guitar intro. He was very good on the guitar and loved the Beatles. He was not unlike George Harrison and his mate, Elay, in his band was the image of Paul Mc Cartney. So at least they had that going. He also worked for the Council, you know, leaning on a shovel all day yapping about shite and no work getting done.

He was not aware that I had escaped and all the talk was about his new band and how they were going to make it big. They were called the Ins and Outs. I wondered was he thinking of me when he came up with that name as it seemed that I was always in and out of trouble.

It wasn't too long before my Nan came in. Now, she was a different story all together. She knew immediately that I had done something wrong as she knew I should have been in prison.

'Frank, my god, what are you doing here?' She bellowed.

Oh shit, I'm in for it now.

'Nothing Nan. I'm on a weekend out for good behaviour' I said.

'Don't lie to me young man. I know you have absconded and you are definitely not stopping here'.

'Ned take a hold of him and we will bring him down to Irishtown Garda station.' She said.

Ned was her husband but we knew very little about him and did not call him Granda. He had been a carpenter on the ships and had made Vincent his first guitar. He was a very quiet man and never said a lot. I did feel sorry for him as he seemed to be treated like a non-person.

'I am not getting involved' Ned said.

'Look Nan, I really don't want to get into a row. I'm ok and can look after myself, so can we drop it please?' I said.

'I have told your mother on numerous occasions that you will never be any good. I know you will never be any good cos you're just like your father. You mother is from better beginnings'.

'Look Nan this is just no good so let's leave it and I'll go ok?'

After a bit of pondering she relented and asked me if I wanted a cup of tea saying, 'I do not want to be involved and wait until I see you mother.'

Vincent and I took ourselves out to the back room where he showed me a long haired black wig he had that they would use on stage.

'You can have this and you can use it to disguise yourself and have a better chance of not getting caught.'

Looking at it I burst out laughing.

'It's too long. I'll look like an old wan in it.'

'No, no we will cut it to suit you'.

With that he placed the wig on my head and took out a scissors and started to cut it into shape. After a while it did not look too bad, almost looked like a Beatle hairstyle. Sitting on the bus back into town I felt that everyone was looking at me and my wig but that was probably just me.

On arrival back to the flat Mike opened the door to start laughing at the look of me.

'Here would you look at this eejit at the door trying to disguise himself. He looks some gobshite'.

I took the wig off but did keep hold of it just in case.

A couple of evenings later we decided that we would try our hand at a robbery and headed out about eleven o clock at night. It was quite cold but no rain.

We were on a street with large tenement houses on both sides. There were some cars parked but not many. Tosser was going along trying car door handles when one started to make a noise of the horn beeping. We ran up the road away from the noise only to find it was a dead end with no way out. The noise of the car had stopped. But we could hear in the distance the squealing of tyres and the noise of a car travelling very fast.

'Fuck, it's the rossers. Run and hide' I shouted out.

The only place to go was to jump over railings to a basement and hide there. Mike and Tosser got over the railings okay, but I misjudged my vault and my right leg got caught on one of the spikes. I fell backward and the spike went into my leg. With my body hanging over backwards my weight caused the spike to pierce further into my leg. I was hanging on the basement railing by my leg and screaming in pain.

Mike and Tosser scaled back up and got hold of me on both sides and lifted my leg from the spike and lowered me to the floor of the basement.

'Shush, shush now. The coppers are nearly here. You will be ok.' Mike said.

We could hear the squad car come roaring up the street then turn around and creep slowly back down the street. We could see the beams of torches shining in the darkness but they passed our hiding spot by. They reached the bottom of the road and we could hear them speed off again into the night.

The boys pulled me from the basement and stood on each side of me as I limped back to the flat. The pain was very severe and I felt as if I was going to pass out. Mike placed me on the couch and Tosser started to rip up a sheet to use as a bandage. The hole in my leg was about three inches long and looked very deep.

'You're going to have to go to the hospital. It is too bad and bleeding' Mike said.

'Hold on' said Tosser as he got the whiskey bottle.

He poured the whiskey into the wound which was very painful. It felt like scalding water had been poured over my leg.

'Don't worry. This is what they do in the cowboy films and it works. You can't go to the hospital cos you're on the run and you will be nabbed. We will take care of you' piped Tosser.

Mike then wrapped the sheets around my leg and also put a tourniquet on the upper part to slow the blood flow. I fell asleep quickly. I don't know if it was from shock or what.

Next morning Mike went out and got bandages and ointment and put them on to my leg. It felt a lot better but I was in bother trying to walk and decided that I would keep my weight off it for a while.

CHAPTER 28

I HAD PHONED ANN WITHIN a few days of getting out of Shanaghan Castle to update her, just in case she would try to come and visit and I would not be there. We had agreed to keep apart until at least Christmas time in case the Gardaí were keeping an eye on her. With my right leg out of action, it would have been difficult to have met up with her anyway as I would have had to go out to meet her. I did not want her to come here to the flat due to the state and smell of it.

I was spending most of my day lying on the couch. The lads were looking after me and I was grateful for that.

The next couple of weeks flew in and I was now able to get around. We decided that we would go up to town for a mosey around. I decided that I would wear the wig in case we bumped into any rossers that we might know.

After a while of walking the streets in drizzly rain, we decided to go into a Cafe in Marlborough Street for a coffee to heat us up. The Cafe was situated upstairs and I was unsure if I should try to walk up but with Tosser at my side I managed okay.

The place was quite dingy and there were few customers there. We ordered three bowls of soup and the two waitresses were quite helpful and polite. After a while we got chatting to them.

One of them remarked that my wig was a bit lopsided. Well, to say I went red in the face was an understatement. I could feel hot all over. I was so embarrassed. The girls decided that they were going to give me a dry wash and set the wig for me. The lads were roaring laughing and thought this was gas.

At this stage we were the only customers in the Cafe and the girls got out the hair spray, brushes and scissors and started to work on the wig. When they were finished I looked in the mirror. I looked like Cilla Black on a bad day.

We paid our bill. Well, Tosser paid our bill and we thanked the girls and headed out into the rain again.

'Let's nip into Cleary's' suggested Mike.

Cleary's was a big department store close by and was a good place to walk around and keep warm. We went from floor to floor but knew that we were being followed by store detectives as they stood out like a sore thumb.

'Let's get out of here. I'm sick of being followed around. Do they not know we might be customers?' said Tosser.

On leaving by the side entrance we bumped into Mickey Finn a detective from Store Street Garda station.

Looking at us he pointed to me and said 'What's the fucking wig for Heeney? Trying to hide yourself or what?'

I nearly died, but we just shuffled away without a reply and he walked into Cleary's. So much for me being worried about the Gardaí staking out my house. It was obvious that they did not know I was on the run, or at least Store Street did not. Still, rather than go to my house I had got word out to tell the family I was okay and living in town and I would get out to them when I could.

'Let's get back to the flat and get dry' suggested Tosser.

We were into December now and everyone was thinking about Christmas and what they were going to do. I knew that the boys, as they were a bit older than me, were getting a dole payment every week so they had some money but Tosser was coming out with all mad sorts of ideas about jobs we could pull off to give us money for Christmas. I had my doubts, and was not up to running if we were to be chased and me driving was out as the leg was not fully mended yet.

It was a Tuesday night 17th December 1968 and we decided that we would go out and see what we could find. We headed up Blackhorse Avenue and came across a butchers shop. It had turkeys hanging in the window for Christmas.

'This is it. Just the job. We can get the turkey and ham for our ma's for Christmas dinner here and we can also sell some' said Mike.

Creeping around and trying to not make any noise we looked to see if there were any alarms on the window. We could see a red box on the front of the shop that we presumed was an alarm.

'Looks like its bugged and that means a smash and grab, and I won't be able for running never mind trying to carry an armful of turkeys as well' I said.

'Look, it's like we can smash the window and grab what we can and leg it into the back of the flats up the road there and hide out and wait for the coast to clear and then we can walk back to the flat. What do you think?' asked Tosser.

I pondered about this, but did not like the idea at all.

With that I heard Shhhhh a sound of air releasing. I looked over to see Tosser putting a knife back into his pocket. He had just flattened a car tyre.

'What the fuck! What are you at? Why are you carrying a knife?' I asked.

'We don't want to get chased by the owners car now do we?' said Tosser.

'I'll go and wait in the back of the flats then, as I'm not into this. Okay?' I said.

'Fuck off then you chicken. We'll do the job but you better keep your eyes peeled for the rossers. Okay?' said Tosser.

I headed up the road and stood on the corner near to the flats and waited. It was not long before I heard this unmerciful crash of glass and shouts and roars coming from the butchers.

With that both Tosser and Mike came running up the road with arms full of turkeys and what a sight that made. We three ran into the flats. There were some sheds that were for bikes or storage there. We found one that was open and bunched inside.

'Shhhh not a word now. Stay quiet' said Mike

It was not long before we could hear the sound of cars driving at high speed out on the street, then shortly after we could hear men's voices.

'The fuckers must be in here somewhere. Let's check out these sheds'.

We could hear them coming along the sheds trying the doors as they got closer we knew that the game was up. Then they were outside our shed we all kind of sunk into each other for protection and you could hear us rubbing off each other. With that Tosser kicked out the door and ran to the right. Mike ran to the left, turkeys flying in all directions as they were thrown into the air.

I just stood still rooted to the spot, but no one came into the shed. I could hear roaring and shouting 'Stop, Stop' in the distance but I was rooted to the ground. The door was flapping over and back. It must have only been one minute since the boys burst out but it seemed like an eternity.

I slowly crept out of the shed and went around to the back of them. Lights were on in a lot of the flats now due to the commotion and noise. I went into the garden and sank into a pool of water. The whole place was waterlogged from all the rain we were having. With that I heard more roaring and shouting and could see the light from torches heading my way. I lay down in the grass and it might as well just have been a river. I just sank into the water. A light came on in the ground floor flat directly above me and I was sure the Gardaí would be able to see my shape lying there. But as luck had it they moved on without seeing me.

With that a door to the balcony opened and I heard 'Son, son come over here.'

I looked up and an old man was beckoning me in to his flat. I stood up and water just poured out of me. I must have looked a sight. I climbed over the balcony.

'I'm soaked to the skin' I said.

'Not to worry. Come in and dry yourself off' said the man.

I was like a drowned rat and was shivering as his wife handed me a towel and said 'Dry yourself son before you get pneumonia'.

'Thanks. Thanks so much.'

'Okay, we don't condone what you might have done, but we also don't condone what the Gardaí do either. So we will help you get dry and then you'll be on your way, okay?'

I just could not believe my luck on meeting such decent and normal people. They must have been in their late seventies, and took a chance in letting me into their home and helping me.

After a while when all had calmed down and a lot of the lights in the flats had gone off again, I thanked the elderly couple and made my way out into the night.

Making sure I did not pass by the butcher shop I took the long way around the block and headed back to the flat in Capel Street. When I got there I stood across the road to see how the wind would lie. There were lights on in the flat and I knew we had left none on when we went out earlier.

After about thirty minutes or so I crept across the road and down the steps to the flat, knocking on the door. I could again hear shuffling inside.

'Who's there'? Mike's voice.

'It's me, Frank.'

With that the door opened and Mike stood there with two bread knives in his hands.

'What the fuck are the knives for? You lunatic!'

'Protection'

'You'll get twelve months for that, some protection. Where's Tosser?'

'Don't know. I think he got caught, thought you had got nabbed also'.

'Better get these clothes off and have a wash. I've been in a lot of water and am freezing.'

I was only just changed when there was a lot of banging on the door.

'OPEN UP! OPEN UP! GUARDS'

'Mike get rid of the stupid knives. Put them in a drawer. The game's up. We were not out of here tonight, right. Got it?'

The game was now up and I knew in my heart that we had a squealer in our little group. I had for a while thought that Mike was the one to be wary of and so I had distrusted him from time to time. But it seemed that Tosser was the Rat, the untrustworthy one, the one that had just led the Garda to our door. The squealer.

I was feeling sick to my stomach and looking over at Mike he looked the same.

'Ok lads the game is up' spouted out a Guard.

They grabbed hold of both of us and we were bundled into the rear of a Garda car that was parked outside on the road. Although it was quite early a small crowd had gathered to see what the Garda were up to. Off we sped to the Bridewell, a Garda station that was positioned to the rear of the Four Courts, Dublin's main court houses.

We were booked in by a Sergeant and placed in separate cells. The layout of the Bridewell was such that the cells were upstairs and not below ground as they would be in many other Garda Stations. Instead there was a tunnel under the Bridewell that led to the Criminal Courts.

I was told I would be held over in the Bridewell until the next morning 18th December 1968 for court after being charged with the Breaking and Entering of the butchers shop and stealing ten fresh turkeys.

At court the next morning Tosser, Mike and I were remanded for one month to further appear in court to answer the charges. Both Tosser and Mike were granted bail and I was sent back to resume my sentence in St Patrick's.

We were taken back underground by way of the tunnel for the two boys to await someone to arrive and sign for their bail, and I was to wait for transport back to prison. I was put back into a cell on my own but the two boys were put in together and I could hear them shouting from the cell window to Tosser's brother who was outside on the Street explaining that Tosser would have to wait until that evening for his Da to get off work so he could come up and bail him out. Tosser's Da worked for a well-known whiskey distiller and had this big blue bulbous nose from his daily free allotment of whisky.

It wasn't too long before I heard the jangling of keys and my cell door was opened inwards.

'Ok Heeney, your transport is here' said the Guard as he held the door open.

I was taken to the Sergeants desk where I signed for my meagre belongings which were then placed in a see through plastic bag and handed to the screw from St. Patrick's that was to bring me back to prison.

My journey did not take long, and my mind just wandered at what was now going to happen to me. I was still upset from the realisation that Tosser, who I looked up to, was a Rat, the worse kind of a friend, or not a friend at all.

Back at St. Patrick's the screws were not the politest to me. As I had escaped from their clutches it would mean my hard time was going to get a lot harder.

The main screw who booked me in was nothing but abusive as he said to me 'You little fucker, we are going to make either a man or mincemeat of you. It's up to you!'

After getting my inmate clothing and bedding I was escorted back to the original cell I was in before being shipped out to Shanganagh Castle.

As the screw closed the door behind me he said. 'You will be before the Governor tomorrow at 10.00 o'clock so be at your best then?'

With that, he closed the door with a bang and I could hear the rattle of keys as he locked it. With no other company than my thoughts I tried to reflect on my life and future, what was to become of me. All my reasoning came back to the same conclusion. I had to make the rest of my time here as easy as possible and to keep my nose clean. My sentence would eventually come to an end. It was only time and time passes. I then would have to reconstruct my life to my own better advantage. No more Mike or Tosser. I would have to leave the family home and start a new beginning I was seventeen years old now and this life could just not carry on.

My tea was brought to my door by a Trustee inmate, tea and bread and jam. That was to do me for my first night back.

Next morning I was taken from my cell to go in front of the Governor. I stood in front of his desk with my hands by my side trying to look as contrite as possible, but not knowing if I did as I could not see my own face.

'Heeney, here we go again with you. You are before me due to horrendous misbehaviours on your part.' He said 'I am not going to ask you why or wherefore I am just going to get on with my job of dealing with your misbehaviours.'

With that he went into a litany of self-importance to a seventeen year old kid. He was flanked by two screws, and had his head honcho also present. I suppose he thought he presided over Alcatraz Prison.

'I am awarding you three days No. 1 Diet. (That was three days in the Chokey or basement cell on bread and water, stripped naked with only a mattress in the night time with no blankets or covering.)

Fourteen days No. 2 diet (which was only tea or water and bread for breakfast and teatime, but lunch allowed.)

Fourteen days loss of remission, with the privileges of recreation smoking and the Hall withdrawn for one month. This meant 24 hours per day lock up in your cell and no cigarettes. For a smoker like me this was paramount to a red flag to a bull.

'You had served 159 days of your sentence of 303 days when you absconded from Shanganagh Castle, leaving 144 days outstanding. Your new release date will be 10th May 1969. Acting on the instructions of the Department of Justice, I intend to place you before the visiting committee at their January meeting on 8th Approx.'

This meeting never took place.

'Take him down.'

With that I was grabbed by the arms on both sides by the two screws and marched down to the basement to start my three days No. 1 Diet. This time they only took my clothes from me but did not put me into the straight jacket.

Immediately the cold struck me and I felt it sink into my bones. There was nothing I could do but walk around the eight by four cell as fast as I could to try to bring some warmth to my body. I would also do press-ups and skipping without the rope anything to distract the cold. Minutes were as long as hours and hours felt as long as days. I looked around me and I felt that god had left this place a long time ago.

It felt like an eternity before the screw came with the mattress and my night time bread and water. I knew that night was to be the worst time. The darkest time.

I lay on the mattress in a foetal position trying to stave the cold off. I knew to cry out or show any weakness would only give satisfaction to the screws. I could hear them come and look through the peephole very often and I did not want to give them anything to talk and laugh about.

CHAPTER 29

I DRIFTED INTO A KIND of never, never land and my dreams took me back to the evening of 17th September 1966 when I was incarcerated in St Joseph's industrial School Letterfrack Co Galway. It had been quite a gruelling Saturday on the farm, up at 05.30 to milk the cows and perform other farming chores. After a long day it was about 6.30 in the evening and the second session of cow milking had been done and the cow sheds had been cleaned out. The cows were back in the fields. We, the farm boys, were back in our washroom at the end of our dormitory. We are all feeling playful and happy as we were about to go to the hall to see a film. It's going to be a cowboy film we were hoping. But we never knew what the film would be until we saw the opening credits, the type and title would be only known by the villagers and the Christian Brothers.

I heard SMACK and turned to see Brother Chinny had just hit a boy on the side of his head.

'I have warned and warned you not to mess about in the washroom' he screamed, as he lashed the kid again to the head.

I could see that he was in a foul mood and we were going to have a hard evening ahead. Our playful happiness stopped like a shot. The silence of us boys was felt in the washroom as we then slowly moved to the dormitory to get dressed in preparation for the film. We were like the quietest of little field mice hoping that our silence would appease Brother Chinny. No one wanted to miss the film.

The young boy's face was roaring red where he had been hit and he was doing all he could to not cry. He stifled his hurt. We eventually filed out of the dorm and down the stairs and into the yard where all the other boys were lined up with readiness to go to the hall.

We took our place at the end of the long queue that wound like a snake across the yard and up the steps turning left towards the hall's main entrance. On entering the hall we boys stayed on the left hand side as the right hand side was reserved for the paying locals. This setup was the same as the church. Locals on the right, boys on the left. As we were last in we were seated in the back row.

Now this could make it quite difficult to see the screen if you happened to be placed behind a bigger boy. There was a bit of jostling and laughter coming from the boys as they were in good spirits because we were to see a film. Brothers Chinny, Titch, and Tea were present in the hall. Brother Friar Tuck was in the projection room. He would normally handle the projector, change the reels and ensure a smooth showing.

Chinny was still in a foul mood as he walked up and down the centre aisle giving bulls looks to any kid who was not sitting straight and looking ahead towards the screen. It did not take him long to have all the boys in complete silence and looking straight ahead like robots.

After a while the locals started to filter into the hall and take their seats. The hall was filling up quickly now when this big fat woman entered. She was dressed like she was going to a wedding hat and all. She was having a bit of bother trying to walk in shoes that had heels so high that if she fell off them she would break her neck. The shoes seemed to be two sizes too small for her.

Dave who was sitting on my right blurted out 'Jaysus has yer one come into the wrong hall? Does she think this is the church?'

Jimmy who was sitting next to Dave replied 'She probably could not get up the hill to the church with them there high heels on.'

With that the lady gave a kind of hop skip and jump and very nearly fell on her arse. Well that was it! I just burst out laughing. I was in fits and could not control myself.

With that Brothers Chinny and Tea started to beat us about the heads with their fists. But the laughing had now spread to other rows of lads and I was just uncontrollable, could not stop and was shuddering from the laughing and the blows to the head. Chinny had started to thump me on my back now to try to stop me laughing.

With that, five of us were dragged out of our row of seats. We were made to kneel down and face the wall of the projection room. We were instructed to stay like this and not to move until the film ended. And then we would be dealt with. Every one of the Villagers had just stared straight ahead as if nothing had happened.

I was in a state as I knew that there would be no mercy shown to us for what had just transpired. We were in for a thorough battering and God knows what else. My head was reeling with fear and also pain from the blows I had received.

We were able to hear the film as it played out behind our backs. It was not a western but about a girl who was travelling around Italy and met a man and they fell in love. As we quietly knelt facing the wall Dave let out this loud fart. It was like thunder in the hall. The laughing started again. I was in stitches with tears rolling down my face. It could not be helped it was contagious.

Brother Tea went berserk, lashing out and kicking us. He seemed to be in a trance. His eyes were screaming from his sockets and he seemed oblivious to the local villagers who were in the hall. I received a kick to my shoulder that resulted in my head bouncing of the wall. This beating lasted for quite a few minutes before sense got the better of him and he calmed down. We boys were in a terrible state of fear now. We were battered and bruised and trying to hold our pain in.

I knew that we were in for a brutal form of punishment when the film was over and we had left the hall. I was worried as I knew that the Brothers were in a state that could not be controlled. They had shown no fear in what they had being doing in the hall with villagers present. What would they do to us where they got us alone?

I feared for my life to be quite honest. I am going to get out of here was running within my mind. 'I'm going to make a run for it before we get back to the dorm.'

The five of us seemed to be lost within our own thoughts and we dared not to speak or communicate in any way to each other. The film ended and we all just waited until all the locals had left the hall for home. Normally some of the lads would stay behind and clean and sweep out the hall. We five boys were the first to leave the hall.

I cannot remember if anything was said among us, all I know is when we got to the yard we just ran together like March hares as fast as we could across the yard and into the side door of the kitchen. Like one we dashed across the stream at the rear of the kitchen. Without saying a word to each other we split up, two running to the right two running straight ahead and me alone turning left.

With my heart in my mouth and my head still thumping from the earlier beating I knew that my route would take me near to the Brother's house but that did not deter me as I assumed that the brothers would be heading to the area of the yard on hearing of our escape. After about a half an hour and badly out of breath I stopped to try and get my bearings and to listen to see if I was being followed. I had cut up to the farm and was now heading around to the rear of Diamond Mountain to the right. This I was hoping would take me to the back of the Diamond.

The ground here though boggy was reasonably flat. I was aware to watch out for pools of water that you could sink into and vanish. There was also quicksand like bog that would suck you down under. After a while I decided that I was not been followed the night was clear and bright and the Moon shone bright and high in the night sky. This was helping me to pick out a safe route across the rugged terrain. I kept running as fast as I could keeping my head held high but also watching my steps so as I would not have a mishap.

The idea was to use the night darkness to put as much space as I could between me and Letterfrack. I was going to escape this time, I was adamant as they would probably kill or seriously injure me if I was captured. I had not planned this escape and my only choice now was just to run and run. After some time I came to a large lake. I had been here before but this time I was on the side that was further away from the road and I was glad of this as it would be harder for the brothers or Garda to see or hear me. The night air was mild, but I was hot and sweating. I was soaked through with sweat and grime from the bogs. My shoes felt like they were small barges as they were full of water and muck.

My head was spinning, 'Why the fuck? Why does this keep happening to me? Why? Why? Why?'

But God only knows why. Your life is laid out for you they say; some life!

After some time I could hear a noise in the distance. It sounded like someone with a bad cough but only amplified. I slowed down to a trot trying to figure out where the noise was coming from. I soon found it was coming from a bank on the lake. This strange noise was not something I had heard before. Was it a sick wolf? I hoped not.

I crept slowly forward keeping as quiet as I could. Eventually I came across a part of terrain that allowed me to look down on the lake shore. There I could see what seemed to be hundreds of frogs. It was them that were making the racket, like dogs barking from the back of their throat. I was happy to see it was just frogs and not the big bad wolf.

There was nothing for me to fear here so I carried on into the night with a spring in my step. I was full of adrenalin and fear was driving me on. It felt like an unseen being had control of my body. Some soul was possessing me and pressing me on.

What if I never make it?

What if I do fall into a bog hole?

What if my mum and da are never to see me again?

What about my brother and sisters?

Would they miss me?

Have they already given up on me?

On and on into the night I ran and ran. I am going to get away. I am the runner.

Pausing to catch my breath and to get my bearings again I started to feel cold. It was now well into the night and the temperature had dropped dramatically. That part of the country tended to get very misty at that time of the year and I could feel the cold mist on my brow. I was finding it difficult to see too far ahead. I was also unfamiliar with the area. Was I heading in the right

Survivor

direction? I knew I was not going in circles but I was unsure of the straight path ahead. But I just plodded on and hoped I was heading in the direction of Galway City.

At first light I should be able to make out my direction. After some time I could see what looked like the headlights of a car off to the left in the far distance. But it was so far away that I was sure that I could not be seen. But to be on the safe side I crouched as I ran. If only my mum could see me now? I was like a big old turkey bent over running. The car lights eventually faded into the night. All around me now was just an eerie silence. I was feeling tired and sat on a rock that was protruding from the earth. It was quite cold to my touch and I began to shudder somewhat.

I was drenched now from top to bottom from the morning dew. I had given up on trying to drain my shoes and was just sloshing along in them. I must keep moving so I headed off again and in the distance now I could see the dawn coming up on the horizon. I would have to be much more careful now as there was a chance I would be seen as I was now in the open with nothing to hide behind. The terrain here was mountainous and sparse and there were no trees or gorse for cover.

I was feeling the pangs of hunger now but put them to the back of my mind. The sun was coming up and this was making the dew rise. Soon it was straddling my waist like a blanket. It was like the scene from some horror picture but in daylight not darkness.

I kept heading in the direction I thought was east. It was not long before I came across a small stream and bending over it I filled my belly with cold spring water. I splashed the water over my head and face and this revitalised me. Shaking my head like a dog I continued my journey.

After a while I came to a spot that I could see a road from. I had not seen or heard another car since the earlier one so I pondered the option of taking to the road so as to make more time. I made my way over to the roadside and kept down in the ditch to see if I could hear any sound of life.

I crept up on to the road and pressed my ear onto the surface like and Indian to see if I could hear any sound. I couldn't hear a murmur so I decided to start running along the road. It was so much easier now and I was making better progress when I came to a bend in the road that I couldn't see around, so I slowed up and crept forward with caution. As I rounded the bend all looked clear ahead so I started to run again. I had not gone 100 yards when I hear a roar of

'STOP BOY! STOP!'

'Shite. Where did that come from'? I looked behind to see a big burly Garda chasing after me with his baton raised above his head.

'STOP! STOP YOU LITTLE BASTARD!' He screamed.

I was in no position to try to outrun him so I came to a stop and fell to my knees and hoped that he did not decide to batter me with his baton. He caught up to me.

'Stay still and do not move a muscle' he bellowed.

I couldn't move anything as I was exhausted. I probably would have only got another ten yards before collapsing. I was all done in. I sat on my backside and awaited the consequences. The big Guard seemed to be all fagged out after only running a short distance. He stood beside my slumped body breathing heavily like a big giant as I stared up at him.

'You're caught now, boyo. Just you sit there and the car will be along shortly to take you back to the school.'

I was thinking 'what is going to happen to me now? My God what is going to happen now that they have caught me?'

It was not too long before the car arrived. It pulled to a stop and out jumped another Garda.

He walked over and then said. 'Oh it's you again have you no sense? You can't get away from here you know and now you're going to be in for a good hiding. Have you not had enough of this running away, young lad?'

With that they both hauled me into the back of the squad car. They took me back to Letterfrack Garda Station and not to the school. They brought me inside and put on a nice demur to me but I can see by them I had upset the daily living and they had probably been on the side of the road all night. They gave me a hot mug of tea and a ham sandwich.

One of them said 'We know you won't get fed when we take you back to the school so eat up. We are going to have to make charges for you as you have been part of a mass escape. We have already caught the other four idiots. They never got very far. You got further probably because you are a habitual.'

I replied 'I don't understand how you can charge me with anything. I'm under sixteen and none of my parents are present. I am also under supervision of the school.'

'Ah sure don't worry about any of that. We can charge you. We can do as we will.'

I was there about another hour to hour and a half before Brother O Shea and Brother Chinny arrived to collect me and hauled me out to the car. I was terrified. Chinny just grabbed me by the scruff of the neck. He pushed me into the back seat and slid in beside me and kept a tight grip of my arms. I was in pain as he gripped my arms in such a way.

We were only a couple of hundred yards from the school and we drove up the lane way to the left hand side of the school. We parked at the top of the yard. Chinny dragged me from the back of the car. I was waiting for the kicks or punches to rain down on me but nothing happened. He just grabbed me by the scruff of the neck, dragged me across the yard and into the shower room. He pushed me into the shower with all my clothes on.

'Wash yourself, you little bastard, wash' he shouted.

I pulled off my clothes as the cold water rained down on top of me. Everything was so dirty and stinking so getting them off me was not a problem. He left the room so I could shower in peace. It was not long before he was back. He threw a towel at me.

'Dry yourself' he muttered.

I dried myself doing all I could to keep my privates from his prying eyes. He then pulled me by the arm. I had only the towel around my waist at this stage, and he dragged me up to the dorm.

'Get to bed.'

With that he turned on his heels and left me to my own devices. I just collapsed onto the bed and fell asleep. I was awakened by the sound of the boys coming into the dorm that evening. Nobody said a word. Everyone just looked at me. I cast my eyes around looking to see the other four escapees but could see them anywhere.

I started to wonder where they might be. They were not here when I arrived. Maybe they were in the other dormitory. I closed my eyes and pretended to have gone back to sleep. Everyone just went to bed. It was about an hour later when I was hauled from the bed and dragged to the washroom. Its brother Chinny.

'Now bend over' He says.

I hesitated so he grabbed hold of me and bent me over and pulled up my night shirt so as I was naked from my back down. With that, he started to flay me with the leather strap. I just screamed and screamed with the shock and the pain. He was like a man possessed. He just kept belting me. He did not say anything. He just kept flaying me. I could hear him sucking in his breath. Hear him groan over my screaming. Was he going to kill me? He just stopped and dragged me by my hair back to my bed threw me onto it. I just lay there whimpering, I could hear other boys whispering and murmuring.

He started to scream and shout 'Shut up. Shut up. Go back to sleep. This does not concern you.'

I just cried and cried within myself for the whole night long. The pain was unbelievable. I had taken beatings from him before but this pain seemed worse than anything before.

Next morning I could hear the boys getting up and getting ready to leave to do their daily dues. I had my head under the blankets and kept it there.

Chinny had come out earlier clapping his hands together and shouting 'Get up' as he usually did but he did not approach me so I assumed I was to stay in the dorm for the day.

So no one came near me all day. I received no food. My pain was so bad I was unsure that I would ever get better. The day passed and the boys came back into the dorm that night and went to bed. No one said a word to me.

Next morning CLAP CLAP CLAP. Chinny came out to waken everyone up. I woke and was feeling somewhat better although the pain in my bum was still unbearable. My head also still hurt unbearably and felt like a little man was inside it with a hammer going knock knock knock. Was I going to survive here? Was I ever going to make it out of here? These were the questions just running around my head.

Brother Chinny was standing by my bed.

'Get up get up now' he demanded. 'You're going back to work'

I crawled from the bed as another boy approached me with a pillow case full of clothes. He handed them to me. I tried to wash and dress the best I could. I went to church and then I went down to the rec and tried to eat my breakfast with the other boys whose eyes were all over me. I looked around but still no sign of the other four boys.

After breakfast at line-up Brother Chinny pulled me from the line 'You are on farm duty until further notice. You will be rock breaking'

When I got to the field I could see that the other four escapes were there. They were picking rocks from the field and carrying them across and stacking them in piles. I was happy to see them but couldn't get to speak to them as Joe Nortimer, the farmer Mike Nortimer's son, was in charge and he was a brute. Joe Nortimer approached me and handed me a sledge hammer.

'Do you see that large granite rock in the field over there?' He pointed to it.

'Yes' I replied.

'Well go and break it.'

With that he shoved me in the direction of the rock.

I was hammering on this rock and as my hammer hit it flakes of rock keep hitting my legs, I was in short trousers and it was not long before blood was seeping from my legs. No matter what way I tried to break the rock I couldn't stop the flying pieces from hitting them.

Joe Nortimer approached me from time to time. He could see the situation I was in but just said 'Hit it harder, much harder. It will make some spunk for you.'

The working day ended, and it took me all my time to walk to the tractor trailer that would take us back to the farm yard. We piled aboard like half dead kids after a gruelling day on the farm.

After supper we went to the hall as it was raining. I was anxious to try to speak to the other boys to see what had happened to them but I didn't get the chance. The brothers present in the hall that evening were Brother Chinny, Brother Tea and Brother Titch.

We were only minutes in the hall when Chinny started clapping his hands to get attention.

'Ok, gather around and look towards the stage.' He demanded.

Titch separated us five escapees from the other boys.

'Go up onto the stage' he said to us.

Some trustee boys brought five chairs up on to the stage. We knew something was about to go down and it was not looking good for us. We five were standing in lines facing out towards the boys who were looking up at us on the stage, Brother Chinny came up. He made a speech about the escape and how it was going to affect the school and how all the boys would suffer for it. There would be no tuck shop for two weeks for anyone.

We five were now going to be punished in front of everyone in the hall. I was terrified and looking around I can see the look of fear and horror on the other four boys faces. With that Chinny demanded that we take our trousers down and bend over the chairs. Chinny had a big stick. Titch had got his leather. Tea had also leather.

They took it in turns walking up and down the line hitting us as hard as they could. They lifted their arms above their heads as far as they could and then lashed down with all their strength on our bums. They just kept going up and down the line. All the other boys were screaming, I was not. I was biting my tongue, anything, but I refused to scream anymore.

I felt like I was going to die with the pain. It was pain on top of the pain I had received in the washroom, but I refused to cry or scream. They could kill me now but I was mute.

Chinny went mad he started hitting me across the back the head with the stick. He was just lashing out. He then grabbed me up off the chair and started punching and kicking me. I was falling around the stage. I was in a mess.

'He is going to kill me but I won't cry, I won't cry' I thought.

He was screaming 'Cry. Cry you bastard. Take your punishment like a man, you bastard.'

He had just gone berserk, had totally lost it. With that the door to the hall opened. I couldn't hear the door open, but I could hear it in the noise from the other boys in the hall. It was Brother O Shea, the head brother, the guardian of us boys!!

He came onto the stage, and stopped the madness that was occurring there. The madness that left me battered and bleeding on the ground and the other four boys also battered and bleeding. This was how we were being educated. This is how we were being looked after. This was St Joseph's Industrial School, Letterfrack in 1966 Ireland.

CHAPTER 30

I AWOKE WITH A START. It was the noise of the keys clanging in the cell door lock. My breakfast of bread and water was shoved in to me and my mattress was dragged out. I was allowed to walk out and empty my chamber pot. The door clanged behind me and I was left with an empty room. I picked at the bread. It was stale. My mind wandered back to my fitful dreams of last night and Letterfrack. This place was no different for abuse except here they use batons and fists instead of leathers.

I started walking around the cell and did some rope less skipping to keep warm. The three days passed, as days always do. Time waits on no one.

The jangle of the keys in the cell door, taken for a shower and then given a pillowcase of clothes and bedding. I was taken back to my cell to spend 23 hours a day for the next 30 days. At least I could get some books to read, but no smokes made it very hard. Now I could hear movement and noise from other inmates, their shouts and screams and laughter, also some far away music from time to time, *Baby come back*, by The Equals this song seemed to be following me around.

Days just slipped in and out. Christmas came and went. I was still under report so it meant nothing to me and I knew I would not have missed much anyway. You were not forced to go to church in here but sometimes it was nice to go just to see and hear other voices, but I gave it a miss, put it down to not needed at this time.

The nights were very cold now and I wrapped the blankets around me as many times as I could to keep warm. Clothes were all kept on in bed also. I just seemed to read, fall asleep, read some more, sleep some more, just to try to get the days to pass.

My thirty days were up and I could go out to the yard and mingle with other inmates, but I just tended to keep to myself. I couldn't be bothered mingling all over again. I just wanted my sentence to finish and get out of here.

Monday 20th January 1969.

We were all in the recreation room, an old school classroom turned into a TV room in the evening for watching TV when a screw decided to turn the TV off for no apparent reason in the middle of a programme. Well, all hell broke loose. Jimmy Murphy started smashing windows while other inmates pulled the TV off its stand and it went crashing to the floor.

Screams of 'it's our rec time' and 'fucking bastard put the TV back on' were being shouted as the room turned into a riot.

Two screws were battering Jimmy Murphy unmercifully with batons as he lay on the ground. I jumped on one of their backs trying to restrain or stop him hitting Murphy. I was immediately dragged from the screws back and battered to the ground. A lot of screws had arrived into the hall by now. Four of them grabbed hold of me, one to each leg and one to each arm and I was dragged from the room down the stairs. Whilst being taken across the grounds, all four of them were punching me into the body and face. I couldn't do anything as they had a tight hold of me. I was supposed to have broken windows whilst being held like this and I was also supposed to have fallen on my face whilst been held like this.

I was dragged down to the Chokey whilst being repeatedly beaten. I was stripped naked and put into a strait jacket and flung to the floor and left there. As the screws left one of them kicked me in the back. I couldn't see who it was. The names of the four who beat me were Officer O'S, Officer N, Officer J.A. F and Officer Vincent McP. It was not long before the door opened and I was pulled from the floor and manhandled onto a chair.

The Senior Screw K was present and he checked my injuries and said 'Get the doctor down here immediately. What has happened to him? Heeney can you speak?'

I just nodded my head as I couldn't open my mouth. My face felt as if it was all blown up like a balloon and the pain was unreal. I was trying to sit on the chair but just kept falling sideways. I felt as if I had no balance.

'Hold him on the chair' said the Senior Screw K.

After some time the doctor arrived and examined me.

'He needs to be taken immediately to hospital. Get him dressed and cleaned up. It's possible his jaw is broken and some ribs also.'

The doctor was Sergeant T. M and he stated in his statement that I was sent to hospital because I informed him I fell off a chair!!! I was unable to speak to him.

I am taken to Jervis Street Hospital by Officers P. N and J.A. F. On arrival the doctor in charge of emergency, after examining me, demanded that the two screws leave the hospital. He also made inquiries to the Garda Station for a Garda to come and see the condition I was in so as someone could be charged with causing my injuries. A Garda did come but as I could not speak I couldn't give him a statement. It was then decided that he might come back in a week or so to speak to me but he did take note of my injuries. I had made a written statement to the best of my ability to him and the doctor that evening but I was in a lot of pain and could not write in a very legible manner.

The doctor said that I would finish my time in the hospital as he would not discharge me back to the Screws as long as he was in charge of me. He said he had never seen such injuries inflicted on a kid before.

The Screws in a statement said that I 'directed arrogance and abuse towards the nurses and doctor that night'. This was made up as I was unable to speak. They also alleged that I smashed windows in the recreation room and en route to the base. This was also untrue and on arrival to the hospital I had no markings or damage what so ever to my hands or fists. But they were trying to deflect from the harm they had done to me by making these accusations. But even if I did 'smash windows' that did not give them the right to batter me in the way they did.

I was in a private room in Jervis St. Hospital. I had been treated by the on-duty doctor throughout the night and managed to get some sleep.

I communicated by writing on a pad to the nurse and asked her if she could contact Ann at Our Lady's Hospital, Crumlin to let her know I'm in hospital. She agreed to do so.

I had been taken for x-rays earlier that morning and was awaiting the results. My face was still badly swollen and I could see my body was black and blue and full of bruises. I had been dosed up with pain killers but was still feeling pain all over. There was now a Garda present outside the room door keeping watch on me. He popped his head in from time to time to check if I was still there. On one occasion he came into the room to try to speak to me but I couldn't answer him as my mouth wouldn't work.

He said 'Some lot them screws giving you such a going over. Did you try to kill one?'

I nodded my head to say no.

'Well all the best to you and I hope you are not too badly hurt' he said.

The nurses and doctors came and went prodding and pulling. I couldn't eat so I was put on a drip to get some fluids into me. I dozed on and off throughout the day. It was evening time when my Ma and Da arrived in.

'Oh Frank what have you done now?' said my Ma.

'It's not what has he done. But what have the bastards done to him' said my Da.

'Jaysus the state of you, can you talk? Your face is like a balloon. Who did this?' my Da ranted.

They both sat down beside the bed and I wrote on the pad and tried to explain what had happened.

'We will get a solicitor onto them and get it sorted' my Da said.

I felt a relief there and hoped that he kept to his word and did that as I feared what might happen to me when I went back to St. Pats. The doctor had said that he would keep me here but I didn't think that was feasible; neither did my Ma and Da.

With that Ann arrived. She was shocked to see the state I was in and tried to give me a big hug but the pain was such she just kissed me on the forehead.

My Ma and Da had brought in some fruit and a bottle of sugary pop for me, leaving them on the bedside locker. They made their goodbyes and promised to be back in the next evening. They wanted to give me and Ann some space. When they had left Ann wanted to know the whole ins and outs of what went on so I tried to jot it down for her on the pad. I was getting better at the writing now.

It wasn't long before the nurse was in telling Ann it was time to go. She again kissed me on the forehead and bid me farewell promising to be back up tomorrow night. I settled in for the night then and was feeling a lot better after having the visit.

Next morning the doctor came in and explained how strong I was. He said the jaw and ribs were not broken and he could not understand why as my body had taken such a beating. It would take time for things to mend but there were no bones broken according to the X-Rays.

He said that he was going to keep me in the hospital as long as he could. He explained I should be able to start moving my mouth and talking in a day or so as the swelling was receding. I felt so much better now and was glad that I was on the mend. I did not feel up to having nuts or bolts put in my jaw.

It must have been about midday the next day when the two screws that had brought me to the hospital arrived into the ward.

The bigger of the two came right up beside me in the bed and bending over me he whispered to me 'You boy better withdraw your accusations of us beating you, because if you don't when we get you back to Pats we will do you and you won't ever again be able to talk to anyone when we finish with you, understand'

I did not answer in any way to him. With that his colleague came up on the far side of the bed and he bent over so the two of them were bending over me and I could smell the stale breath from both of their rotten mouths.

The second one, the skinnier one said 'We have ways of making things happen to gurriers like you, a slip in the shower, a fall off a landing, things can be arranged, so withdraw the shite you are saying about us, hear.'

I was so fearful that I nodded my head to say 'yes.'

I felt I did not have much choice in the matter. They both went about leaving the room but as they got to the door they turned and looked at me and in unison said.

'Remember, it's our playground you'll be coming back to.'

With that they left the room banging the door shut behind them.

The Garda who was outside came into the room then. He looked at me in a funny way. I don't know why. Maybe he saw the fear on my bruised face, I don't know, but he said.

'Dangerous lot that crowd. They don't know if they are guardians or owners, be careful son.'

With that he left. Again my head was spinning, why me. As if I wasn't in a bad enough state, now threats from the screws to set my mind on another escape. I was going to have to run again, what other choice did I have? Who would help me back in St. Pats?

Evening time came around and Ann arrived up first. I had decided that I was going to try and make a break for it regardless. I was beginning to be able to speak in a whisper as my mouth seemed to have opened a bit now.

'Ann, I am in a bit of a quandary' I explained, as she leaned closer to me and I was able to whisper in her ear and proceeded to tell her about the threats made by the two screws earlier in the day.

She was perplexed and asked in what way she could help.

'Clothes are what I need. I have shoes here. Can you maybe bring up some clothes tomorrow night?'

The words were not out of my mouth when my Ma and Da came into the room.

'Clothes for what?' my Da said. 'He could hear grass grow; you are not thinking of doing a runner from here are you?'

'No. No I'm just thinking of when I can get up and about I can have some clothes here.'

'I hope that is the case' my Da said.

The visit was now under a bit of a strain and Ann decided that she had to get back to her job as she had some work to finish. She bid her good byes.

'I hope that you are not going to get that girl into trouble' said my Ma.

Looking at my predicament I did not want them to know of the threats that had been put on me so I tried to convince her all was fine. But I knew by the look on her face that she was not convinced.

With that the nurse came in and announced visiting time was over. I wished my parents good bye and I said I would see them tomorrow night. I fell into a slumber, a kind of half sleep; I was starting to feel much better now and could speak in more than a whisper. I awoke with a start, to see a vision sitting on the end of the bed.

It was a nurse dressed in an all blue uniform. There seemed to be a glow from her. It looked like she was shining in the dim light, but she looked too young to be a matron. She had the bluest of eyes, and jet black hair tied up behind her hat.

She saw that I was startled and said 'it's ok I won't bite you. How are you feeling? Doctor says that you can talk now and are mending very quickly, this is a very good sign.'

I was quite taken back by her beauty and honesty and just nodded my head.

'It will all be fine for you. You will leave here very shortly and have a marvelous life. Things will get much better for you and you will live a charmed life.'

I shook my head. Was I dreaming? Or was she there?

'Frank remember you have a guardian angel that will look after you and take care of you.'

I closed my eyes tightly and paused my brain for a moment. Is this really happening? When I reopened my eyes the room was empty. There was no matron there. The hair stood up on the back of my neck and I started to shiver inside. Had I just seen a ghost? Surely not! I tossed and turned all night and the next morning I was unsure if I had seen a ghost or had a dream. But it still looked in my mind that I had seen a young matron who spoke to me.

During the day I plucked up the courage to ask one of the nurses about my late night visit.

'Do you have a young matron with black hair and very blue eyes on the night shift?' I asked.

The nurse looked at me in a very strange way and replied 'Young matron? No. Not to my knowledge.'

Her reply only made matters worse for me. Was I losing it from the beating I had taken or was I hallucinating from the drugs that were being pumped into me? Only time will tell.

The day passed without any more frights, and there were no more visits from the screws. The Garda outside the door changed all the time but each one threw their eyes in every half hour or so to check on me.

Visiting time came around and Ma and Da were up first tonight. I asked about a solicitor and Da explained that he had gone to Bowler Gerathy but to no avail as the lady there Susan had told him that the prison service were a law onto themselves and have full backing of the government on internal issues. She added that it would take too much money for a case to be fought against them. No, it was a no brainer. They will get away with whatever they say and do. This only frightened me more and hastened my thought of escape.

Ann arrived and I saw she had only a small bag of goodies for me, some grapes and other fruit. Where were the clothes I was wondering?

Da was no fool and handed me £5 saying 'Just in case you need anything from the shop.'

As soon as my Ma and Da left, Ann started to peel off her jeans.

As I looked on in horror she said 'I've got two pairs on and two tee shirts. I did not want to carry in a bag of clothes in case the Garda got suspicious.'

She also had socks and underwear in her handbag. I put the clothing under the blankets in the bed to hide them out of sight.

'I have some money for you also.' She handed me £5.

'I will wait for you on Rathmines Road near the church. Try not to make it too late. The last bus leaves town about 11.45 pm.'

'Ok. I should be able to do that, but I don't have a watch to tell the time.'

'I'll leave you mine it won't fit you so hide it under the pillow and don't forget to take it with you. I'm going to leave now ok, see you later, be careful.'

So, off she popped.

I pretended to be asleep and could hear the Garda look in a couple of times then he stopped, maybe he has gone for a snooze.

I pulled the jeans up on me under the blankets, slipped the socks on and then the tee shirt. Checking the watch I saw it was 11.15 and decided to make a move. Slipping from the bed, I approached the window in silence, hoping it would open. Pulling the catch across, the window slid up noisily. I put my leg out first and then dragged all my body out. I closed the window. I had placed the pillow in the bed hoping it acted as a decoy so as I could make some distance from the hospital before it was discovered that I had gone.

The room was on the ground floor so I had no problem there. I approached the main gate that was closed but the smaller door was open so I just walked out as if I had come from the emergency department. There was a porter at the gate but he paid me no heed. I turned right and headed up Abbey Street, turned left onto Jervis Street and left again onto Ormond Quay. I crossed the Ha'penny Bridge and cut up through the side streets until I got to the bus stop that would get me to Rathmines. Once on the bus I paid my fare to the conductor and knew now that all would be well. I had gotten away.

Hopping off the bus I saw Ann standing in the shadows. She ran to me and we embraced, but tenderly as I was still in some pain from my injuries.

'I have a flat now with a friend. We share it. I don't think that she will mind you staying for a few days but please don't tell her about your escape or that you were inside. Just say that you are going through some problems at home and need somewhere to stay until you can sort things out' Ann said.

Again I felt like I did not fit in anywhere but was prepared to go along with Ann's little story as I had no choice in the matter.

We came to a big house after a short walk. It was made into five flats and Ann and her friend's flat was on the top floor. It was a one room flat that included a small kitchen area. It was bright as it had large windows that looked out to the front of the building. It was a typical bedsit of that time but had two single beds crammed in. All the more for the landlord to cream in some more money.

I was exhausted and still unwell and in pain. Ann offered me some painkillers and I took four at once to try and numb the pain. I took to the bed as Ann waited for her friend to return. Immediately I fell into a deep sleep and only awoke to the sound of the girls getting up for work. The bathroom and toilet were down the hall and shared by other bedsits. Ann explained that it would be better for me to wait until everyone had gone to work before venturing down the hall to use the bathroom.

Ann introduced her friend to me. Her name was Joan and she was also from the country. She was similar in build to Ann but had red hair all in curls and she had a pretty smile. I found her quite easy to get along with.

Ann explained that it would be best to stay indoors for a couple of days to let the dust settle and get stronger. I agreed as I did not think I was in a fit state to go out. I realised that I was not as recovered as I might have thought. The girls set off and I passed the day in the blissful freedom of being cooped up in a small flat.

After a while of trying to read girlie magazines, I got quite bored and did a recce around the house to familiarise myself with it. There were two flats to each storey and it was a three storey house. The hallways and stairs were very well kept and it looked in quite good shape for a house of bedsits. I just kind of dozed and listened to the sounds that the house made.

After some time I could hear the other tenants returning from work and I could make out their idle chatter as they moved from room to room. There seemed to be a lot of men living here. On Ann's return she explained that she and Joan were the only girls occupying the house but the lads were no problem and kept to themselves. There was no knocking on doors looking for a cup of milk so far.

This easy life style continued for about another three weeks and I started to become very restless and felt cooped up in the small flat. Ann had gone out to my house in Coolock and my Ma had given her some clothes that she had come by for me, but I knew I could not spend the rest of my life cooped up here. Joan had been so good letting me stay but of late she was staying out of the flat for longer times each day and sometimes not coming home at all. Ann was afraid that she might leave and Ann would be in a quandary with the rent as she would not be able to maintain the flat on her own and I was a nil contributor.

We decided that I would go and try to find Tosser and see if he could put me up for a while. I headed off to Sheriff Street to Tosser's mothers house.

On arrival she told me where he was staying. It was near to the Five Lamps, Amiens Street area. I headed up there as it was only five minutes away.

Knocking on the door I heard Mike's voice 'Who's there?'

'Sure it's only me.' I called out.

With that the door opened and there stood Mike with a big grin on his face.

'Well I heard you had done a runner and knew it would be only a matter of time until you arrived on the doorstep. Come in.'

This room was very basic not as salubrious as the Rathmines flat. It was more rundown and old. There was the same small kitchen area and two single beds but there also was a couch and I had my eye on that. Tosser was out somewhere but Mike said there would be no problem me sleeping on the couch, the more the merrier.

After thanking Mike I headed back to Rathmines to give Ann the good news. On arrival at the front door I realised that I had no key to get in. After a bit of looking around I could see that the bathroom window was opened on the second floor so I shimmed up the drainpipe and climbed in the window. Then I had to sit on the landing as I had no key to get in to Ann's flat. I had not thought this through when I had left earlier. I was on the stairs and it had been dark for a while now when I heard the lads come in downstairs. I decided to hide in the bathroom as sitting on the stairs was too open. It seemed like hours before Ann arrived home. The lads in the flat next to her had been in for hours and I was fearful that they would need to use the bathroom and catch me there. I crept up to her door and softly knocked on it. She opened it and looked at me in a funny way.

'What are you doing here?' she said.

Pushing my way in, I asked her what did she think I was doing there.

'I was under the impression that you would stay with Tosser' she replied.

Well that was not the way we had left it this morning but I did not want an argument. As a matter of fact we had never had an argument as such.

I explained about my visit and what Mike had said. I had not seen Tosser but Mike did not think there would be any problem with him on the issue. She said that she just had gone out for a drink with some friends not thinking that I would be back that night. I left on good terms the next morning and we said we would meet up over the weekend.

On arrival at the two boys flat, the place was laden down with bags of clothes and other bits and pieces.

'We got lucky last night. A truck parked over the road and was packed to the hilt with clothes. Everyone in the area now has new clothes. It was an English truck that had come off the ferry and the driver had gone into the pub for a pint, not knowing the area. He was cleaned out.' Mike explained.

'Will the Garda not know that you are living here?'

'No they wouldn't have a clue to who lives here.'

The days just seemed to fly by then with me coming and going between the Five Lamps and Rathmines. I felt in my head that this could not go on forever. There was going to have to come a time that I would be caught, or I would give myself up but I knew that this life would not be sustainable.

CHAPTER 31

14th March 1969.

I LEFT THE TWO LADS in the Five Lamps flat and headed over to Ann's place in Rathmines. It was a lovely spring day so I decided to take a walk over instead of getting the bus. Things were not good with Mike, Tosser and I at the present time as I was not up to their lifestyle any more. I just wanted to try and somehow get my sentence in St. Pats finished and over, so I had decided to go over and speak to Ann about it.

I meandered across town as there was no rush to get to Ann's so I went via St Stephens Green. All the young girls and lads were out in their spring finest and it was a lovely sunny day, one of the days that made you feel alive and part of life.

On arrival at the flat I had to go in through the bathroom window again as I still had no key. Even though I had been many times to Ann's flat and stayed for days on end I had never bumped into any other of the tenants. So in the window I went and took my place on the stairs, not knowing that there was a man home in the flat next to Ann's. After a while a door opened and I had no chance to duck into the bathroom. I was caught red-handed sitting on the stairs.

'Oh, you gave me a start, what are you doing sitting there?' this man said.
'I'm just waiting on my girlfriend.' I replied.
'From in there?' and he pointed towards Ann's door.
'Yes'
'Oh ok. I'm just going out to the shop' he replied.

It was not long after that he returned but he was not alone. He had this big burly man in tow.

'That's him' he said pointing at me. 'He got in the bathroom window. I don't know who he is. I have never seen him before.'

'What's your name boy? And what are you doing here?'

Before I could answer Ann and Joan arrived up the stairs. Without saying a word they passed us by and opened their door.

The man from the flat next door piped up 'He said that his girlfriend lived here.'

With that the big man took me by the arm and marched me into Ann's flat.

'Do you know this lad?' he asked Ann.

As I was out of his sight I nodded to Ann to say no, but the Garda turned and caught me nodding.

'I won't ask you again.' he said to Ann.

I knew the game was up and I did not want Ann to get into trouble so I said 'I don't know her. I don't know either of them.'

The Garda knew I was telling lies. I could see it on his face, but I felt I just wanted this to end now. I did not want Ann to take any of the blame and I just wanted to finish my sentence, just get it over with regardless. I could see by Ann that she was relieved by me not implicating her.

The Garda took my by the arm and marched me out of the house to his car. He had a mustard coloured Renault 4 parked at the footpath.

'You are going to be charged for breaking and entering, as your girlfriend did not live there. Do you still deny that that girl was your girlfriend?'

'Just charge me. Do what you like.' I replied.

On arrival at the station I was led into a room and the door locked behind me. After about twenty minutes the big Garda came back.

'Are you sure you are Heeney?'

'Yes.' I said.

'Well I would have been under the impression that you would not have been a skinny kid as St. Pats have you down as a hardened criminal. I am going to take you back to St. Pats now. Are you okay with that?'

'Yes'

'Okay then.' And he led me out to his car.

'I won't be charging you with breaking and entering. You seem to have enough on your plate and you have been no trouble for me.'

'Thanks.' I said.

I kept looking out the window of the car soaking up my last bit of freedom. It was an odd type of a car and the gears were on the dashboard. The Garda was giving it Fucks every so often when it refused to go into gear for him. I was smirking at him thinking of my Morris Minor foray when I could not select the gears.

Well here we go again as we approach the gates of St. Pats, for the last time I hoped. The next time I want to see these gates is when they close behind me.

I was taken into induction again. No one was abusive I was glad to see. My new clothes and possessions were put into the bag that is already there with my earlier possessions. These ones were just pushed into the bag on top, I had sixteen cigarettes and a box of matches on me, and the screws allowed me to hold onto them.

I was placed back in my cell and locked in there without being allowed out for any recreation for four days. The only time I left my cell was to empty my chamber pot and to then throw water over my head and face. All my meals are brought to my cell and no screw was saying why this was happening or how long it was going to last for. It was a type of isolation punishment but not in the chokey and with food allowed. I was glad that I had been left with my cigarettes and matches.

I heard a rattling of keys in the door and it swung open.

'Okay, you are up before the governor. Come along.'

So I was led to the governor's office without notice or warning. I was in a bit of a state as I did not know what fate awaited me.

On arrival at the office I was told to wait outside for a minute, the screw stood by my side.

'Okay, bring him in now.'

In I went to see the Governor, the head screw and another screw, so in total four screws and myself.

The Governor spoke the following.

'You gave yourself up to the Garda at Rathmines Garda station on Saturday 15 March 1969 and you were readmitted to St Patrick's Institution. At the point in time when you were transferred to Jervis Street Hospital your date of discharge on remission was 10th May 1969. Between 23rd January 1969 and your arrest on 15 March 1969 you were actually 49 days at large. This means that having to serve that 49 days your remission date of discharge now reads 28th June 1969. And your expiry date is 25th July 1969. Are you prepared to settle down and cause no further trouble?'

'Yes sir.' I replied, hoping that my punishment was going to be lenient.

'If you as stated are prepared to settle down and cause no further trouble, under prevailing circumstances, I propose, at this stage, to defer imposition of any punishment in respect of your behaviour on 20th January 1969.'

'Yes I promise.' I replied.

'Okay then that will be all. Take him back to his cell and he is to be treated as a normal prisoner from now.'

I could not believe my luck. Or was it luck or were they afraid if they were to start abusing me again would my family try to intervene with a solicitor, or had they even received a solicitor's letter. I did not know, but their tune had dramatically changed and I was glad it was so. But alas things were to take a turn for the worse in no time.

I had not been very well and seemed to be run down. After a visit to the doctor he prescribed that I should have milk instead of tea and a double ration of bread and butter at all meal times. This was to try to build me back up as I had lost quite a lot of weight and with me not being of big build in the first instance it showed. My clothes although never a good fit were now hanging off me like rags.

All went well with the new diet for about 3 days, however on the evening of 10th April at the supper time queue the screw in charge, a tall skinny one, would not allow me milk or double bread and butter rations. The trustee who dished out the supper told him I was on a special diet and I also explained to him I was on this diet.

Well, he was having none of it and just lost it saying 'You will be getting no supper at all tonight now get to your cell.'

Well, I thought, if I'm getting no supper then no one else is either. With that I gripped hold of the table with two hands and toppled it over. Tea and bread went everywhere. The place was awash with hot tea and everyone was yelling and running in all directions. I ran to my cell and got hold of the chair and smashing it on the wall. I grabbed hold of a leg of it to defend myself as best I could with four screws coming towards me batons drawn.

Well I tried to hold my own but I was no match for the screws. The only consolation this time was they did not hit me in the face or the head just the body, arms and legs. I was dragged screaming and fighting with all my might to the Chokey. When there I was stripped naked and the straight jacket put on me again.

I went through another three days of bread and water and no sleep or blankets, just soiling myself constantly, and freezing cold. Was I to blame for my behaviour? Or was it the screw who denied me my diet? Who knows but it was not again a very pleasant experience. Again I was not taken to the Governor for this misdemeanour. This was probably to keep it out of the records so there would be no trace of it.

It was like before, taken from the Chokey after three days and thrown into the shower and then taken back to my cell and locked up for 24 hours with no yard or recreation time. This continued for a week and this time I had no cigarettes and was going slowly mad in my cell, chewing my nails and just not being in a nice frame of mind. My head was spinning and my thoughts were now for revenge and mayhem. This was not good I knew but as each day passed I got more distraught. Not having cigarettes was driving me up the wall.

Then out of the blue the morning screw just opened the door and left it open. I peeped out and he was going along the landing opening all the doors, so I was being allowed out again. This was that really hard part as one would not be sure how long you would be allowed stay out. The screws would keep moving the goal posts to control and try to break you. They took delight in seeing you being miserable, hungry and cold. From what I could see they were outcasts themselves, maybe would not able make it into the Garda or mainstream employment, but one thing for sure they were sadistic in their treatment of kids.

I was, at this stage, taking the stance now that I had taken in Letterfrack with the brothers. I was no longer going to cry or take abuse. They refused to give me cigarettes so I went back to my cell that evening. I had matches so around 11 o'clock I set fire to my mattress and then started to smash the small windows in my cell with my fists. Now this was no mean feat as the glass was half an inch thick, but I had had enough. I was at my wits end.

The screws did not come quickly so I was nearly suffocated in my stupidity to cause mayhem. I was dragged back down to the Chokey, stripped and put into the straight jacket again. Except for some beating on my legs they held off on the brutality that night. I hardly slept. I just did not want to be here anymore. I just did not want to live. I wanted out of this life. I could see no end to the madness; it just seemed to go on and on and on.

After a while I calmed down and my thoughts went back to that Matron in the hospital with the bright blue eyes. Was she right? Would things be better for me? It just did not seem so at this time. Maybe if I could just keep myself calm, maybe just ignore the screws, keep to myself. Keep calm.

I was going to try to make her words come true for me. I was going to make a life that was better. My luck was going to get better. I was going to make it get better; I fell into a shallow sleep, but kept these thoughts in my head. It was up to me, no one else. I would do it.

Next morning I was taken in front of the governor again. But on the way there I was taken to see the doctor. He checked me over and announced me fit for punishment. So they were worried about what they had done to me in January as this is not normal procedure.

The Governor did seem the best pleased to see me. I was informed that I was being charged by Officer R. Q with the following charges.

1. Setting fire to the mattress in my cell.
2. Breaking all the panes of glass in my cell.
3. Causing a disturbance in the institution at 11 o'clock at night.

When asked if the charges were correct, I nodded.

'Do you have an explanation to offer?'

'No I don't have any explanation to offer.' I replied.

He then said.

'See my reports from 27th January and 20th March concerning this youth's general conduct and behaviour. He gave a verbal undertaking that he was prepared to settle down and cause no further trouble following his return to the Institution on the 15th inst. He is an unpredictable scoundrel.'

He continued 'I award 3 days No 1 diet. [Bread and water in the Chokey, 14 days No 2 diet, 14 days loss of remission, 14 days loss of privilege of recreation and smoking. I also order that 30 Shillings be deducted from his gratuity to pay for the mattress and the breaking of the glass. His new remission discharge will be 5th October 1969.

Take him away.'

So off we went back to the chokey for 3 days bread and water. But this time I will just take it on the chin and it will be the last time that they get me down to this hell hole.

I just became one into myself and didn't in any way mix or speak to screw or inmate until my date of discharge came around. I thought I can be a better person, I know this and I will strive to do so in this life, I shall leave behind my dark memories.

CHAPTER 32

On my last day in St. Pats I had butterflies in my stomach. I was anxious about 'a gate arrest.' That was when the Garda have other things against you and they arrive up at the prison gates to arrest you. I only had the Rathmines breaking and entry on my mind as it had never come up, but I was okay on the morning as there were no Gardaí outside waiting on me.

I was as free as a bird and my intention was to stay that way. I held onto my plastic bag of meagre belongings and headed home to Coolock and the family home.

On arrival there, Ma welcomed me with open arms, and I promised to her that it is all over now. My first priority was to get a job and start to build my life. She told me Ann had come out a few times on the bus, as she was not able to get into the prison to see me. She had tried on a few occasions to no avail. I had thought that she had got on with her life when I had not seen her come up on a visit, I explained. But Ma said no, she wanted to see me as she was very fond of me. I decided that gaining employment was now the first choice and that I would need money if I was to start taking Ann out.

Within days I had secured work in a factory in Santry. It was a long walk twice a day but it was a job and it suited me.

After a week or so on a Saturday I went in to see Tosser to get an update on how he was doing. He had met a girl and was working in the Whisky plant with his Da. I could see the blue hint on his nose. His intention now was to go straight also. He invited me out with him and the girlfriend that night for a few pints. I agreed.

During the course of the evening when a few pints had been had and his girlfriend had gone to the toilet Tosser looked at me with a sorrowful look and said.

'I don't know how to say this.'

'Just say it' said I not realising the blow I was about to receive.

'Well I was up in Pats one day to visit my brother and Ann was there to visit you, but they would not let her in. She was very distressed about not being able to see you so I went with her to Rathmines to her flat. Now it was only to console her, but things got a little bit out of hand and you know, well, we, you know.'

'YOU FUCKING KNOW WHAT' I shouted.

I could see other revelers looking at us now when Tosser said 'I'm sorry I never meant it to happen and I only saw her three or four times since.'

I just looked at him, some fucking friend I had there.

I got up and left the pub never looking back. I decided then and there to split from Ann. When I told Ma about my decision to split from Ann she decided to tell me the secret herself and Ann had together. She told me that Ann had confided in her that she was three months pregnant when we met; she had become pregnant by a business man in her small town in the country. Whilst in Our Lady's Hospital Crumlin Ann had been a domestic worker. She was working for her sins under the supervision of the Nuns for bed and board and a small weekly sum of money. She was never a trainee nurse as she declared to me. As she got nearer to her time of giving birth she was taken out of Crumlin hospital and placed in the Mother and Baby home on the Navan Road in Dublin where she gave birth to a baby girl. The baby was immediately taken from her at birth by the Nuns. Ann had kept this secret from me from the start, and my being in prison helped her to keep the secret safe as my being locked up kept me unaware of her life on the outside.

I never saw Tosser or Ann again. Sure who needs friends like that? This was to be my moment. This was to open my eyes. This was to tell me that my life must change for the better. My blue angel was going to help me change. She was sitting on my shoulder guiding me and I would change. No more the wild one, no more the miss-behaving. Time would sort things out. Time would be all I had. Time for me for my life ahead. My time - not the prison's time, not the Government's time, not the judiciary's time. My time, my life.

With special thanks to Dr S O Donnell.
And Caranua.

About the Author

R.F. HEENEY ENCOUNTERED NUMEROUS HORRORS during his years as a child prisoner in Ireland in the 1960s. Born into poverty, he found himself caught up in a cycle of crime and punishment that took a tremendous toll of his mental and physical health. He eventually left Ireland in the early 1980s.

After spending many years abroad, he moved back to Ireland. He realized that little had changed in the country. The abuse was still happening to children, and too many men were eager to cover it up instead of changing the system. Heeney became inspired to write his story as a condemnation of the government's failure to take responsibility and a call to arms to reveal past injustices.

Heeney now lives in Dublin. He has also written *In My Own Words (Still Running)* under the pen name Mickey Finn and is currently working on a third title.

Made in the USA
Columbia, SC
29 October 2017